D0241142

Christoph D. Walser

Industrial Policy in the Process of Transition

Christoph D. Walser

Industrial Policy
in the Process of Transition

Verlag Paul Haupt
Bern · Stuttgart · Wien

Christoph D. Walser (1968) studied economics at the University of St. Gallen. He specialised in transition economics and development economics. Following his graduation, he worked as a research assistant for Professor Dr. Jean-Max Baumer in the field of development economics. On the awarding of a Fellowship for Prospective Researchers by the Swiss National Science Foundation he then studied as a visiting research student for a year at St. Antony's College, University of Oxford. On his return to St. Gallen in 1996 he became research assistant to Professor Dr. Alfred Meier who works in the areas of economics and public finance. In 1998, after having concluded his dissertation which is presented in this book, the author joined the Zurich Financial Services Group in Zurich.

Die Deutsche Bibliothek – CIP-Einheitsaufnahme

Walser, Christoph D.:
Industrial policy in the process of transition /
Christoph D. Walser. –
Bern ; Stuttgart ; Wien : Haupt, 1999
Zugl.: St. Gallen, Univ., Diss., 1999
ISBN 3-258-06017-7

http://www.haupt.ch

Two roads diverged in a wood, and I – I took the one less travelled by,
– and that has made all the difference.

Robert Frost

Contents

Overview

List of Tables, Boxes and Figures   xv

Glossary   xvii

Preface   xxi

Acknowledgements   xxiii

1 Introduction   **1**

    1.1 Definition of Research Objective 1

    1.2 Delimitation and Presentation of Topic 4

    1.3 Clarification of Basic Terms 8

2 The Transition to a Market Economy   **29**

    2.1 The Economics of Transition 29

    2.2 The Political Economy of Transition 45

    2.3 Synthesis I 52

3 Industrial Policy and Economic Theory   **57**

    3.1 Orthodox Approaches 60

    3.2 Heterodox Approaches 73

    3.3 Critical Assessment 89

    3.4 Synthesis II 98

4 Western Industrial Policies   **103**

   4.1 The European Union 103

   4.2 The East Asian NIEs 117

   4.3 Synthesis III 135

5 Early Experiences – The Leading Countries in Transition   **149**

   5.1 The Czech Republic 150

   5.2 Hungary 162

   5.3 Poland 173

   5.4 Slovenia 186

   5.5 Synthesis IV 202

6 An Industrial Policy for Countries in Transition   **213**

   6.1 The Policy Agenda 213

   6.2 Policy Areas and Instruments 227

   6.3 Institutional Aspects 243

7 Conclusions   **255**

Appendix   263

Bibliography   271

Detailed Overview

List of Tables, Boxes and Figures xv

Glossary xvii

Preface xxi

Acknowledgements xxiii

1 Introduction 1

1.1 Definition of Research Objective 1

1.2 Delimitation and Presentation of Topic 4

1.3 Clarification of Basic Terms 8

    1.3.1 Transition 8

    1.3.2 Industrial Policy 19

2 The Transition to a Market Economy 29

2.1 The Economics of Transition 29

    2.1.1 Financial Intermediation 32

    2.1.2 Corporate Governance 37

2.2 The Political Economy of Transition 45

2.3 Synthesis I 52

3 Industrial Policy and Economic Theory 57

3.1 Orthodox Approaches 60

    3.1.1 Neoclassical Theory 60

        3.1.1.1 Market Failures 61

        3.1.1.2 Barriers to Market Entry 64

    3.1.2 Neoliberalism 68

3.2 Heterodox Approaches 73

  3.2.1 Infant Industry Argument 73

  3.2.2 Information Economics 78

  3.2.3 New Evolutionary Economics 83

3.3 Critical Assessment.. 89

  3.3.1 Orthodox Approaches 89

    3.3.1.1 Neoclassical Theory... 89

    3.3.1.2 Neoliberalism.. 91

  3.3.2 Heterodox Approaches.. 93

    3.3.2.1 Infant Industry Argument 93

    3.3.2.2 Information Economics 94

    3.3.2.3 New Evolutionary Economics 96

3.4 Synthesis II... 98

  3.4.1 Justification 98

  3.4.2 Policy Areas 99

  3.4.3 Institutional Aspects 100

4 Western Industrial Policies   **103**

4.1 The European Union.. 103

  4.1.1 The Phare Programme.. 104

  4.1.2 The Union's Industrial Policy Approach 109

4.2 The East Asian NIEs.. 117

  4.2.1 Fundamentals 121

  4.2.2 Interventionist Policies 123

  4.2.3 Institutional Arrangements 129

4.3 Synthesis III 135

  4.3.1 The Rapprochement with the European Union 135

    4.3.1.1 General Lessons... 135

4.3.1.2 Industrial Policy Areas 137

4.3.1.3 Institutional Aspects 138

4.3.2 The East Asian Experience 139

4.3.2.1 General Lessons 139

4.3.2.2 Industrial Policy Areas 141

4.3.2.3 Institutional Aspects 144

5 Early Experiences – The Leading Countries in Transition   149

5.1 The Czech Republic 150

5.1.1 Policy Areas and Instruments 151

5.1.2 Institutional Aspects 159

5.2 Hungary 162

5.2.1 Policy Areas and Instruments 164

5.2.2 Institutional Aspects 171

5.3 Poland 173

5.3.1 Policy Areas and Instruments 175

5.3.2 Institutional Aspects 183

5.4 Slovenia 186

5.4.1 Policy Areas and Instruments 190

5.4.2 Institutional Aspects 199

5.5 Synthesis IV 202

5.5.1 General Lessons 202

5.5.2 Industrial Policy Areas 206

5.5.2.1 Crisis Management 206

5.5.2.2 Privatisation 206

5.5.2.3 SME Policy 207

5.5.2.4 Competition Policy 207

5.5.2.5 Investment Promotion 207

5.5.2.6 FDI 207

5.5.2.7 Export Promotion... 208

5.5.2.8 Science and Technology Policy.............................. 208

5.5.2.9 Regional Development Policies 208

5.5.2.10 Employment Measures 209

5.5.2.11 Environmental and Energy Policies 209

5.5.3 Institutional Aspects 210

6 An Industrial Policy for Countries in Transition   213

6.1 The Policy Agenda... 213

6.1.1 The Basic Rationale for Industrial Policy..................... 214

6.1.1.1 Market Failures 214

6.1.1.2 Market Structure and Barriers to Entry 217

6.1.1.3 Political Economy of Transition......................... 217

6.1.1.4 De facto Industrial Policy 219

6.1.2 The Foundations of Industrial Policy 219

6.1.3 Objectives... 221

6.1.3.1 Short-Term Objectives...................................... 222

6.1.3.2 Medium- to Long-Term Objectives.................... 223

6.1.4 Constraints 224

6.2 Policy Areas and Instruments 227

6.2.1 Industrial Policies in the Short Term 227

6.2.1.1 Financial Intermediation................................... 228

6.2.1.2 Small- and Medium-Sized Enterprises.............. 229

6.2.1.3 Competition Policy 230

6.2.1.4 Labour Market Policies..................................... 231

6.2.1.5 State-Owned Enterprises 232

6.2.1.6 Privatisation 233

6.2.2 Industrial Policies in the Medium- to Long-Term..........................234

    6.2.2.1 Investment Promotion...234

    6.2.2.2 Export Promotion...235

    6.2.2.3 Education and Training 236

    6.2.2.4 Infrastructure..237

    6.2.2.5 Science and Technology Policy............................237

    6.2.2.6 Foreign Direct Investment..................................239

    6.2.2.7 Regional Development Policies 240

    6.2.2.8 Environmental Policies.......................................240

6.2.3 Convergence of Industrial Policies....................................241

6.3 Institutional Aspects 243

6.3.1 Principles..243

6.3.2 Designing an Industrial Policy Strategy 245

    6.3.2.1 Institutionalised Dialogue..................................246

    6.3.2.2 Long-Term Vision 247

    6.3.2.3 Comprehensive Approach 248

6.3.3 Implementing Industrial Policy 249

    6.3.3.1 Institutional Consolidation 249

    6.3.3.2 Learning 251

7 Conclusions **255**

Appendix 263

Bibliography 271

List of Tables, Boxes and Figures

Tables

1.1: Matrix of transitional change 15

2.1: Private sector share in GDP and employment in Eastern Europe, 1994 32

2.2: Concentration of banking sector in selected countries in transition 33

2.3: Areas of industrial policy 54

3.1: The neoclassical paradigm 64

3.2: Contestable markets 67

3.3: Neoliberalism 72

3.4: The infant industry argument 78

3.5: Information economics 83

3.6: New-evolutionary economics 88

4.1: Key elements of the European industrial policy 111

5.1: The industrial policy of the Czech Republic 159

5.2: The industrial policy of Hungary 171

5.3: The industrial policy of Poland 183

5.4: The industrial policy of Slovenia 199

5.5: Cross-country comparison of state activity in industrial policy areas 203

6.1: An industrial policy framework for countries in transition 253

A.1: Priority sectors and support of Phare 263

A.2: Macroeconomic data for the Czech Republic 1990-1996 266

A.3: Macroeconomic data for Hungary 1990-1996..........................267

A.4: Macroeconomic data for Poland 1990-1996............................268

A.5: Macroeconomic data for Slovenia 1990-1996.........................269

Boxes

1.1: The phases of economic transition and respective key reforms..................18

1.2: Definition of transition...19

1.3: Definition of industry...19

1.4: Definition of industrial policy I......................................23

2.1: Definition of industrial policy II.....................................56

Figures

1.1: The location of industrial policy within economic theory.........................22

1.2: Industrial policy and overlapping policy areas............................25

1.3: Taxonomy of industrial policy..28

4.1: The pillars of the European Union's pre-accession strategy....................105

4.2: The European Union's approach to industrial policy..............................116

4.3: The East Asian NIEs' approach to industrial policy.............................134

5.1: Pattern of emergence of industrial policy in the transition process.........204

6.1: The pillars of industrial policy in transition.............................221

6.2: Hexagon of industrial policy principles in transition.............................245

6.3: The pilot agency's position within government administration................250

Glossary

AMO	Anti-Monopoly Office
CCET	Centre for Co-operation with Economies in Transition (OECD)
CEC	Commission of the European Communities
CEE	Central and Eastern Europe(an)
CEEC	Central and Eastern European country
CEFTA	Central European Free Trade Agreement
CEPR	Centre for Economic Policy Research
CIS	Commonwealth of Independent States (the countries of the former Soviet Union excluding the Baltic states)
CMEA	Council of Mutual Economic Assistance (former)
COFACE	Compagnie Française pour l'Assurance du Commerce Exterieur (French export credit guarantee company)
CPI	consumer price index
CSFR	Czech and Slovak Federal Republic (former)
e.g.	*exempli gratia*, for example
EBRD	European Bank for Reconstruction and Development
EC	European Community
EGAP	Export Guarantee and Insurance Company
EIB	European Investment Bank
ERG	Exportrisikogarantie (Swiss export credit guarantee)
etc.	*et cetera*, and all the others
EU	European Union
f.	and following page
FDI	foreign direct investment
ff.	and following pages
Ft	forint
GDP	gross domestic product
GDR	German Democratic Republic
HERMES	Hermes-Kreditversicherungs-AG (German export credit guarantee company)
HIDB	Hungarian Investment and Development Bank

HSHC	Hungarian State Holding Company
i.e.	*id est*, in other words
ibid.	*ibidem*, in the same place
IBRD	International Bank for Reconstruction and Development
IFIs	international financial institutions
IMF	International Monetary Fund
km	kilometre (s)
mill.	million(s)
n.a.	not available
NATO	North Atlantic Treaty Organisation
NBER	National Bureau of Economic Research, Cambridge, Mass.
NCTD	National Committee for Technical Development
NEO	National Employment Office
NGO	Non-Governmental Organisation
NIE	Newly Industrialising Economy
NIF	National Investment Fund
NPF	National Property Fund
OECD	Organisation for Economic Co-operation and Development
OPC	Office for the Protection of Competition (Slovenia)
p.	page
Phare	Poland and Hungary Aid for the Reconstruction of the Economy
pp.	pages
PSE	post-socialist economy
R&D	research and development
S&T	science and technology
SAP	Structural Adjustment Programme
SEC	Slovene Export Corporation
SEZ	special economic zone
SHPA	State Holding and Property Agency
SKLAD	Development Fund of Slovenia
SME	small- and medium-sized enterprise
SOE	state-owned enterprise
SPA	State Property Agency
sq	square
UK	United Kingdom

UNCTAD	United Nations Conference on Trade and Development
UNIDO	United Nations Industrial Development Organisation
US	United States
US$	US dollar(s)
USSR	Union of Soviet Socialist Republics (former)
VAT	value added tax
WTO	World Trade Organisation

Preface

This thesis is on industrial policy in the Central and East European transition process. It ultimately centres on the question of what role the state can and should play in transforming former command economies into market economic systems. When the initial euphoria regarding the fall of the iron curtain and the newly reunited Europe had just begun to settle, Western mainstream economists were surprisingly quick to offer a simple policy advice to the new governments: let the market play. To bring about a market economy for the state, all there remained to be done was to create a legal framework guaranteeing private property rights and to liberalise both prices and trade. If rapidly implemented, this shock therapy, it was believed, would eradicate the remnants of central planning and foster the emergence of a competitive economy based on private initiative and entrepreneurship. The new system would arise like a phoenix from the ashes of real socialism.

Yet, some years into the transition process, there are reasons for serious doubts about the simplistic neoliberal policy advice. The scope and dimensions of the requisite structural change are far too big to be entirely entrusted to the emerging markets. It turns out that a crucial task of systemic transformation is the modernisation of the role of the state. This background is the starting point for our analysis in which we scrutinise the role of industrial policy in the transition from a planned to a market economy.

Acknowledgements

Without the generous financial and moral support of my parents I could not have written this thesis. They gave me the chance to study and, after my graduation, encouraged me to make my doctorate in economics. I would like to thank Professor Jean-Max Baumer at the University of St. Gallen who offered me the opportunity to work for him as a research assistant in the field of development economics for two years (1993-4). He, moreover, agreed to examine my thesis as the co-supervisor. I am gratefully indebted to the Swiss National Science Foundation which granted me a Fellowship for Prospective Researchers. With this most generous funding I had the invaluable opportunity of studying at the University of Oxford for one year (April 1995 - April 1996)

There, at St. Antony's College, Professor Michael Kaser supervised my research progress. I would like to thank him for his valuable comments and support. I would also like to express my deep gratitude to Professor Alfred Meier at the University of St. Gallen. Although the topic of my thesis does not fall into the realm of mainstream economics he, nevertheless, encouraged me from the beginning to go ahead with this project and agreed to supervise it. He went on to back my application for the Swiss National Science Foundation fellowship and employed me as his research assistant after my return from Oxford in 1996 until the completion of this work in spring 1998. For all this, and for his fatherly advice, I am very grateful.

I would like, too, to express my gratitude to Dr. Thomas Fuster and Dr. Bernhard Günther who both agreed to read the manuscript and to comment. And I thank Ms. Gillian Rathbone for her meticulous editorial work. Last but not least I am greatly indebted to Andrea who accompanied me through the final stages of my thesis. I thank her for her patience and for the energy she has given me. Finally, I would like to acknowledge the help and support of those whom I do not mention here. All conclusions and remaining errors are mine.

St. Gallen / Zurich, Switzerland
CHRISTOPH D. WALSER

1 Introduction

The purpose of this introductory chapter is threefold: first, we define the objective of our research and formulate the working hypotheses. Next, the thesis' topic is delimited and its construction is explained. Finally third, the two core expressions 'transition' and 'industrial policy' are both clarified and defined.

1.1 Definition of Research Objective

The 'theory of systemic transformation' hitherto has dealt with the issue of industrial policy only in passing, if at all.[1] Instead four questions have thus far received prominence in the theoretical discussion on systemic transformation: first, how best to tackle the problem of severe macroeconomic imbalances that paralysed the economies in Central and Eastern Europe (CEE) at transition's inception. Second, whether to liberalise a centrally planned economy overnight (i.e., the so called shock therapy) or to choose a more gradual approach.[2] Third, what institutional framework is needed for a market economy to emerge. Finally which of the proposed privatisation methods or combination thereof ought to be applied to transfer state-owned assets from the public to the private sector.[3]

---

[1] The 'theory of systemic transformation' is not to be thought of as a coherent body of theorems derived by way of logical deduction. It is rather a patchy collection of ideas relating to the transition from a centrally planned to a market-type economy. Some of these notions belong more to the realm of ideology than to economic reasoning, while others are empirically won insights based on the experience of developing countries or advanced industrial economies and, to an increasing extent, on the early experiences of leading transition economies.

[2] On the issue of the appropriate speed and sequence of systemic reforms see, for example, Aghion and Blanchard (1993), Dewatripont and Gérard (1992), Funke (1993), Lösch (1992b), Lipton and Sachs (1990), Newbery (1991), and Roland (1994a).

[3] The mainstream interest in the phenomenon of transition may be summarised under the headings, stablisation, liberalisation, privatisation, and restructuring. See, as an example, the programmatic approach of Blanchard, Dornbusch, Krugman, Layard and Summers (1991).

Yet some years into the transition process it emerges that in order to transform a socialist economic system into a modern market-based economy far more is required than macroeconomic stabilisation, the liberalisation of prices and foreign trade, institutional reforms, and the privatisation of state-owned assets. To arrive at an advanced industrial economy far-reaching structural reforms are necessary. The need for restructuring is particularly acute in the industrial sector where large conglomerates and outdated production capacities as legacies of the socialist development strategy predominate. Given the dimensions of prerequisite change on the one hand and the fact that markets in the region only begin to emerge and can be expected to function poorly for years to come on the other, the state will have to play a significant role vis-à-vis the industrial sector.

Hence, the fact that the issue of industrial policy is largely left out by the mainstream debate on systemic transformation in Central and Eastern Europe has to be deemed a major shortcoming. Not only does the theoretical discussion miss a central element of transition strategies it also leaves in the lurch CEE governments looking for advice on the design of an industrial policy strategy. Against this background the *core goal* of this thesis is twofold:

1. given the historical and socio-economic realities of countries in transition an attempt is made to show the *desirability of an explicit industrial policy* under the prevailing circumstances of systemic transformation;

2. we aim at developing a *general industrial policy framework* for the transition from a centrally planned to a market-type economy.

In more general terms, we hope with our thesis to make a contribution to the debate about the appropriate role of government in the transition process. Moreover, by developing an industrial policy framework for transition economies we intend in particular to help close the existing gap in the theoretical discussion of systemic transformation in Central and Eastern Europe. We thus address those scholars and students in economics, comparative economic systems and political science who show an interest in the governance of the transition process from an interdisciplinary perspective. At the same time, this thesis is also meant for politicians in transition countries who are involved in the design of industrial policy strategies. It is hoped that the present paper may offer them some helpful hints or at least encourage them in their endeavour to master the challenge of structural transformation.

Having defined the core goals of this paper and identified those whom it attempts to address we are now in the position to formulate the *working hypotheses* as follows:

1. The *theory of systemic transformation* has not yet satisfactorily dealt with the issue of industrial policy. This gap should be closed since industrial policy ought to be a key element of transition strategies.

2. The transition from a command economy to a market economy that is internationally competitive requires a *process of far reaching economic restructuring*.

3. The need for restructuring is especially pressing in the *industrial sector* where socialist production structures and state-ownership have to be overcome.

4. This enormous task and the as yet underdeveloped nature of emerging markets require an *active role of the state*.

5. For state action to be predictable, goals and the measures to attain them need to be explicitly outlined. An *industrial policy strategy* has to define the role of the state in this field.

6. Guidelines for the *design* of such a strategy can be eclectically derived from economic theory, from industrial policies of advanced industrial countries and, finally, from the early industrial policy experiences of leading countries in transition.

1.2 Delimitation and Presentation of Topic

Industrial policy in the transition from a command to a market economy being the topic of this thesis, we focus on formerly socialist countries which after 1989 embarked on a process of large-scale systemic reforms. Systemic transformation is an all-encompassing process and entails radical political, social, institutional and economic change. As will be explained below, industrial policy becomes relevant only when substantial progress with political and particularly economic reforms has been achieved.

We therefore focus on the leading countries in transition which are already well advanced with macroeconomic stabilisation. These post-socialist economies (PSEs) have entered the second phase of economic transition[4] where economic restructuring stands at the top of the policy agenda. The term 'leadership' in transition is understood here in a comprehensive sense including criteria such as macroeconomic stability, restructuring and privatisation, integration in international organisations, institutional reforms, the transition towards a pluralistic democracy, etc. In accordance with these criteria we concentrate on the *Czech Republic, Hungary, Poland* and *Slovenia*. This geographical delimitation, however, is not to say that the findings arrived at would be irrelevant for those countries which are still at an earlier stage in the transition process. They may learn from the experiences of the leading countries and so avoid costly mistakes. For practical reasons we consider developments in the countries under scrutiny until the end of 1997.

After having delimited the topic of our research we now delineate the construction of the analysis that follows. The remainder of the *introductory chapter* is devoted to the semantic clarification of the terms 'transition' and 'industrial policy' respectively. An explanation of these terms is prerequisite since they form the common basis from where to start our discussion.

Chapter two attempts to show the desirability of an explicitly formulated industrial policy strategy in the transition process from a command to a market economy. Economic aspects of the transition process form the core preoccupation of the first part of this chapter: we focus on two fundamental economic

---

[4]   For the delimitation of transition phases see Section 1.3.1.

problems, namely financial intermediation and corporate governance. The second part discusses political economy aspects which corroborate the notion of industrial policy in the transition process. The concluding section then joins together the economic and socio-political arguments presented in the chapter and develops as a first intermediary result a number of pointers for the design of industrial policies in transition economies.

The *third chapter* deals with the issue of industrial policy from a theoretical perspective. After having shown in the previous chapter that the concomitant challenges of structural reforms may require an active role of the state, we now turn to the question of whether economic theory does support such policy interventions. Since a coherent theory that would justify industrial policy interventions does not exist, we have to resort to an eclectic analysis of different theoretical approaches. In our discussion we make a distinction between orthodox and heterodox approaches. First we analyse their respective position with regard to policy interventions in general and industrial policy in particular. In addition the different theoretical approaches are examined with a view to the design of industrial policies and institutional arrangements for their implementation. Next the arguments brought forward by the different approaches are critically assessed against their applicability to the context of CEE transition. The concluding section, Synthesis II, gives an overview of our findings: we derive a number of lessons pertaining to the theoretical justification of industrial policy interventions, the design of respective policies, and institutional aspects.

Due to the lack of firm theoretical foundations for industrial policy in general, and for such policies in the context of CEE transition in particular, we examine in *chapter four* the industrial policy approaches of advanced industrial economies. As a first reference we analyse the industrial policy of the European Union (EU). This policy conception is important for our discussion for two reasons: first, the CEE transition economies under consideration have all applied for full EU membership and are eager to comply with the Union's body of regulations and directives (i.e., the so called 'acquis communautaire'). Second, with its Phare-programme the EU possesses an important leverage on the industrial policy design in PSEs. The second section of the chapter deals with the East Asian newly industrialising economies' (NIEs') industrial policy approach. Against the backdrop of unprecedented growth rates witnessed in the region over two decades and the concomitant rapid catching-up with advanced industrial countries, the NIEs' industrial policies are often considered as a prime example for successful policy interventions.[5] The concluding section combines the insights won into Synthesis III. For each of the analysed industrial policies we first derive a number of general lessons before we turn to lessons relating to particular policy areas and institutional arrangements respectively.

After having treated economic aspects of CEE transition economies in more abstract terms in chapter two, we next look at concrete country examples: the assessment of the industrial policies of the Czech Republic, Hungary, Poland and Slovenia forms the frame of *chapter five*. Beyond theoretical considerations and industrial policies conducted in advanced industrial economies, we examine the industrial 'Realpolitik' operated in these countries. For each of the PSEs under scrutiny we first sketch the development of the respective policies over time and analyse the official government stance regarding industrial policy. Next we delve into the different policy areas and instruments used. As Synthesis IV, the final section summarises and elaborates on the insights imparted by the country analysis. First we comment on *de-facto* industrial policies in transition economies before we extract pointers for the different policy domains. The chapter concludes with a discussion of institutional aspects.

In *chapter six* we amalgamate the hitherto eclectically derived lessons and insights into an industrial policy framework for countries in transition. We develop a number of guidelines that cover key aspects of industrial policy under the circumstances of market-oriented systemic transformation. Although our framework is supposed to be committal, in that it covers pivotal policy areas that apply to transition economies in general, it ought, nevertheless, to leave ample room for the idiosyncratic historical, social and economic characteristics of an individual country in transition. It is precisely in this respect that our framework differs from some blueprint or simplistic policy advice such as 'let the market play'. We neither intend to design a master plan that claims to offer the ultimate solution to the challenges faced by PSEs nor do we present some kind of magic formula. Both would necessarily fall short of reality. Our policy framework should rather be seen as a benchmark or a starting point for the design of industrial policy in the process of transition. Against this background we

---

[5]   This holds despite the recent severe financial market crises in East Asia.

first discuss the policy agenda. The section is structured as follows: first, the rationale for industrial policy in the transition from a command to a market economy are explained. Then we broach the policy foundations before the overall policy objectives are discussed. Finally we present those factors which constrain industrial policies in the transition process. In Section two are presented the different policy areas and instruments. We make a distinction between the short- and the medium- to long-term in order to reflect different priorities attributed to the respective policy areas. In the final part of this section we briefly comment on the long-term convergence of PSE industrial policies with the EU approach. The final section is devoted to institutional aspects. The principles that ought to guide industrial policy in the transition are elaborated. Then we explain the aspects that should be considered both for the design and implementation of industrial policy strategies.

In *chapter seven* we return to the working hypotheses that were formulated in the introductory chapter to see which of them have to be verified or falsified against the background of our analysis. Then we sketch an image of the state as it emerges from our industrial policy framework. Finally we raise a number of issues for further research.

1.3 Clarification of Basic Terms

In what follows we try to elucidate two basic terms which are central to our discussion, namely 'transition' and 'industrial policy'. Since for neither expression does there exist a generally accepted definition, it is vital that we determine their meanings before we embark on our analysis. All the more so since the semantic delimitation of both expressions largely lay out the horizon and scope of our research.

1.3.1 Transition

Due to its scope, depth and sequence the systemic change that started throughout Central and Eastern Europe towards the end of the 1980s and the beginning of the 1990s has no historical equivalent or precedent. The transition process affects virtually all aspects of a given socio-economic system with revolutionary change. A distinctive feature, moreover, is the sequence of CEE transition relating to the different speed of political and economic reforms: "[g]iven the largely simultaneous beginnings of the political and economic transitions, this asymmetry in speed produces a historically new sequence: mass democracy [...] first, and market capitalism later."[6]

The *start* of the transition process may be linked to the fall of the socialist power monopoly. Despite the abrupt and radically initiated systemic change, however, this starting point must not be seen as a *tabula rasa*, i.e., as an immediate complete break with the past. It is patently not the case that the new system will arise like a phoenix from the ashes of the socialist system. The legacies of the past substantially determine the feasible options for the transition and will continue to influence the political, economic and social development for a long time to come.

Thus the *initial conditions* of transition economies, despite country-specific differences[7], show various common characteristics which can be traced back to

---

[6]   Balcerowicz (1995), p. 146

[7]   These relate to whether or not reforms were initiated under socialist rule, the extent of macroeconomic imbalances, and other historical and cultural factors.

six basic features of the socialist system which we discuss in turn:[8] first, classical socialism[9] is essentially a *one-party system*. Regardless of whether *in concreto* there may exist other political factions it is the Communist party and its ideology that dominate. The indivisibility of power and the totalitarian nature of communist rule are thus distinctive characteristics of the socialist political system. Although the separation of powers formally exists, in reality it is the all-powerful party-dominated 'apparatus' (i.e., the set of agencies comprising party functionaries, the bureaucracy, the mass organisations, and the managers of state owned enterprises) which decides everything. The party as the "vanguard of the working class" and so ultimately of the whole society "stands *in loco parentis*: all other strata, groups, or individuals in society are children, wards whose minds must be made up for them by their individual adult guardians."[10] This paternalism penetrates many aspects of everyday life under the classical system and sways significantly the expectations that a post-socialist government sees itself confronted with by its electorate.

Second, given *socialist ownership* of the means of production firms are owned by the public. Nominally it is the state represented by the government who owns these enterprises. According to the official ideology it is the society as a whole who is ultimately the owner. In reality, however, the "depersonalizing of property becomes extreme [...] State property belongs to all and to none."[11] The right to use property, i.e., to effectively control it, is exercised by the party apparatus by means of mandatory planning.

The residual income of the state owned enterprise arbitrarily set by bureaucracy goes entirely to the state budget. The profit motive, which the Communist ideology contends to be one of the major evils of capitalism is completely eradicated. Deprived of its major driving force, entrepreneurship cannot foster profitability and innovation. Worse, since there is no clearly identifiable owner or group of owners who feel responsible for their property and could be held li-

---

[8] On the bases of the socialist system see Brown and Neuberger (1979), Kornai (1992) and Lavigne (1995).

[9] The term 'classical socialism' stands for the period between the consolidation of Communist political power and the onset of reform socialism.

[10] Kornai (1992), pp. 56ff.

[11] Kornai (1992), p. 75

able for it, the maintenance of plants is neglected and environmental damage caused by production is totally disregarded.

Third, socialist *economic planning* is the attempt to substitute centralised vertical bureaucratic control for the decentralised horizontal co-ordination of the market. Every aspect of the allocation and production process is subject to rigid plan commands. A national planning office faces the gigantic task of elaborating minutely detailed plans for the entire economy. Bureaucratic co-ordination of the economy eliminates freedom of enterprise, autonomous actors in a market environment and the competition between them. They are replaced by the centralisation of both decision making and information, by hierarchical dependence, the mechanism of bureaucratic control and execution of plan commands.

Fourth, an important element of socialist ideology is the promise based on the belief in the system's superiority to catch up with the developed capitalist economies and even to overtake them in terms of growth and living standards. A strategy of *forced growth* is pursued to achieve this goal. This strategy has two key elements: (1) a specific set of development priorities and, (2) extensive methods of growth.

The socialist development strategy is based on priorities which reflect the dominance of political and ideological criteria over economic considerations. Central planners prioritise in the first place the production of investment goods over consumers' goods. The industrial sector and in particular heavy industry enjoy priority at the expense of both services and agriculture.

To overcome economic backwardness methods of extensive growth are applied. This means that the exploitation of existing resources is virtually brought to the physical limit. The active labour force is increased to the point of full employment. Working hours and shifts are extended as much as is feasible. The boundaries of arable farmland are pushed outward and more and more reserves of raw materials are tapped. This strategy both reduces personal consumption and is costly in environmental terms. Early results are quite impressive: the economy grows at unprecedented rates. But soon growth rates start to stagnate and then even to decline. With the available technology and resources growth cannot be longer sustained.[12]

---

[12]   Lavigne (1995), p. 54

Taken together with the forced growth strategy ensues an unbalanced and disharmonious structure of the economy. The socialist planners' priorities lead to a 'hypertrophic' development of heavy industry.[13] Mining, steel industry, heavy machine building and chemical industry receive strong support. The gigantic industrial conglomerates and the almost total lack of small and medium enterprises, which contribute substantially to the flexibility and dynamism in a market economy, pose one of the most difficult problems for post-socialist managers of the transition process.

Fifth, the classical socialist economy is essentially *closed* revealing the primacy of domestic economic considerations over the exigencies of foreign trade. As with any other economic activity, the latter is subject to bureaucratic planning. The state holds a complete monopoly over trade which is controlled by its foreign trade organisations. Experience shows that within the framework of the Council of Mutual Economic Assistance (CMEA) – which accounted for 60-70 per cent of its members' trade volume – political considerations stood above economic reasons. The official ideology sought for bloc autarky among CMEA countries.

Sixth, as chronic economic problems become increasingly felt central planners resort to half-hearted and often ill-conceived *reforms*. The socialist economy seriously lags behind the capitalist West in terms of technical and economic development. Rampant shortage threatens to paralyse production and bears the risk of social unrest. To the leadership it becomes apparent that the strategy of forced growth has come to a dead end. The hitherto neglected sectors (i.e., housing, infrastructure, services, etc.) become a growing burden on the entire economy.

Public dissatisfaction increases and protest is voiced. Those in power realise that, given the enormous sacrifices demanded from their people by the methods of extensive growth, concessions to the consumer are inescapable to secure their political survival. Central planners, however, find themselves in a serious dilemma: the production of consumer goods must be urgently increased but at the same time the strategy of forced growth demands further investment. These difficulties are further compounded by the decentralisation of investment decisions

---

[13]   Lavigne (1995), p. 51

which contributes to the already critical overheating of investment demand. Foreign loans offer a seemingly convenient way out of this deadlock. However, it soon becomes clear that external borrowing leads only to a postponement of the problems to be tackled. The macroeconomic imbalance grows as foreign debts are accumulated.

Reform socialist systems tend to run a persistent budget deficit. Notwithstanding economic reforms, the state must heavily subsidise loss-making state-owned enterprises (SOEs) and the consumer goods sector. It even has to increase its financial support to promote exports: to generate hard currency central planners have to turn to price competition as a means to penetrate Western markets. Given decreasing tax revenues[14], on the one hand, and a rising fraction of available funds that has to be set aside for debt service, on the other, investment projects and expenditures both on the bureaucracy and the armed forces become a serious burden on the budget. As a last resort, monetary policy hitherto kept under strict bureaucratic control is made instrumental to the financing of the budget deficit and further fuels inflationary pressures.

In sum, on the eve of the breakdown of the socialist system the economy is in complete disarray. High inflationary pressures, persistent budget deficits and substantial external debt stand for severe macroeconomic imbalances. Huge industrial conglomerates being the result of excessive vertical and horizontal integration dominate the structure of the economy. The service sector is underdeveloped and the number of small- and medium-sized enterprises (SMEs) negligible. The infrastructure, above all telecommunication and transport, is in deplorable condition and environmental damage is vast.

After more than forty years of socialist rule individuals have little to no familiarity with the market economy. The implicit social pact guaranteeing employment, social security and personal safety from the 'cradle to the grave' in exchange for system conformity has left its traces on individual behaviour (i.e., lack of self-responsibility, unwillingness and incapability to take individual risks, etc.). It also created deep-seated expectations with regard to the role of the state. Firms have no experience of a competitive market environment and their

---

[14] This is a direct result of relaxed mandatory planning and controls over the economy. High inflation rates, in addition, substantially devalue actual tax yields.

management is largely unfamiliar with modern business practices. Production facilities and technologies are outdated. Productivity compared to advanced industrial economies is low.

When these starting conditions are confronted with the primary objectives of economic reforms commonly shared across CEECs, namely marketisation (i.e., replacing central planning for the decentralised co-ordination of economic activity through the market price mechanism), privatisation (i.e., the transfer of state-owned assets to the private sector) and finally the integration with the European Union, it emerges that the transition from a planned to a market-type economy requires fundamental systemic changes. The transition pertains not to economic phenomena alone: Table 1.1 on page 15 reveals that CEE transformation involves radical change at all systemic levels. Narrowing the analysis to economic aspects means not to comprehend the transition process in its totality. It, moreover, entails the risk of neglecting important reinforcing and countervailing interactions between the subsystems. To illustrate this contention one may think of the interplay between social, political and economic change. The restructuring and privatisation of SOEs result in rising unemployment figures. The unemployed, due to the democratisation of the political process, may express their complacency and exert considerable pressure on the government. Seeing its political survival endangered the latter may revise its reform course and slow down the pace of economic transition.

Table 1.1 distinguishes three *phases* of the transition process. It goes without saying that the stylised time phasing is a great conceptual simplification and as such cannot be more than a rough approximation to reality. This holds in particular for the given start and termination date of each phase. Bearing these caveats in mind the table shows that:

– the three phases overlap;

– systemic transformation describes a multi-track process of reforms at different pace;

– from a mixture of theory and experience a sequence of reform steps (e.g., macroeconomic stabilisation before privatisation and economic restructuring) may be derived.[15]

Each cell of Table 1.1 identifies the essential *key reform measures* for a given phase and subsystem. As to the *economic transformation* severe macro-economic imbalances require fast action up front. To unleash the emergence of markets both prices and foreign trade must be liberalised. At the heart of phase two stand the privatisation of shops and other smaller assets, the creation of an independent central bank and separate commercial banks, and the breaking-up of market dominating SOEs into smaller units. In phase three large SOEs are privatised and restructured. Moreover, a process of rapprochement with the EU is initiated ultimately aiming at full membership. The final destination of economic transformation is a market-type economy. The attribute 'market-type' indicates that the process is not deterministic, i.e., that it would head on to some pre-ordained type of market economy. The latter cannot be expected to develop into a copy of a Western market stereotype (i.e., along the lines of the Anglo-Saxon capitalism or the 'Rhenish model'[16]) but rather will evolve as an idiosyncratic mix of systemic features.

The emphasis of *institutional reforms* in the first phase lies on the introduction of a market-oriented legal system, particularly on private property rights and a commercial law. The adoption of a new constitution, tax reforms *inter alia* aimed at establishing a value added tax and building a social safety net are key issues of phase two. The reform of the state administration, i.e., the reorganisation of ministries and state agencies falls also in this period. The longest term objective of the institutional reform process is the redefinition of the role of the state vis-à-vis the economy and with regard to society at large. The overall goal of the institutional transition is it to lay the foundations for a democratic constitutional state.

---

[15] Gelb (1994), p. 114

[16] The 'Rhenish model' describes a bank-based financial system of the German and Swiss type. See Albert (1992). See also Csaba (1995), pp. 286ff. and Armstrong, Glyn and Harrison (1991).

Systemic transformation			
Subsystem / Phase **Economic**	**Institutional**	**Political**	**Social**
I Year: 1 - 5+	• Macroeconomic stabilisation • Liberalisation	• Market-oriented legal system	• Democratisation • 'Honeymoon' phase[17]	• Change of behavioural patterns
II Year: 3 - 10+	• Small-scale privatisation • Two-tier banking system • Demonopolisation	• New constitution • Tax reforms • Social-safety net • Reform of the administration	• Change of government • Decentralised regional self-government • Stable democratic coalition	• Emergence of winners and losers • Stratification
III Year: 5 - 15+	• Large-scale privatisation • Restructuring • Rapprochement with the EU	• Redefine the role of the state	• Formation of stable democratic parties • Establishment of democratic political culture	• Emergence of a middle class • Entrepreneurship
Aim	Market-type economy	Democratic constitutional state	Pluralistic democracy	Civil society

Note: The period given for each transition phase relates to the start of the transition process: e.g., phase I begins in the first year and ends approximately (+) in the fifth year after transition's inception.

Table 1.1: Matrix of transitional change

---

[17] The 'Honeymoon' phase in the transition process stands for a period of popular euphoria over the newly won freedom. This atmosphere may be seized by politicians to push through highly unpopular reform measures (e.g., the liberalisation of prices to neutralise the monetary overhang in the population). On this type of policy making under exceptional circumstances see Section 2.2 on the political economy of transition.

Phase one of the *political transformation* is primarily devoted to the democratisation of society. After more than four decades of autocratic communist rule initial change in politics is revolutionary. Virtually overnight the old regime is swept away by mass demonstrations. The euphoria over the newly won political freedom, together with not yet organised interest group representations, allows for a short period of almost unrestricted policy making by the initial democratic coalition for change. During this so-called 'honeymoon phase' radical and highly painful macroeconomic reforms can be pushed through in no time.[18] Phase two sees the political backlash against the initial leaders of the reform process since the deep transition recession dashes early hopes for a rapid improvement of general living conditions.[19] The decentralisation of political power and the emergence of a stable democratic coalition are further issues at this stage. The formation of stable democratic parties and the establishment of a democratic political culture are central to the final third phase. The political transformation is ultimately tending toward a pluralistic democracy.

The transition process entails also far-reaching *social change*. Economic, institutional and political reforms require a fast adaptation of individual behavioural patterns since the population has no practical experience of the market economy and knows little of its functional requirements.[20] The second phase of the social transition stands for the increased stratification. Whereas the socialist society was largely egalitarian, economic reforms lead to an increase in poverty and widening disparities in income. At this stage of the transition process a small class of 'nouveaux riches' is met by an increasing number of 'losers', i.e., people who lose their jobs and income due to the closure, privatisation and restructuring of SOEs. Only later, in phase three, do a middle class and genuine entrepreneurship emerge. The ultimate goal of social transformation is the civil society, i.e., a set of institutions that are neither governmental nor private enterprise, including political parties, voluntary organisations, religious groupings and la-

---

[18] The 'shock therapy' or big bang approach meant the almost immediate liberalisation of commodity prices and foreign trade. The sweeping price liberalisation led to a swift eradication of the monetary overhang in CEECs which was a result of forced savings under the previous system.

[19] On the interplay between economic and political transition see also Balcerowicz (1997) and Roland (1997).

[20] Lösch (1992a), p. 260

bour unions. The development of a genuine civil society may be considered as a key to the success or otherwise of political and economic transition.[21]

Compared to the temporal subdivision of the transition process it is even more difficult if not impossible to identify its *end*. First there would have to be agreement reached on observable parameters by which to measure the progress of systemic reforms. Such an attempt has been made by the European Bank for Reconstruction and Development (EBRD). In its Transition Reports the Bank has developed a classification system of transition indicators which are summarised in five groups: (1) enterprises (large-scale privatisation, small-scale privatisation, corporate governance and restructuring); (2) markets and trade (price liberalisation, trade and foreign exchange system, competition policy); (3) financial institutions (banking reform, securities markets and non-bank financial intermediation); (4) legal transition indicators; and finally (5) environmental reforms.[22] Although these indicators encapsulate important aspects of the transition they nevertheless capture only a fraction of the entire process and thus cannot give more than an incomplete image of it. Notwithstanding that EBRD transition indicators may be used for a rough comparison of achieved reforms across CEECs, their usefulness is qualified by the fact that they are ultimately based on the judgement of the Bank's Office of the Chief Economist. Against this background it emerges that the end of the transition can at best be determined by way of approximation: "The transformation process can [...] be considered complete only when the adjustment requirements caused by the old inefficient system and revealed by the new economic system have been fulfilled".[23]

The transition process as shown in Table 1.1 presents itself as a *complex multidimensional matrix of change* over time and across subsystems. It is important to keep this complexity and the various interrelations in mind before we turn to the issue of industrial policy in the transition. Although our topic primarily touches upon economic transformation, institutional, political and social aspects have also to be considered.

---

[21] On issues of civil society in the transition see EBRD (1997b), pp. 5f. and Dahrendorf (1990).

[22] See EBRD (1994), pp. 9ff. and EBRD (1997b), pp. 15ff.

[23] Lösch (1992a), p. 235

For the sake of clarity, we use in what follows a slightly different time phasing of the transition process as a point of reference. From an economic perspective we may distinguish the following three phases with the respective key reforms:

Phase I:	*macroeconomic stabilisation*
Phase II:	*large-scale privatisation and restructuring*
Phase III:	*consolidation of reforms and take off to sustained growth*

Box 1.1: The phases of economic transition and respective key reforms

The sequence can be summarised as stabilisation - transformation - consolidation. For our analysis, phases two and three are of primary interest since it is not until the second phase of the transition process that industrial policy becomes an issue. Three factors corroborate this contention: first, given acute and severe macroeconomic imbalances inherited from the socialist past at the inception of the transition process policy efforts are bundled at macroeconomic stabilisation. Low inflation, low fiscal deficits and sustainable current-account deficits in the balance of payments are all necessary conditions to spur private investment demand, productivity gains and economic recovery.

Second, to operate an industrial policy a stable system of state administration is prerequisite. The collapse of the socialist system meant that most of these institutions (i.e., ministries, government agencies, etc.) had to be either rebuilt from scratch or thoroughly reformed or even to be founded.

Third, industrial policy is primarily related to structural change.[24] This process cannot be expected to gain ground until the transfer of the means of production from the state to the private sector, i.e., until large-scale privatisation is well advanced and substantial progress towards macroeconomic stability has been achieved.

After having analysed the transition process in CEECs we are now in the position to define the term as follows:

---

[24]   Refer to the following Section 1.3.2 where we clarify the term 'industrial policy'.

Definition

The Central and Eastern European transition is a process of revolutionary and multi-track change permeating all levels of a given socio-economic system. In its course a post-socialist system is ultimately transformed into a market-type economy, a democratic constitutional state, a pluralistic democracy and civil society.

Box 1.2: Definition of transition

1.3.2 Industrial Policy

In the context of the present discussion the semantic delimitation of industrial policy is very important. In the sometimes fiercely led discussion on the subject matter this central question is all too often either not addressed satisfactorily or even left out altogether. What is industrial policy all about? This section tries to answer this question. The general definition of industrial policy elaborated here, however, has to be seen only as a *first step* in an attempt to come to terms with the issue at hand. Since this paper is about the role of industrial policy in the process of transition from a planned to a market economic system, later chapters refine and adapt the definition to the present discussion.

Yet, before we turn to the issue of industrial policy, we ought briefly to clarify what is understood by the term *industry* in the present paper. In contrast to the Anglo-Saxon area, where the term is used in a broader sense and encompasses *inter alia* the service, banking and transport industries, we more narrowly define industry as it is commonly referred to in the German language area:

Definition

The term industry primarily stands for manufacturing industries (i.e., industry in the narrow sense) and also subsumes mining and energy industries.

Box 1.3: Definition of industry

The search for a clear-cut definition of industrial policy in the relevant literature is frustrated quite quickly. The number of different authors is mirrored by the variety of their definitions of industrial policy. In addition, the standard reference book in economics the *New Palgrave Dictionary of Economics* does not even make an attempt to come to grips with the concept of industrial policy. One looks in vain for an entry on this topic.

Against this backdrop, individual authors have the freedom to choose or fabricate a definition of industrial policy according to the needs of their respective discussion. In what follows the issue of industrial policy is first situated within the field of economics. This helps the general understanding in that it gives initial insights into what industrial policy is about. Next, the desirable properties which the definition of industrial policy should have for the present purpose are elaborated. Having defined the terms industry and industrial policy we then relate industrial policy to other areas of economic policy. Next, the approaches to industrial policy are presented and the different orientations they can take are discussed. To conclude this section we elaborate a taxonomy of industrial policy bringing together policy approaches and policy orientation.

Within economic theory the discussion of industrial policy belongs to the sphere of microeconomics and here to the field of industrial economics. The latter applies microeconomic theory to the analysis of firms, markets and industries.[25] Industrial economics has two branches. The first, *industrial organisation*, is mainly concerned with the structure of industries at a particular point of time. *Industrial dynamics*, the second branch, focuses on the development of industries over time. Its main concern is *structural change*. It analyses the dynamics of supply, the change of interdependence between firms over time, the determinants of technological change and factors conducive to technological progress. As against industrial organisation, the perspective of the investigation widens because industrial dynamics examines the adjustment of the economy to changing micro- and macroeconomic circumstances both at a domestic as well as an international level. It is here where the theoretical discussion of industrial policy has to be located (see Figure 1.1).

---

[25] See Ferguson and Ferguson (1994), pp. 1ff.

Given the spectrum of definitions of industrial policy, the research objective of this paper has to be kept in mind before making a choice or formulating yet another definition of the term. Since it is the declared goal of this paper to examine the role of industrial policy in the process of transition from a planned to a market economic system, it seems reasonable to start with a more general interpretation of the term. The following discussion thus allows the narrowing of this circumscription to a definition which, at the end of the first part of this paper, establishes the meaning of industrial policy in Central and Eastern European transition economies.

Which then are the desirable properties of this first definition? To begin with, as has just been said, it should not be too narrow. Industrial policy can be understood as industry related government action which is an integral part of an overall industrial policy strategy. The problem with this interpretation at this stage of our discussion is that it *a priori* precludes the analysis of a variety of industrial policy measures which form part and parcel of real world economic policy making. This applies in particular to the phenomenon of *de facto* industrial policy, an important aspect of our discussion. In reality, declared policy strategies (e.g., a complete industrial policy abstinence) tend ultimately not to coincide with enacted policy measures. Everyday life of economic policy making, and this holds especially for industrial policy, is often dominated by *ad hoc* measures.

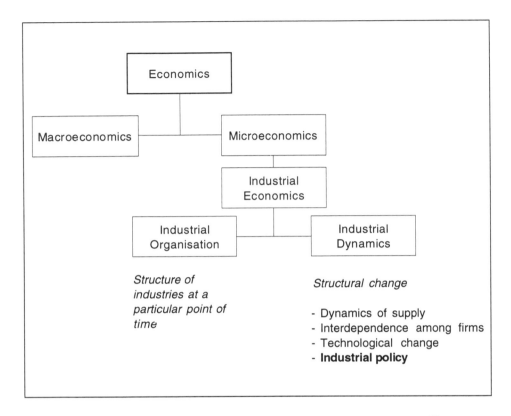

Figure 1.1: The location of industrial policy within economic theory[26]

The circumscription of industrial policy should moreover be manageable or in other words not be too detailed. Brabant (1993) gives a very minute description of his industrial policy concept:

> A strategy formulated, and possibly initiated, by the state (or on its behalf) that encompasses mechanisms by which the actions of various layers of decision making about resource allocation in an economy can be coordinated, monitored, evaluated, and fine-tuned with a view to influencing, by direct or indirect means, static resource allocation in and among economic sectors and especially the pace and composition of dynamic economic expansion through the selective commitment of resources to particular activities with a view to facilitating, accelerating, or retrenching their growth path.[27]

---

[26] Our representation based on Ferguson and Ferguson (1994), pp. 1ff.

[27] Brabant (1993), pp. 16f.

This definition certainly points to a number of important aspects of industrial policy. It is, however, long-winded and for the present purpose not very helpful. Such a detailed definition is even counterproductive at this juncture because again it does not leave enough room for discussion.

In addition, the definition should not yet lay down any specific task and/or objectives of industrial policy. A definition which establishes that the objective of modernising production technology is central to industrial policy obviously does not leave any room for discussing industry-relevant government initiatives aiming at safeguarding jobs. This is, however, a prominent motive for industrial policy interventions.

Finally, neither should the definition be too wide. In a most general way industrial policy can be interpreted as "any policy which affects industrial activity".[28] Put this way, industrial policy encompasses the whole range of economic policies. The two, indeed, overlap in many ways and it may be sometimes difficult to draw an exact line between them. However, to treat industrial policy and economic policy as synonyms goes too far. Such a definition is obviously not very fruitful.

Against this background as a starting point the following definition seems to be adequate:

Definition

Industrial policy embodies measures formulated and implemented by the state which are targeted at industry to achieve given sector specific objectives.

Box 1.4: Definition of industrial policy I

This approach to industrial policy is open enough to allow for a whole range of government interventions whether they be part of an overall coherent policy strategy or are makeshift. The given definition, furthermore, determines industrial policy objectives only insofar as they must be sector specific. Under the condition that they are industry specific, the above formulation leaves room for

---

[28]   Hare (1995), p. 6

a variety of objectives whether they are primarily socially motivated or whether they aim at an industry-wide productivity increase.

As already has been pointed out, the dividing line between industrial policy and other areas of economic policy is often blurred. Industrial policy as a mesopolicy (i.e., it deals with industries, that is to say with the economy at a 'medium' level of aggregation[29]) is interrelated and overlap with other policies in various ways. Industrial policy applies a number of instruments which taken alone would fall into another policy area. Thus, as an example, the setting-up of trade barriers to protect domestic industry from foreign competition makes instrumental trade policy in order to achieve industry specific goals. This example, together with our definition of industrial policy, make it clear that it is ultimately *the motivation behind the use of a policy instrument* which decides whether or not to classify a given policy (strategy) as industrial policy. Figure 1.2 (see next page) shows the major policy areas with which industrial policy is interrelated.

Based on the intensity of state intervention, four different *approaches to industrial policy* can be distinguished: (1) laissez-faire, (2) the supportive approach, (3) the active approach, and (4) the planning approach. Pivotal to the *laissez-faire approach* is a strong trust in the market mechanism. The free flow of information is the best guarantor for an optimal co-ordination of economic activity. As an arbitrator of desirable economic developments the market is doing far better than any government agency. Against this backdrop industrial policy has no role at all to play. All that remains for the state to do is to allow the natural course of market forces to evolve unrestrainedly and consequently to see to a competitive environment.

The *supportive approach*, while still basically convinced of the underlying superiority of market forces, recognises the existence of information imperfections and transaction costs. Thus, given unfavourable external constraints, government interventions to foster economic change (e.g., measures to improve the allocation and the enforcement of property rights) may be justifiable, even if this means that only second-best solutions may be achieved.

---

[29] Elsner and Huffschmid (1994), p. 343

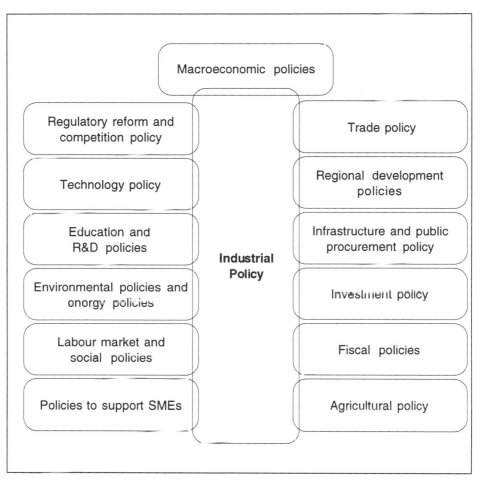

Figure 1.2: Industrial policy and overlapping policy areas[30]

The *active approach* to industrial policy differs crucially from the previous two in that the co-ordination mechanism of the market is often superseded by government decisions. Wider and more direct involvement in the industrial sector is supported. The policy instruments typically applied under this approach range from selective financial support for individual companies to promote restructuring to the protection from foreign competition by tariff and non-tariff barriers. At the same time, however, steps would be taken to nurture domestic competition.

---

[30] Based on Holzem (1995), p. 16

Yet a more extreme version is the *planning approach*. This approach is founded on the rationale that welfare can be enhanced through central planning. It is argued that policy makers have superior economy-wide information and that the answer to the co-ordination problem is the solution of a number of algorithms. Industrial policy interventions are consequently far-reaching and are much more comprehensive than under the active approach. The planning approach is an attempt to replace the market mechanism by the centralised decision making of some planning agency.

From what just has been said there emerges a *basic dichotomy* between the advocacy of non-interference (i.e., the laissez-faire and supportive approaches) on the one hand, and the advocacy of a large element of government intervention (i.e., active and planning approach) on the other. These varying attitudes to industrial policy are determined by the belief or otherwise in the efficiency of markets and in the ability of governments to intervene successfully:

> The greater the belief in the efficacy of the market and in the impotence of government agencies, the greater the tendency to reject intervention and to favour an essentially 'hands off' industrial policy. [...] The choice between the laissez-faire-supportive approaches and the active-planning approaches therefore turns on views as to which uses information more efficiently, state agencies or the market.[31]

Depending on its orientation, an industrial policy can have two basic *policy forms*: a horizontal (also indirect or neutral) and a vertical (also direct or proactive) industrial policy. A *horizontal industrial policy* is framework-oriented: leaving the specific intra- and inter-industry developments to the market it seeks to improve the framework within which economic agents operate, i.e., to improve the functioning of the market process itself. The laissez-faire and the supportive approaches to industrial policy fall into this category. Horizontal industrial policies are now clearly *en vogue* and propagated by the OECD:

> The appropriate policies are, therefore, those that encourage technological innovation and diffusion, and increase productivity and investment, including in infrastructure. These largely entail *horizontal policies* to ensure a stable macroeconomic environment, a realistic exchange rate, a sound education and

---

[31]   Ferguson and Ferguson (1994), p. 150

training system, a solid technological and scientific establishment, and favourable treatment of firms' R&D.[32]

A *vertical industrial policy*, in contrast, aims at individual industries or at the structure of the entire industrial sector. Taking up a proactive stance, a government directly interferes with the market and attempts to partially or even, as in the case of the planning approach, to completely replace its mechanism. With regard to structural change, a distinction has to be made between an accelerative and decelerative vertical industrial policy. *Accelerative* policies try to speed up the process of structural change by providing financial support to the most promising firms. Some government agencies take the initiative and attempt to identify those companies or industrial sectors (so called 'sunrise industries') on which according to their estimates the future competitive advantage of the economy will rest. Once these 'winners are picked' their development is fostered by a variety of means, ranging from credits on preferential terms to public procurement measures.

Decelerative industrial policies, on the other hand, try to slow down or even suppress structural change. By supporting 'sunset industries' and thereby keeping them (temporarily) alive, governments try to avert their falling prey to the evolutionary selection of the market. The motives behind such policies can be various. Whereas the German shipbuilding industry was rescued primarily on social grounds, US firms in the aircraft industry were saved from collapse because they were of 'strategic national interest'. These two examples indicate that decelerative industrial policies are particularly sensitive to the exertion of influence by well organised interest groups (i.e., unions in the case of Germany and industry associations in the US). Decelerative industrial policy can take two forms: in the case of a *conservation policy* structural change is impeded. Industries, which would not survive without public support, are kept afloat. Confronted with rapid structural change governments may also seek to cushion its negative effects by phasing the closure of companies which face bankruptcy. This *phased closure* means giving companies some temporary breathing space to allow for retraining of their staff and the establishing of new firms in the region. The active and the planning approach are both primarily vertically oriented industrial policies.

---

[32] OECD (1995), p. 19

Figure 1.3 brings the policy approaches and their orientation together and summarises our discussion. The bottom shaded area should not be misinterpreted in the sense that in practice there exist four always clearly separable approaches to industrial policy. There is rather a *continuum* of industrial policy approaches between laissez-faire and planning, spanning from purely market-driven change at one extreme to a complete replacement of the market mechanism by the state at the other. Moreover, the distinction between the horizontal and the vertical policy orientation is merely analytical since in reality an industrial policy strategy usually includes a *combination* of horizontal and vertical policy instruments.

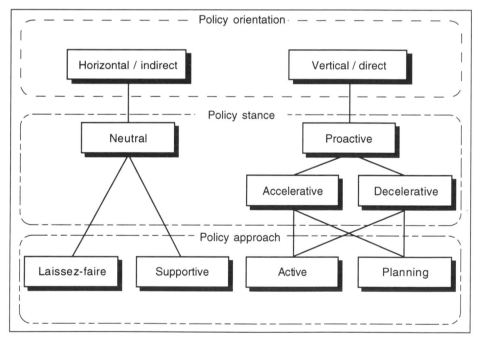

Figure 1.3: Taxonomy of industrial policy

2 The Transition to a Market Economy

The goal of this chapter is to show the desirability of a coherent industrial policy strategy for countries in transition from a command to a market economy system. To this end, we first elaborate on economic problems endemic to the second phase of the transition process. At the heart stand fundamental stock-flow problems which obstruct the process of Schumpeterian creative destruction. We focus our discussion on the two central aspects, namely on the deficient financial intermediation and corporate governance problems.

In Section 2.2 we broaden the scope of our analysis by investigating political-economy aspects of systemic transformation. Issues of distributional justness have long been neglected by the academic debate of the transition process. Hitherto its primary concern focused on issues of allocative efficiency. Our analysis of socio-political developments in Central and Eastern European countries (CEECs) reveals, however, that sustained political stability as a *conditio sine qua non* for the success or otherwise of systemic transformation should be made a corner-stone of an overall industrial policy strategy.

Synthesising the economic and the political-economy arguments discussed in this chapter, the concluding Section 2.3 vindicates the notion of industrial policy in the process of Central and Eastern European (CEE) transition. As a first intermediate result we outline an industrial policy framework for countries in transition.

2.1 The Economics of Transition

The task in hand in post-socialist economies is vast: The transition from a planned economy to a market economic system requires far-reaching and fundamental change both at micro and at macro levels. Individual behavioural patterns have to be adapted to the new economic regime. Existing institutions must be adjusted to the market environment and others have to be brought into being. The role of the state and its policies have to be redefined. The direct control of central planners is replaced by the indirect co-ordination of the market mechanism.

From an economic perspective, the objectives of reforms in Eastern Europe can be reduced to marketisation and privatisation. *Marketisation* refers to the change in the allocation mechanism from the politico-bureaucratic co-ordination of economic activity to the price-led allocation of resources in a market environment. A key feature of the transition from a planned to a market economy is *privatisation*. The latter has to be interpreted not only in terms of pure ownership transfers but also encompasses, above all, the restructuring of state-owned enterprises (SOEs), i.e., the prerequisite changes in management methods, incentive systems, wage setting, scope of vertical and horizontal integration, financial structures, physical and human capital, etc.[33]

Reforms in the leading post-socialist economies (PSEs) are now well under way. The *first stage* of the transition process, *macroeconomic stabilisation*, has already been accomplished to a great extent. The liberalisation of prices and trade meant that shortages, a hallmark of the planned economy, vanished virtually overnight. Despite continuous upward pressure on both consumer and producer prices (wage-price spiral, product market monopolies, etc.), inflation could be contained yet still stands at a two-digit level. Beyond macrostabilisation, an impressive reorientation of trade has been achieved after the collapse of the Council of Mutual Economic Assistance (CMEA) system. Foreign direct investment and private commercial activity, above all small-scale trade and distribution, have grown steadily although their growth rates have not yet met the initial (over-) optimistic expectations. A key element of systemic transformation, legal and regulatory reforms, have been initiated and in some areas considerable progress has already been made.

Despite the advances realised in the first phase, a plethora of challenges remain to be tackled in the *second stage of transition*. All Eastern European PSEs have been hit by sharp declines in measured output (over 20 per cent in 1991 for the better performers), particularly in industrial production.[34] The collapse of

---

[33] Aghion and Stern (1994), p. 4

[34] EBRD (1995); On the alleged causes for the transition recession see e.g., Blejer, Calvo, Coricelli and Gelb (1993) and Kornai (1994).

CMEA trade and the inflow of imports from Western markets have certainly contributed to this decline.[35] Governments have run into serious *fiscal difficulties*. Tax receipts have experienced a sharp decline due, above all, to falling profits of SOEs. Privatisation revenues which turn out to be much smaller than expected, tax concessions to the private sector and widespread tax evasion further exacerbate the situation. On the other hand, the support for declining (state) sectors, the recapitalisation of the banking sector and the social safety net, to name but a few, put a great strain on expenditures. Large-scale privatisation has proceeded only slowly and enterprise restructuring has so far been much too sluggish to support a speedy transformation. Against this backdrop, it becomes clear that the rapidly rising unemployment will pose a very serious long-term problem to the reform process.[36]

Given the level of already achieved macrostabilisation, the *restructuring of enterprises and the completion of large-scale privatisation form the core preoccupation of the second stage* of the transformation. At the heart of this restructuring process stands what Landesmann labelled the *fundamental stock-flow problem*[37] of transition or – as Schumpeter called it – a process of *creative destruction*.[38] As a result of the past allocation mechanism of central planning, the stock of existing resources is stuck in the existing physical and human capital of SOEs. Notwithstanding the growing shares in GDP and in overall employment of the private sector (see Table 2.1), these enterprises continue to contribute substantially to gross domestic product and are still among the biggest employers in the region. The employed resources are to a large extent misallocated and the assets obsolete. The application of strict market criteria would lead to a dramatic closure of plants and enterprises with the concomitant large-scale shedding of workers in a very short time. The 'flow' part of the stock-flow problem relates to the building-up of new capacities and skills as well as to the reallocation of those resources allocated in the state sector which could be made vi-

---

[35] The issue is still subject to an ongoing debate in the transition literature. A detailed discussion of this topic, however, is not within the compass of this thesis.

[36] Gelb (1994), pp. 116ff.

[37] See Abel and Landesmann (1994), Landesmann (1993), Landesmann and Székely (1995), and in particular Landesmann and Ábel (1995).

[38] Schumpeter (1943)

able in a market environment. Against this background it becomes clear that the surmounting of the stock-flow problem will be a time-consuming process and that, for a transition strategy to be socially and politically sustainable, 'stocks' have to be kept in operation which under strict market criteria would not be viable.

Which then are the obstacles that obstruct the process of restructuring and compound the stock-flow problem? The stumbling blocks that hinder the progress of transition can be reduced to two interrelated areas: financial markets and corporate governance problems. In what follows both are discussed in turn.

Private sector share (%)	in GDP	in employment
• Bulgaria	40.2	34.7
• Croatia	44.9	46.6
• Czech Republic	56.3	n.a.
• Hungary	n.a.	n.a.
• Poland	56.0	59.8
• Romania	35.0	51.4
• Slovak Republic	43.8	31.9
• Slovenia	n.a.	n.a.

Source: EBRD (1995), Table 1, p. 28

Table 2.1: Private sector share in GDP and employment in Eastern Europe, 1994

2.1.1 Financial Intermediation

To overcome the stock-flow problem and to effectively restructure the economy vast investment finance is prerequisite. To attain medium- to long-term growth rates of 5 per cent, or higher, investment finance of about 20 per cent of GDP is required.[39] In this respect financial markets are paramount for the successful completion of the second transition phase. As a transmission mechanism financial intermediation has to efficiently mobilise and allocate investment capital in

---

[39] EBRD (1995), p. 5

the economy. The underdeveloped nature and the imperfect functioning of the financial system in PSEs therefore has to be seen as a major obstacle to the efficient allocation of resources, the inflow of foreign capital and rapid growth.

Commercial banks are the key to well-functioning financial markets. In Eastern European PSEs the banking sector is characterised by high concentration and little foreign competition (see Table 2.2). A highly concentrated banking sector does not by itself cause concern. On the contrary, the potential advantage of a small number of big players becomes apparent in the German-Japanese type of banking system. However, if one considers the legacies of the socialist monobank system which are persistently prevailing in and dominating commercial banks in PSEs the matter is an altogether different one.

Shares (%) of total banking assets held by top five banks, by ownership in 1994:			
	State	Former state (privatised)	Private banks	Total
• Belarus	0	54	21	75
• Czech Republic	0	65	0	65
• Hungary	49	8	6	63
• Latvia	6	0	21	27
• Poland	66	0	0	66
• Romania	74	0	0	74
• Russia	21	6	6	33
• Slovak Republic	36	40	3	79
• Slovenia	48	22	0	70
• Ukraine	11	59	0	70

Source: EBRD (1995), Table 10.2, p. 161

Table 2.2: Concentration of banking sector in selected countries in transition

At the outset of the reform process commercial banks in Eastern Europe continued their symbiotic relationship with large SOEs. "This meant not only that they tended to follow the old lending patterns, but also that their managers viewed their interests as analogous with those of the *nomenklatura* managers of the industrial firms." [40] The continuation of this collusive behaviour becomes evident once the amount of bad debt banks had accumulated is taken into consideration. The fate of SOEs and commercial banks became inevitably interconnected. Bank managers had every incentive to recycle SOE debts. As long as (privatised) state banks are not restructured and their books cleaned of bad loans this lending pattern can be expected to be preserved.

The *malfunctioning of credit allocation* in PSEs has two major implications both detrimental to the progress of transition. First, banks become the main substitute for the previous subsidies under central planning. The budget constraint of SOEs essentially continues to be soft.[41] Enterprise managers have little incentive to use resources efficiently and to restructure their business. Second, banks can be expected to try to recapitalise themselves by extending interest spreads and thus pushing up real interest rates.

Underdeveloped lending expertise and the problem of business evaluation under the circumstances of transition further compound the situation. Given little experience with modern market accounting methods, the lack of historical enterprise track records and inter-enterprise debts, the evaluation of the worth and performance of business often transcend the abilities of analysts and accountants.[42,43] In their lending practice banks thus tend to favour large SOEs due to their large fixed assets which can serve as collateral. In so doing, they have in mind the idea that these companies are simply too big to fail and that, in other words, the state would have to bail out these firms in the case of failure. The

---

[40] Frydman and Rapaczynski (1994), p. 130

[41] The term 'soft budget constraints' goes back to János Kornai (1986). Under classical socialism the budget constraints of SOEs were not binding, i.e., these firms when faced with liquidity problems could always count on the state for additional fresh capital. With the start of systemic transformation, (state) banks stepped in and provided ailing, state-owned enterprises with new finance. This meant that the budget constraints of state firms, even after the beginning of economic reforms, remained soft. Soft budget constraints entail serious moral hazard problems since enterprise management has no incentive whatsoever to increase business performance.

[42] Frydman and Rapaczynski (1994), pp. 130ff.

[43] Interenterprise debts were accumulated when new governments cut subsidies and enterprises short of liquidity stopped paying their suppliers. This makes the evaluation of SOEs even more difficult since intercompany debts came to constitute a substantial portion of the assets of most state enterprises.

continued imprudent lending and adverse selection of customers poses a substantial threat to the stability of the entire financial system of transition economies.

Against the backdrop of SOEs facing the likely prospect of liquidation and claiming the major share of the loan market *new business*, particularly small and medium enterprises, is starved of credit. Banks are very strict with new companies in terms of interest rates and collateral requirements. Private entrepreneurs are deterred from profitable investment since, regardless of their long-term creditworthiness, they find it next to impossible to obtain the much needed financial means. This *credit squeeze* substantially exacerbates the flow problem of transition. The importance of small- and medium-sized enterprises (SMEs) for economic development cannot be overstated: the dynamic sector of SMEs is the competitive backbone of every advanced industrialised economy. Thus, to further stimulate the development of the private sector and to enter on a path of sustainable growth at an adequate pace, it is vital for countries in transition to grant SMEs access to investment finance and to foster their formation.

Given the credit misallocation in the loan market, the question of alternative sources for enterprise investment becomes all the more pressing. For at least three reasons *domestic savings* have yet played but a minor role: first, the monetary overhang that existed as a result of forced savings under central planning at the outset of the transition was neutralised by the early price and currency reforms that were initiated in an attempt to stabilise the macroeconomy. Second, throughout Eastern Europe a strong tendency towards 'consumerism' can be observed. After forty years of shortage economy[44] people spend a large fraction of their disposable incomes and savings on Western consumer goods. Third, rising consumer prices together with falling average real wages means that the fraction of savings in national income will remain low for several years to come. Clearly this situation must change in the future. For the mobilisation of savings an efficiently functioning financial intermediation will be crucial.

Another potential source of finance is *foreign direct investment* (FDI). FDI has a number of advantages in addition to the needed financial means from which

---

[44] On the notion of the 'shortage economy' see Kornai (1980) and Kornai (1995).

enterprises in PSEs can greatly benefit: improved monitoring of management, transfer of production skills and management know-how, access to Western markets, etc. On the other hand, the involvement of foreign investors can also turn out to be problematic when xenophobic sentiments are stirred up. Except for Hungary, the inflow of foreign investment into the region has so far remained very low: "In 1994, the total FDI into eastern Europe, the Baltics and the CIS, a region with a population of 400 million, was similar to that into Malaysia with a population of 19 million."[45]

The reasons for the *reluctance of foreign investors* are various: first, uncertainty caused by the volatile macroeconomic environment and political risks and rudimentary markets resulting in high transaction costs work to the detriment of FDI. Second, when change is as drastic as in transition economies coordination failures emerge. Any productive activity is part of a network of suppliers and clients and interlinked with the service of utilities, distribution systems, business services, infrastructure and so on. An investment which has a high potential may then be postponed for the lack of complementary investment and for the fear of being left out in isolation.[46] Third, when the financial system is dysfunctional and capital markets are shallow, the reallocation of investible funds across sectors to the highest yielding uses is prevented. This makes investment opportunities in PSEs less attractive. Finally, despite the acknowledged importance of FDI, unnecessary or arbitrary government regulations (e.g., limiting foreign majority shareholdership to certain sectors or even preventing them altogether) and the tax system often hinder the inflow of foreign capital. From what has been said, it emanates that as long as these obstacles remain untackled no major increase in FDI is to be expected; indeed, as long as no efficiently operating financial system is in place external funds will not improve the situation:

> [U]nless domestic accumulation is secured, and unless the domestic system of intermediation allows for scarce resources to be allocated efficiently, no amount of external financing will be of much help: indeed, the more it is forthcoming, the more it will be wasted.[47]

---

[45] EBRD (1995), p. 6

[46] EBRD (1995), p. 86

[47] Csaba (1995), p. 109

Against this background, enterprises in PSEs have to resort to *internal financing* as the primary source for their investment. As a consequence, investment activity is both determined and constrained by the amount of retained earnings. It goes without saying that this constitutes a major impediment to economic growth and the recovery of PSEs. From our discussion it thus emerges that the dysfunctional financial intermediation in PSEs is a major stumbling block for the reform process in Eastern Europe. It adds substantially to the fundamental stock-flow problem of transition:

> Without clean portfolios and adequate capital, banks do not face the appropriate incentives to operate prudently in competitive financial markets, and cannot be privatized. On the other hand, a lack of effective financial markets and institutions while state enterprises are being restructured will impede the potentially faster emergence of private business.[48]

2.1.2 Corporate Governance

The issue of corporate governance is the second pivotal factor compounding the stock-flow problem. Corporate governance refers to arrangements by which enterprise owners (e.g., shareholders) monitor the management so that it acts in accordance with the proprietors' interests. *Agency problems* of this kind are also endemic to advanced market economies.[49] They are, however, particularly acute in transition economies and constitute a major obstacle to the successful restructuring of the remaining SOEs. In what follows, the reasons for the severe corporate governance problems encountered in PSEs are elucidated.[50]

The *state* as the *de iure* owner of SOEs has neither the expertise nor the necessary manpower to control enterprise management and is consequently more of a *de facto* absentee owner.[51] Also, since the short-run social costs of bankruptcy enforcement and liquidation of SOEs are likely to be much higher than the revenues derived from the sale of public assets, governments have no incentive

---

[48] Gelb (1994), p. 126

[49] Formal study of agency problems began with Arrow, Ross, Stiglitz, Grossman and Hart, and others. See, e.g., Grossman and Hart (1988) and Ross (1973).

[50] On the issue of needed corporate governance mechanisms see also Frydman, Phelps, Rapaczynski and Shleifer (1993).

[51] Aghion, Blanchard and Burgess (1993), p. 3 and Aghion, Blanchard and Burgess (1994).

to monitor the management of public enterprises.[52] This situation puts SOE managers in a potentially powerful position because they possess superior insider knowledge of 'their' firms and because, under the previous system, they already enjoyed quite a considerable autonomy in their decision making despite central planning. The shortage economy, moreover, let managers adopt a strategy of keeping information on economic performance from the planning administration and gave rise to widespread shirking and illicit appropriation of state property. Thus old habits are preserved and continue to dominate, as yet another legacy of the past, current behaviour. Information asymmetries standing at the heart of every agency problem, thus, are even more accentuated under the conditions prevailing in Eastern Europe.

The lack of effective outside control creates an *incentive structure for SOE managers* which is highly detrimental to the restructuring process. Given that their large idiosyncratic knowledge in an underdeveloped and depressed labour market yields only a low outside wage, they act in a very short-term and risk averse way. This is even more the case since the risks associated with restructuring are particularly high in an unstable macroeconomic environment prevalent in transition economies. The situation is further aggravated because efficiency-improving measures are met by costly opposition from workers and since there is no reward for managers when they adopt them. Thus the temptation to 'play safe' and to avoid enterprise restructuring altogether by adopting muddling-through strategies is great, even if this leads to the slow erosion of the firms' physical and human capital.[53] Against this backdrop and because misbehaviour is not sanctioned "a perverse incentive structure results in which economic actors play end games, merely looking at maximising the chances of immediate survival."[54]

A key feature of the Eastern European transition is the strong *influence of workers* on the corporate decision making process. In this context a clear distinction has to be made: it is one thing if profit-sharing schemes are in place in which workers are taking part. Such arrangements may definitely affect the average employee's performance in a positive way. It is, however, an altogether

---

[52]   Raiser (1993), pp. 177ff.

[53]   Carlin, Reenen and Wolfe (1994), p. 62

[54]   Raiser (1993), p. 176

different matter if workers under the prevailing circumstances have a dominant say in the enterprise management. The strong position of labour in the governance structure of enterprises qualifies managerial power to a large extent. There exists by now general agreement that an influence of workers on management in the process of transition beyond the German-type factory committee "creates a very powerful conflict with the goals of postcommunist restructuring."[55] The restructuring of SOEs requires massive increases in productivity. Since most state enterprises are overstaffed this entails massive lay-offs. It is easy to see that this is diametrically opposed to the interests of workers. Their primary goal is the maintenance of employment directly followed by the interest in rising real wages.

The workers' attitude towards their workplace is a result of a peculiar 'social contract' that was struck under socialism: "[i]ts main features were a trade-off between political passivity and the security of every single work-place, low rates of inflation, and, last but not least, very lax labour discipline for most of the masses."[56] Consequently, employees perceive their jobs as an acquired right largely independent of their actual work performance. The tendency of securing jobs at all costs and despite urgent adjustment needs is reinforced by the underdeveloped *labour markets* and the nature of unemployment in transition economies. The deficient institutional infrastructure of labour markets makes an assessment of the actual situation a tricky task, let alone the formulation and implementation of labour-market policies. Even with statistical data leaving much to be desired in terms of reliability, early available empirical evidence suggests that a stagnant pool of unemployed is a distinctive characteristic of PSEs.[57] The low 'turnover' in labour markets, i.e., the fact that those losing their jobs face the high likeliness of becoming the chronic unemployed substantially increases the social, economic and psychological costs of joblessness. This further intensifies the resistance of workers to restructuring plans.[58]

---

[55] Frydman and Rapaczynski (1994), p. 147

[56] Csaba (1995), p. 61

[57] See Carlin, Reenen and Wolfe (1994), pp. 63ff. and Brabant (1996), pp. 37ff.

[58] On the interrelations between unemployment, restructuring and the pace of transition see also Commander and Tolstopiatenko (1997).

It turns out that SOE management and workers do indeed have common inter-ests. Both resist change and restructuring. Due to the lack of effective owner-ship control and their highly uncertain personal future, managers have an extremely short-term time horizon and adopt a wait-and-see strategy. To pre-vent disruptive conflicts with employees their demands for wage increases are met. The collusion between management and workers means not only that re-structuring is not initiated but, more importantly, entails a rapid erosion of the firm's remaining assets and skill base. Available scarce funds instead of being invested are used to pay the salaries of the firm's overstaffed workforce. Thus, *insider control* constitutes a major impediment to economic reforms in the transition process.[59]

This gives rise to the question of how then could the management of SOEs be better monitored and their eventual misbehaviour be effectively sanctioned. In other words, how can the deadlock with regard to restructuring created by in-sider control be surmounted and corporate governance of state enterprises be improved. Under the prevailing conditions, the *creditors of SOEs* cannot be ex-pected to discipline management. The state, as has already been said, has nei-ther the prerequisite skills and manpower nor an incentive to monitor economic activities in SOEs more closely. Banks, on the other hand, as was shown in the previous section are the main ally of SOEs in resisting change:

> [They] have inherited the *modus operandi* of their communist predecessors and quickly became entangled in a process of spontaneous evolution that, far from enabling them to function as genuine monitors of corporate performance, made them into the main tool in the state enterprises' strategy of resistance to significant departures from the status quo.[60]

Accumulated inter-enterprise debts finally point to the SOE suppliers. In a process where firms short of liquidity simply stopped paying their suppliers the latter became involuntary creditors of the former. However, since these compa-nies in turn no longer settle their liabilities they have no incentive whatsoever to pressurise their customers. As long as none of them rocks the boat there is still

---

[59] On the interplay between privatisation and insider control see also Frydman and Rapac-zynski (1993).

[60] Frydman and Rapaczynski (1994), p. 130

hope that the system will not yet collapse. Against this backdrop, 'debt' mechanisms as a control device for SOEs cannot function.[61]

In the context of corporate governance issues the chosen *methods of SOE privatisation* are vital in tackling the problem of dominant insider control.[62] The early Polish experiences with *traditional sales of shares to the public* were, not surprisingly, rather disillusioning. In the absence of a financial market infrastructure and given the endemic lack of capital only five out of twenty firms initially selected to be sold in this way were divested. The revenues from sales were almost entirely used up by the costs of administering the divestiture. This privatisation method, moreover, contributed little to the solution of corporate governance problems since ownership remained dispersed. Another method rather unsuccessfully experimented with at the inception of the reform process were *trade sales*, either through public tenders, auctions, or negotiated private placements. Since buyers were dominantly foreign companies this method promised the advantage of improving the balance of payments and an influx of foreign expertise. In principal, foreign investors can also be expected to defuse corporate governance problems because they have clear investment goals and are prepared to closely monitor enterprise management. However, it came out that trade sales could at best be a solution for a few hand-picked SOEs. Foreign investment, moreover, also entails the concomitant risk of provoking xenophobic resentments among the population in Eastern Europe, a point that has already been referred to above.[63]

Given the failure of sales, and feeling the need to quickly proceed with the divestiture of state enterprises, governments throughout Eastern Europe finally resorted to a range of *give-away proposals* as the primary privatisation method. These various schemes promised to achieve a number of aims pursued by privatisation programmes:[64] first, the political goal of transferring assets from state

---

[61] On this see also Begg and Portes (1992).

[62] On the interplay between privatisation and corporate governance see also Aghion and Carlin (1997) and Frydman and Rapaczynski (1997).

[63] Frydman and Rapaczynski (1994), pp. 156ff. For a concise overview of the main issues of privatisation in PSEs see Lavigne (1995), Table 8.1, pp. 156ff.

[64] For a discussion of privatisation goals see Bornstein (1994), pp. 234ff. and Lavigne (1995), p. 158.

ownership to the private sector (i.e., depoliticisation) could be achieved quite rapidly and support for the privatisation among the population be secured.[65] Second, by evenly and (almost) freely distributing shares (or coupons for that matter) among citizens this method does justice to equity considerations. Critiques, however, see give-away privatisation as an attempt to create capitalism without capital and without capitalists.[66] This is a valid point since privatised enterprises are quite likely not to receive the enormous investment finance necessary for their successful restructuring. On the other hand, mass privatisation does little to remedy corporate governance problems. In the case of the direct distribution of shares to the broad masses, ownership is dispersed in such a way that next to no disciplining effect on managerial practises is the result. This is all the more so because secondary trading due to underdeveloped markets is very low.

To build core investors, and thus to tackle the problem of *dispersed ownership*, some countries created *investment funds* which hold a major fraction of total enterprise shares. Although these intermediary institutions are certainly superior to the direct distribution variant with regard to the control of enterprise management they too are deficient: first, fund managers tend to show a short-term attitude towards the firms in their portfolios which does not work to the advantage of enterprise restructuring. This lack of long-term commitment is well known from the Anglo-Saxon type of capitalism which has to be seen as the driving force behind the idea of investment funds.[67] Second, since banks are often major owners of investment funds a potential conflict of interests arises: a bank's desire to initiate bankruptcy of a firm may run counter to the interest of its investment fund which holds shares in this company: "[t]he phenomenon may be serious enough to account in part for the lower volume of bankruptcies in Slovakia and the Czech Republic than for instance in Hungary and Poland."[68]

---

[65] On political economy aspects of privatisation schemes in PSEs see Rausser and Simon (1994) and Thomas (1992).

[66] Amsden (1994), p. 12 regards this 'pseudo-privatization' as "an attempt to create capitalism without any capital, or without the credit, skills, and expertise necessary to restructure now 'private' enterprises hindered by long-term bottlenecks." (ibid.)

[67] Albert (1992)

[68] Svejnar (1994), p. 16

It emerges that the *design of privatisation strategies* has a strong effect on corporate governance structures and thus on the speed and scope of restructuring. If perceived indispensable for political and, or social justice reasons, mass privatisation schemes should at least provide for block-share holders counteracting the inherent risks of dispersed ownership. In the case of investment funds, it should be ensured that banks are prevented from acquiring major shares in these intermediary institutions. Due to its long-term commitment and the close link between ownership and control, a banking system along the lines of the German model would certainly be advantageous for corporate monitoring and the restructuring of privatised enterprises in Eastern Europe.[69] However, the fact that domestic banks in PSEs are yet to be restructured and their books to be cleaned of bad loans precludes, for the time being, that they step in as responsible and far-sighted co-ordinators of economic restructuring.

In advanced industrialised economies, *competition in product markets* has a disciplining effect upon management and thus exerts a positive effect on productive and allocative efficiency. Industry structure in PSEs, however, preempts such positive effects to a large extent. Notwithstanding liberalisation of prices and trade and despite attempts to break up large SOE conglomerates, there is evidence for persistent monopolies and highly concentrated industrial sectors.[70] Empirical data shows that those branches affected most by high concentration are fuel, energy and basic metal industries. These sectors are dominated by large state enterprises, 'white elephants' which have not yet been privatised. Their market power enables them to charge higher prices for their products. Since energy and basic metals are major inputs for downstream production processes, higher prices may drive buyers which face fierce competition in their respective markets out of business. The lack of competition points to the existence of major barriers to entry and calls for an effective competition policy. Yet governments in Eastern Europe tend to give in to pressures from foreign companies that are very reluctant to invest unless they are granted substantial market power. The resulting protection from imports further reduces competi-

---

[69] On the applicability of the German model of corporate governance see also Nunnenkamp (1995).

[70] See Carlin, Reenen and Wolfe (1994), pp. 68ff. and Pinto, Belka and Krajewski (1993).

tion. Thus product market competition obviously can hardly be expected to discipline SOE management.[71]

---

[71] On the role of competition in economic transition see also Saunders (1993).

2.2 The Political Economy of Transition

This section is devoted to the political economy aspects of transition. It attempts to answer the question of whether the desirability of industrial policy in the transition process can be justified on the basis of arguments which transgress the narrow boundaries of economics. Issues of political economy ultimately centre upon *distributional concerns*. In the context of transition they pertain to the question of how the sacrifices of transition are distributed across society.[72]

Welfare economics – particularly the second fundamental theorem – suggest that the issues of efficiency and distribution can be neatly separated. Western advisors and politicians in post-socialist economies not only designed their strategies along these lines, they also concentrated almost exclusively on ways and means to efficiently allocate resources. The view held in this section, however, sees the *neglect of distributional concerns as a major shortcoming of transition strategies*. In real-life policy making, socio-political realities constitute a constraint which cannot be ignored.[73] When dealing with the systemic transformation in Eastern Europe economists have to transgress the narrow "Pareto-efficient boundaries of microeconomics"[74]:

> Economists cannot luxuriate in political agnosticism, telling themselves self-righteously that they have done their duty once they have offered a menu of policies to politicians. Rather, they must be concerned with the conditions under which their advice is followed, and this implies a need to concern themselves with questions of political economy.[75]

It is argued that for the successful consolidation of economic reforms a *social consensus on the transitional strategy* is prerequisite. This consensus has particularly to be explicit about the distribution of transition sacrifices over time and across social groups. Only in this way can a solid political base be achieved

---

[72] On political economy aspects of transition see Haggard and Webb (1994), Haggard and Kauman (1995), Hillman (1994), Somoguyi (1993) and Wagener (1994) and Wyplosz (1993).

[73] Rodrik (1996)

[74] Brabant (1993), p. 68

[75] Haggard and Williamson (1994), p. 531

and sustained which ultimately decides the success or otherwise of a reform program.

The early years of transition are characterised by an *elite-manufactured transitional pact.*[76] Politicians and their Western advisors took advantage of the 'honeymoon period' to push through their reforms.[77] These top-down style policies were predominantly aimed at the urgently needed macroeconomic stabilisation. Empirical evidence on successful transition suggests that, given certain extraordinary economic conditions (e.g., extreme shortages, hyperinflation, extreme balance of payment crisis) which require urgent and timely remedial action, a strong and autonomous leadership may be advantageous.

However, this vertical policy making which bypasses citizens and is based on an *ex post* social consensus for cases where policy measures turn out to be successful can only be temporary. The reason for this is that the transformation process has not only an economic (i.e., the transition from plan to market) but also a political dimension, namely the transition to a pluralistic democracy. This simultaneity of the fundamental change both in the economic and political sphere is a constituent and genuine characteristic of PSEs. The two dimensions cannot be separated. Marketisation and democratisation are two processes that happen at the same time and that are interlinked. Once the 'honeymoon period' is over and people begin to realise that despite the radicality of reforms a quick turn-around is not yet in sight they will begin to voice their disenchantment via the new democratic institutions.[78]

The different time-frame of sacrifices and benefits of transition is one of the gravest problems of the entire process. The costs of reform are readily evident and often concentrated, whereas the benefits are diffuse and only gradually begin to emerge. The latter, in addition, are subject to substantial uncertainty since they accrue mainly in the longer run. Against this background the initial social consensus notably and in some countries even dramatically has begun to erode:

---

[76] Kaase (1994), p. 95

[77] The *honeymoon hypothesis* holds that economic reformers enjoy more room to manoeuvre immediately after they take office, when painful policy measures can be blamed on the previous regime. See Haggard and Williamson (1994), p. 571.

[78] For a first-hand account of the uneasy tensions between economic reform programmes and social stability see Balcerowicz (1993), pp. 27. Also Roland (1997).

> Politicians and sociologists observe that people are losing the enthusiasm and willingness for sacrifice which they felt immediately after the breakdown of the communist dictatorship. It is no exaggeration to say that the original consensus has been shaken by the negative economic and social consequences of the transformation strategy based on the conventional concept of stabilisation.[79]

This development is mirrored in the Central and Eastern Eurobarometer surveys conducted by the European Commission which is the most extensive available opinion poll in the area.[80] The 1996 report (Central and Eastern Eurobarometer No. 6, March 1996) firstly shows that in the ten Europe Agreement countries the majority of citizens think their respective country is not going in the right *direction*. The approval of the adopted course is highest in Estonia (57 per cent) followed by the Czech Republic (55 per cent) and Slovenia (45 per cent). The strongest disapproval is found in Hungary (79 per cent) and Lithuania (71 per cent).

The second indicator of the survey measuring the *support for the market economy* is less dramatic but still not satisfactory by far. Here 53 per cent of all citizens from Europe Agreement countries support the creation of a market economy against 26 per cent who oppose it. Those countries where support is strongest are Romania (64 per cent) and Poland (62 per cent). The opinion on the market economy is still very divided in Slovakia, Latvia and Slovenia. These figures, however, become worrying when compared with the available data for 1991 when the approval rate was still 79,5 per cent in Bulgaria, 75,3 per cent in Czechoslovakia, 85,5 per cent in Hungary and 73,7 per cent in Poland. Thus the important question has to be raised as to how long the supportive attitude will prevail when people are no longer convinced that things change for the better.

Regarding the *progress of democratisation* one can note an overwhelming dissatisfaction across Central and Eastern Europe. In the Europe Agreement coun-

---

[79] Levcik (1995), p. 26

[80] CEC (1996); The survey includes four indicators: *country direction, support for market economy, democracy satisfaction* and *human rights*. The latest report covers nineteen Central and Eastern European countries: Albania, Armenia, Belarus, Bulgaria, Croatia, the Czech Republic, Estonia, Georgia, Hungary, Kazakhstan, Latvia, Lithuania, the Former Yugoslav Republic of Macedonia, Poland, Romania, Russian Federation, Slovakia, Slovenia and Ukraine.

tries 55 per cent of the populace expressed their disapproval with the way democracy is developing in their respective country. Only 38 per cent are satisfied. The highest approval rates were reached in Poland (50 per cent satisfied
compared to 38 per cent dissatisfied) and the Czech Republic (46 per cent satisfied compared to 50 per cent dissatisfied). This situation is further exacerbated
when the opinion of the interviewees on the *respect of human rights* is considered. Here in the ten Europe Agreement countries 53 per cent think that there is
"not much respect" or "no respect at all" for human rights compared to 40 per
cent who maintain that there is "a lot of" or "some respect" for these rights.

In sum, it seems that the democratisation of post-socialist societies is a cumbersome and only gradually emerging process. The data suggest that Central
and Eastern European citizens' hopes rest on the transition to a market economy
and not on the political system as such. On the latter, people remain highly
sceptical. In this situation the question has to be raised as to "[...] whether the
transition by elite pact will really turn out to be such a stabilizing factor in the
long run as the transition literature claims it should."[81] The position held most
prominently by Jeffrey Sachs that politicians in post-socialist economies must
not worry about an *ex ante* social consensus seems to be out of place once the
initial deep stabilisation crisis is overcome. His politician "heroes"[82] fighting
against the odds of political and public opposition and trying to push through
their reform programmes must give way to more integrating characters with the
ability to moderate between diverging interests. This mediating function calls
upon the government as a co-ordinator in the transition process.

Generally speaking, current transition programmes are predominantly concerned with efficient resource allocation and therefore tend to neglect *questions
of distribution*. For two reasons this is considered a shortcoming: first, because
of the inseparability of efficiency and distribution issues and second, due to the
inherent risk of political instability. The first argument is based on information
economics: when information is imperfect redistributive taxation is inevitably

---

[81]   Kaase (1994), p. 109

[82]   Sachs (1994), p. 504; In an after-dinner speech at a conference sponsored by the Institute
       for International Economics, Jeffrey Sachs called politicians, such as Leszek Balcerowicz,
       the former finance minister of Poland his 'heroes'.

distortionary. It can be shown[83] that, given a society's preferences regarding equality, the extent of initial endowment differentials determines the extent to which government must make use of distortionary taxes to attain the desired final distribution of wealth. In other words, the initial distribution of wealth lastly determines the magnitude of the loss of society's welfare which results from redistributive taxation. Efficiency and distribution considerations can no longer be separated. The exact relationship between distribution and efficiency depends on the magnitude of initial endowment differentials of resources and the nature of the information problem prevailing in the economy.

Once this connection between distribution and efficiency has been acknowledged it becomes clear that from an economic perspective the predominant focus of reform programmes on allocative efficiency may have damaging consequences for the long-run development of transition economies or, in Joseph Stiglitz' words:

> I stress the results on the link between issues of distribution and issues of efficiency, because some of the recent discussions of reform within Eastern Europe have stressed efficiency concerns, with limited regard to the consequences for distribution. Years from now this lack of concern for distribution [...] may come to haunt these economies, not just in the form of social unrest, but more narrowly in terms of *long-run economic efficiency*.[84]

Political economy arguments help to further elucidate the risks which may result for the entire transformation process if the question of distribution is not sufficiently addressed. In particular the widespread discontent ensuing on the *performance-expectations trap*[85] is worrying. As in the course of transition it becomes increasingly obvious that the emergence of functioning markets and a pluralistic democratic order may still take decades to come, widespread disillusionment and impatience are growing. Because of the different time-frame between the closure of old capacities and the creation of new businesses due to the stock-flow problem, and because of defective labour markets particularly, long-term unemployment can become a serious problem. The extent to which individuals will have to face extended unemployment will considerably determine

---

[83] See Stiglitz (1994), pp. 45ff.

[84] Stiglitz (1994), pp. 49f.; emphasis added.

[85] Blommestein and Steunenberg (1994), p. 11

their willingness to support the reform process. "This fear [of unemployment] is pervasive, and much will depend on the number of people who will suffer extended unemployment and who, for lack of resources, cannot be properly supported by the state or other agencies (like trade unions or churches)."[86]

  This situation is exacerbated by a plethora of attitudinal *legacies of the socialist past*[87]. The image of the state who severely limits personal freedom, but at the same time in a paternalistic way automatically provides for extensive social security, is deep-seated. Those who conformed with the socialist system had a guaranteed job and, on the whole, could take for granted considerable security in terms of medical care, education and pensions. This concept of substantial social security still continues to form the bases of the expectations of broad layers of post-socialist societies.

  If, against this background of increasing unemployment and of frustrated expectations it becomes a widely held belief in the population that it is labour who has to bear the major burden of transition sacrifices and, if the speed of economic recovery is perceived as being too slow people may begin to voice their protest. Given that Central and Eastern European governments are generally held in low esteem by their electorate, it becomes evident that this situation holds major risks for the transition process. Under these circumstances, reactionary nationalist parties with their populist rhetoric may easily become a melting pot for discontented citizens. If these backward oriented political forces are strengthened to the point where they manage to get into parliament, the consolidation of transformation might seriously be jeopardised. Their obstructive strategy may lead to a substantial slowing down of reforms and to political destabilisation, with the immanent negative consequences for the economy.

  From the political-economy analysis of transition it becomes apparent that social and political concerns impose binding constraints on reform strategies. Given growing popular dissatisfaction with the speed of economic recovery and increasing discontent with the progress of democratisation a re-orientation of transition policy seems mandatory:

---

[86]   Kaase (1994), p. 94

[87]   See Brabant (1993), pp. 63ff. and Lavigne (1995), pp. 13ff.

Acknowledging the existence of political and social constraints means that they may jeopardize the transition process when overlooked or incorrectly analyzed. Transition is therefore not a period when policy objectives can be neglected or simply reduced to 'exchange of coordination mechanisms.'[88]

Top-down style policy making by elite pacts which bypass the electorate seems no longer feasible as soon as the "economic emergency room"[89] has been left and the consolidation of structural reforms stands at the top of the agenda. Once it has been recognised that political-economic feedback may ultimately endanger the entire reform process a strong case can be made for an *ex ante* social consensus on the transition strategy. A solid political base is prerequisite for the social and political sustainability of reform programmes, particularly for their consolidation.

---

[88] Alter (1994), p. 119; on the role of political constraints in transition strategies see also Roland (1993) and Roland (1994b).

[89] Sachs (1994)

2.3 Synthesis I

From the overall image of the transition process that has been sketched in the previous sections, it emerges that the role of the state with regard to structural change has to go well beyond the mere dismantling of former state control and the reliance on spontaneous market forces alone. The transition from a command to a market economy system is not simply a matter of replacing one economic co-ordination mechanism for another, i.e., central planning for the indirect co-ordination of free market prices. Even within the boundaries of economic analysis such a perspective would fall short.

The scope of prerequisite change and given that the market economic system in PSEs is yet in *statu nascendi*, i.e., that a number of key markets is only about to emerge and still rudimentary in their functioning, means that a strategy of 'deserting' the state at this stage of the transition process is not a feasible option. Reducing the economic function of government to a mere regulator of the rules of the game seems as much premature as our discussion of the fundamental stock-flow problem for advanced transition economies has indicated. Regarding the stock element of the problem, the state acting as a *de facto* absentee owner leaves ample room for insider control. This enables both SOE management and workers to resist change. The precluded restructuring, however, leads to a rapid erosion of the SOEs' skill base and the depreciation of their assets. Mass privatisation schemes, the privatisation method most frequently resorted to across Central Europe, does little to resolve this corporate governance problem.

Turning to the flow part of the fundamental stock-flow problem, the dysfunctional financial intermediation in transition economies poses a major impediment to the reallocation of resources. The continuing interdependence and collusion between SOEs and (privatised) commercial banks both ossifies previous lending patterns and acts as a high barrier to entry for new business, particularly for SMEs. Entrepreneurs in need of venture capital to start up new operations are driven out of the domestic capital market. Since the propensity to save in PSEs remains low and FDI has not come up to early expectations, investment finance has to be primarily generated through retained earnings. The deficient functioning of labour markets further exacerbates the flow problem in that it adds to the resistance to restructuring by job holders and the reallocation of labour across the economy is hindered. Finally, the lack of competition under the prevailing circumstances also works to the detriment of structural change.

In sum, the stock-flow problem implies a substantial retardation of the potential pace of economic restructuring. As our examination of political economy aspects has highlighted, it is this slow-down of economic reforms which causes growing impatience and disillusionment among the population. Responding to the popular discontent for governments in PSEs, however, is a tightrope walk: the acceleration of reforms would in the short run require a number of highly unpopular policy measures, such as the rapid closure of nonviable (parts of) remaining SOEs with the accompanying rise in unemployment figures and public protest. Thus, confronted with the choice of either taking up an active lead in economic restructuring or remaining in a wait-and-see attitude, politicians in transforming countries are quite likely opting for the apparent lesser evil, i.e., for the latter.

It turns out that during the second stage of the transition process political economy considerations might call for policies running counter to the precept of allocative efficiency. It has been shown that the focus of reforms on economic efficiency alone represents a major shortcoming both from an economic and social-political perspective. Transition policies have to account for distributional concerns and must be explicit about who has to bear the major burden of transition sacrifices. Given the socialist past of these societies they must also include political-historical experiences, even if this means a loss of economic efficiency. The state, as an example, may have to keep capacities in operation which were strict market criteria applied would not survive. The prerequisite pragmatic compromise that has to be found between allocative efficiency on the one hand and the distribution of the cost of transition over social strata and time on the other calls for a social consensus.

To speed up the process of economic restructuring, a comprehensive strategy must be defined that simultaneously tackles the existing obstacles to a successful consolidation of economic reforms. An industrial policy strategy that incorporates these findings could play a key role in building a bridge between concerns for allocative efficiency and socio-political issues. Hence we arrive at the *interim result* that *a coherent industrial policy in the transition from a command to a market economy system may be desirable*. Its function would be *catalytic*, i.e., to speed up restructuring and thus accelerate the entire economic transformation. By integrating both economic and social-policy issues it defuses potential conflicts and consequently *preserves political stability*, thereby securing the consolidation of economic reforms.

Table 2.3 identifies the basic policy areas and fields of the proposed industrial policy strategy which have been elaborated in this chapter. Improving allocative efficiency is the benchmark of the *restructuring* process. To successfully conclude the second phase of the transition to the market it is necessary to resolve the fundamental stock-flow problem. As to the stock part privatisation has to be completed. For those SOEs remaining in state ownership appropriate management structures have to be devised to remedy excessive insider control. Competition policy is called upon to stimulate rivalry particularly where market concentration is high. Finally, the vicious circle of soft budget constraints ensuing on inter-enterprise debts must be cut short.

• Area	**Restructuring**		**Political economy**
• Central issue	Allocative efficiency		Distribution
• Target	Stock	Flow	Political stability
• Fields	– Completion of privatisation – SOE management – Competition policy – Inter-enterprise debts	– Banks – Domestic savings – FDI – SMEs – Labour markets – Infrastructure	– *Ex ante* social consensus – Social safety net – Labour markets and services – Phasing out of non-viable SOEs

Table 2.3: Areas of industrial policy

On the flow side financial intermediation has to be urgently reformed. Banking and credit policy reforms stand at the top of the agenda. Since FDI across PSEs has remained comparatively low, and due to the experience of Eastern European governments having to grant over-generous concessions to major foreign investors, efforts to mobilise domestic savings must be stepped up. A substantial increase in the propensity to save is vital to generate the much needed investment capital. However, because domestic sources cannot be expected to furnish capital markets with sufficient resources and despite the risks attached to foreign capital it will nevertheless be necessary to attract FDI. Foreign investors are not only an additional source of capital but also transfer know-how to transition economies. Labour market institutions must be capable of absorbing those who lose their jobs and have to maximise the turnover rate in the unemployment pool in order to minimise long-term unemployment and associated costs. Competition policy has to be linked to the promotion of small and medium enterprises which have been identified as the competitive backbone of advanced industrialised economies. Finally, infrastructure (roads, railways, telecommunication, etc.) plays a key role in supporting the reallocation of resources in the restructuring process.

At the heart of *political economy* considerations, the other major area for industrial policy stands the question of distributing the sacrifices of restructuring. Political stability is the *conditio sine qua non* for a successful economic transformation. To attain this goal an *ex ante* social consensus has to be built which incorporates major interest groups. To cushion the adverse effects of restructuring on employment both a comprehensive labour market infrastructure and social safety net have to be institutionalised. For those SOEs for which no new owner can be found in the course of privatisation and which do not have any chance of survival in a market environment a binding arrangement for a gradual phasing out have to be found.

The predominantly transition-specific nature of the issues at hand suggests an analytical distinction is to be made between the role that the government must play during the transition process and policy interventions in long-established market economies in cases where markets are known to be defective.[90] The *transitional element of industrial policy* is limited to the period of systemic transformation and more precisely to the second stage of the transition process, namely to restructuring. The gradual phasing-out of this policy strand and the concomitant rolling back of the state depends on the extent to which the stock-flow problem can be resolved, i.e., on the speed with which the obstacles to effective restructuring can be removed.

---

[90]   Hare (1995), p. 5

Against what has been said, we come to the seemingly paradox conclusion that in order to arrive at the decentralised co-ordination mechanism of the market and thus reduce the role of the state, governments first have to play a pivotal role in co-ordinating the transition process: "to compress government tomorrow, more of it today may be just the recipe."[91] It has been shown that this holds in particular for industrial restructuring and the political sustainability of the transition. Accordingly, we can now refine the definition of industrial policy which was given in Chapter 1.3.2 (see Box 1.4):

Definition

*Industrial policy in the transition from a planned economic system to a market economy comprises a range of **temporary** (or transitional) policies. They primarily relate to the crisis management of state owned enterprises, privatisation and institutional reforms. Transitional policies are determined by obstacles to industrial restructuring and the political sustainability of the transformation process. The application of temporary policies coincides with the second phase of the transition process.*

Box 2.1: Definition of industrial policy II

---

[91]   Brabant (1993), p. 67; On this specious paradox see also Fuster (1998), pp. 47ff.

3 Industrial Policy and Economic Theory

In the face of the extent to which industrial policy has been and is still practised in the industrialised world as well as in developing countries, it is rather surprising to find that there is no coherent theory on which these policies are based. This lack of a sound theoretical foundation of industrial policy results "partly because [its] proponents [are] more interested in practical policy issues, but mainly because there [is] very little in conventional economic theory that could justify such a policy."[92]

The absence of a theoretical foundation of industrial policy is especially unsatisfactory in transition economies of Central and Eastern Europe which have already embarked on industrial restructuring. There, policy makers faced with the orthodox advice of International Financial Institutions (IFIs) and mainstream economists of Western universities are often left alone with the design of such policies.

This chapter attempts to trace the theoretical foundations of industrial policy. The question it hopes to answer is what justification can be found from different theoretical perspectives for government intervention in the market. Special interest is taken in the applicability of these theories in the context of industrial policy. The result of this discussion is "unlikely to be a single unifying idea – such as the invisible hand".[93] The aim is rather to condense a number of theoretical guide-lines. To achieve this goal an eclectic approach to the different strands of economic theory is used.[94]

In our discussion we make a broad distinction between orthodox and heterodox theoretical approaches. Orthodox or mainstream approaches propagating the unhindered play of market forces have until recently dominated the political debate. They built both the theoretical and ideological foundations of 'Reaganom-

---

[92] Chang (1993), p. 4

[93] Murrell (1991), p. 73

[94] For an overview of theoretical approaches to industrial policy see Dietrich (1992), Grossmann (1990), Sawyer (1991) and Sawyer (1992).

ics' and Thatcherite economics in the 1980s. Towards the end of the decade, their influence culminated with the fall of the 'iron curtain' and the beginning of the Eastern European transition process.

Yet economic orthodoxy had little more advice to offer to Central and Eastern European (CEE) governments than to propagate the unrestricted play of market forces:

> Regrettably economic science – at least until recently – has had very little to say about these fundamental matters, and even less to say about the important issues of transition. The typical advice of the visiting consultant making a hurried trip to one of the economies embarking on a transition path is to emphasize repeatedly the importance of markets, a lesson seemingly by now well learned (though market advocates would say that it is a lesson that cannot be repeated too often and, as simple as it may seem, the full import of which seems difficult to absorb – even in economies long accustomed to markets).[95]

A growing number of heterodox economists feel dissatisfied with this simplistic policy advice. They base their respective dissent from the mainstream on different arguments and, on the whole, are more pro-interventionist in tone.

In what follows we first discuss the orthodox theories before section two turns to the heterodox approaches. For each approach we first briefly broach its basic arguments and then analyse it with regard to its implications for government intervention in general and for industrial policy in particular. The presentation of each theoretical position ends with a tabular overview that answers the following questions:

1. What is the perception or image of the state portrayed?

2. Can state intervention be justified?

3. What is the justification for government intervention or what are the reasons against it?

4. Is the state basically able to intervene successfully?

5. What role, if any, is there for industrial policy?

Section three, next, evaluates the different theories based on their plausibility and applicability to the context of Eastern European transition. The concluding

---

[95] Stiglitz (1994), p. 3

section, as a primary result extracts from the discussed theories a number of guidelines for the design of industrial policy.

3.1 Orthodox Approaches

Although based on rather unrealistic assumptions and despite the little guidance it has to offer to countries embarking on the transition from one economic system to another, the neoclassical paradigm has for long dominated the policy debate. Why then did the neoclassical paradigm hold such a influential position at the beginning of the transition in Eastern Europe and still continues to do so, although to a lesser extent? For one reason, neoclassical economics being the most developed economic theory conveys a clear message: let the market play. Secondly, welfare economics shows with its decentralised solution of 'getting prices right' a seemingly simple and convenient way to a market economy.

A third reason for the neoclassical dominance is the orthodox position of international organisations (IMF, IBRD, EBRD and OECD). There the "widespread belief [was held] that the task of reforming the communist systems of political economy was basically analogous to that of implementing 'structural adjustment and reform' programmes in developing countries."[96]

Neoclassical economics reduced to the notion of perfect competition (i.e., leaving out the more pro-interventionist arguments of welfare economics), together with neoliberal ideas, lead to calls for rapid liberalisation and unrestrained markets in Eastern Europe.

Against this background the terms neoclassical and neoliberal are often used synonymously. However, in what follows, we will show that the two approaches ought to be distinguished due to the different messages they convey with regard to the role of government in economic development. We, thus, first present the neoclassical (competitive) paradigm and then turn to the neoliberal position.

3.1.1 Neoclassical Theory

Within neoclassical theory we first consider the notion of market failures as the justification for government intervention. We then treat an extension of the

---

[96] Chang and Nolan (1994), p. vii

competitive paradigm: contestable markets. This approach shifts the focus of attention to barriers to market entry and exit respectively.

3.1.1.1 Market Failures

The neoclassical framework assigns governments in the first place the task of redistributing wealth where the market outcomes lead to an undesirable income distribution. Secondly, given market failures the state is supposed to intervene by means of provision of public goods, taxation or subsidies in the case of externalities or by setting up a legal system that clearly defines property rights. "The government simply needs to correct the well-defined market failures, which it can do with simple tools having minimal effects on the mode of operation of the market economy."[97] In all this the yard-stick for government intervention is the normative principle of Pareto efficiency.[98]

Where the central assumption of welfare economics, the so-called duality theorem asserting a correspondence between Pareto efficiency and market performance, fails rationally behaving individuals may accept the restriction of their activities by coercive measures of a democratic government.[99] The concept of market failures stands for the "failure of a more or less idealized system of price-market institutions to sustain 'desirable' activities or to stop 'undesirable' activities."[100]

The neoclassical theory originally differentiates three different types of market failures: (1) public goods, (2) technical externalities, and (3) ownership externalities.[101] *Public goods* are characterised by jointness in supply (i.e., once the good is supplied it costs relatively little or nothing to make its benefits available to an additional consumer), non-rivalness in consumption (i.e., the consumption of the public good by one individual does not affect the consumption of that

---

[97] Stiglitz (1995), p. 7

[98] I.e., government interventions must make somebody better off without making anybody else worse off.

[99] Baumol (1993), p. 180. This is essentially the contractarian notion of the state. See Section 3.1.2 on Neoliberalism for further details on Contractarianism.

[100] Bator (1958), p. 351

[101] For this classification see Bator (1958).

good by other individuals) and non-excludability (i.e., it is not feasible to exclude any market individual from consumption). If the supply of such goods is left to the market alone this leads to either its inadequate provision or even to its not being provided at all. To overcome the free-rider problem inherent in public goods, the state has to supply it and tax the individuals accordingly to finance its provision.

Technical externalities are caused by nonconvexities in production and result in non-competitive markets with a monopolistic or oligopolistic structure. Under such circumstances, profit-maximising competitive producers are going to provide an output lying below that of the competitive equilibrium.[102] In this situation the state is supposed to induce the monopolist producer by fiscal means (taxes and subsidies) to provide the Pareto optimal output level.

The third category of market failures are *ownership externalities*. These externalities are the result of nonappropriation, the divorce of scarcity from effective ownership[103] or, in other words, of not clearly defined property rights. They exist where there are some non-accounted-for spillover effects from an individual's activities to those of others, leading to a discrepancy between the private and the social cost - benefit structures. Neoclassical theory offers two solutions to the problem of ownership externalities: (1) a Pigovian fiscal approach (i.e., taxes in the case of negative externalities like environmental pollution and subsidies in the case of positive externalities) or (2) appropriate Coasian legal entitlements.[104] The second solution prevents the state from intervening directly in the market process. The government is merely responsible for the definition of clear-cut property rights. In the absence of transactions costs these legal entitlements will lead to a privately negotiated market solution.[105]

The individualistic notion of consumer sovereignty standing at the heart of the concept of Pareto optimality demands that government interference with the individual's sphere has to be supported by a majority vote. A democratically

---

[102] Arrow and Debreu (1954)

[103] Bator (1958), p. 364

[104] Feldman (1987), p. 891

[105] This property rights solution to market failures goes back to Ronald Coase. See e.g., Coase (1988), pp. 187ff.

elected government is therefore legitimised to intervene on the assumption that it will benevolently work to the advantage of society as a whole.[106] Given market failures, a government is supposed to step in and to find a remedy. Even in the absence of such distortions government intervention can be justified: in the event that the market outcome leads to an undesirable income distribution or undesirable resource allocation, the state is allowed to use corrective measures. The yard-stick for such policies again has to be a social consensus on what is desirable and what is not.

In sum, a government is able to intervene because welfare economics assumes that it has the required information to analyse market failures correctly and to design the right strategy to correct them.[107] Moreover, it has the political power to implement its policies and is immune to particularistic interests. Against what has been said, one may therefore conclude that the image of the state as portrayed by neoclassical theory is that of "omnipotent benevolent guardian"[108] which is constantly and selflessly concerned about the maximisation of some social welfare function. There are basically two justifications for state intervention: one is concerned with allocative efficiency, the other with distributional 'justness'.

Turning to industrial policy, welfare economics equips the state with an apparatus of instruments which it can legitimately use on a number of occasions. It thus opens the door for quite extensive (in comparison to the other orthodox theories discussed) government activity. On the basis of neoclassical economics environmental legislation, monopoly- and anti-trust legislation and social policy can be justified. All these policies can be applied to realise an industrial policy strategy.

---

[106] Baumol (1993), p. 180. This is essentially the contractarian notion of the state. See Section 3.1.2 on neoliberalism for further details on contractarianism.

[107] On the policy implications of welfare economics refer also to Hennipmann, Walker, Heertje and Doel (1995).

[108] Chang (1994b), p. 295

Criteria	Position
Image of the state	Benign, omnipotent social guardian
Can state interven-tion be justified?	Yes, on the basis of market failures and distributional 'justness'
Justification for or reasons against state intervention?	Democratic legitimisation of government activity and social consensus; market failures without government intervention lead to Pareto inefficient outcomes
(In-) ability of state to intervene	State has necessary information, skills and instruments
Industrial policy	Apparatus of instruments which can be used for industrial policy
Central argument	Market failures justify government intervention

Table 3.1: The neoclassical paradigm

3.1.1.2 Barriers to Market Entry

The competitive equilibrium theory suffers from its unrealistic assumption of perfect competition as the model for market behaviour. Therefore the model's applicability is limited if only as an idealised benchmark. It is this deficiency which the contestable market theory tries to overcome by focusing on barriers to market entry and exit.[109]

---

[109] A *contestable market* is defined as a market "into which entry is completely free, from which exit is costless, in which entrants and incumbents compete on completely symmetric terms, and entry is not impeded by fear of retaliatory price alterations." Baumol, Panzar and Willig (1982), p. 349. In a contestable market there exist no barriers to entry: potential entrants do not have to bear any costs that are sunk and there are no legal restrictions that would impede their entry. At the same time, exit is supposed to be completely free (i.e., capital assets are perfectly fungible and there are no shut-down costs). The assumption of complete symmetry between incumbent firms and potential entrants entails that the latter have the same techniques of production available to them, that they face the same market demand as the former, and that they do not have to bear any entry costs which the incumbents do not. Finally, potential entrants do not fear any retaliation from the incumbents should they enter the market by undercutting the current price.

One of the principal policy insights of the contestable market approach is that "if an industry is structurally contestable and is behaving accordingly, and if, in addition, it has sustainable configurations available to it, and if none of these involve any significant welfare problems, then that industry is best left to its own devices with no government interference [...]."[110] Since many of the traditional indicators do not automatically call for government intervention in this framework, the contestable market theory leans more to the side of laissez-faire than does the neoclassical paradigm. Under certain conditions an oligopolistic industry structure in a contestable market can be perfectly consistent with the Pareto optimal allocation of resources and its welfare implications. There is simply no need for regulatory government intervention: "Small numbers of large firms, vertical and even horizontal mergers and other arrangements which have traditionally been objects of suspicion of monopolistic power, are rendered harmless and perhaps even beneficial by the presence of contestability."[111]

Despite these general policy implications, the contestable market approach does not put the case for unrestrained market forces solving all economic problems automatically and for the redundancy of government regulation in general. It is rather that such interventions have to be designed and applied very carefully because they can themselves erect new barriers to entry with all their damaging effects on an industry's efficiency and the resulting welfare losses.

Consequently, the most promising starting point for government intervention lies with the identification and removal of any artificial entry barriers impeding contestability. In the first place this concerns the deregulation of industries, i.e., the removal of regulatory constraints imposed upon entry. This hints in the direction of the theory's intrinsic suspicion towards government regulation:

> [It] immediately suggests some appropriate changes in current public policy. Legal impediments to entry like those that, until recently, characterised almost all regulated industries, are simply the reverse of what is called for by the public interest. Special licensing requirements and other preconditions for the launching of operations must be eliminated unless fully justified by clear dangers to health or public welfare.[112]

---

[110] Baumol, Panzar and Willig (1982), p. 466

[111] Willig (1987), p. 622

[112] Baumol, Panzar and Willig (1982), p. 360

Another artificial barrier to entry may stem from incumbents' predatory behaviour and their threat of retaliatory action in the case of entry. These entry barriers erected by incumbents are quite likely to lead to monopoly profits, resource misallocation, and inefficiencies. Here the government has to intervene in order to prevent potential entrants being deterred by incumbents. These two cases are characterised by incumbents behaving in a way that is not to be expected under the conditions of contestable markets and where there seem to be no structural impediments justifying such behaviour.

So where then can direct government intervention in the context of contestable markets be justified? Above all in the case of natural barriers to entry which stand in the way of contestability. If market entry and/or exit is connected with costs that cannot be recuperated (i.e., if sunk costs are prevalent), then there is not going to be enough pressure from potential entrants exerted on the incumbent firms to minimise total industry costs. This will lead to suboptimal market results. Although sunk costs ask for government intervention, since contestable markets are not able to deal with them, such policy has to be designed with great care. Those activities that are associated with non-recuperable costs are to be isolated in order that they can be tackled directly. It is important to "[draw] a regulatory net over only the segment of the activities of the industry that are inextricably associated with heavy sunk costs."[113] In this way it is hoped the majority of an industry's economic activity can be left to the free market. Among the specific measures suggested by the proponents of contestable markets are tax advantages for rapid depreciation, tax reductions for retooling of plants, and tax incentives for re-use of old plant in new activities.

The contestable market theory pictures the state as judiciously guarding the proper functioning of markets. Although the approach basically accepts the legitimacy and necessity of government interventions in the case of barriers to market entry, it approves state interference to a lesser extent than neoclassical economics. Political interventions potentially run the risk of erecting additional entry barriers and therefore have to be designed very carefully.

Since in the contestable market framework a market structure where perfect competition does not prevail is not – as in welfare economics – an *a priori* case

---

[113] Baumol, Panzar and Willig (1982), p. 483

for government intervention, policy making is much more information intensive. Even in the presence of monopoly a market can be perfectly contestable.
Thus, before a government becomes active it has to analyse very carefully
whether a market structure comes close to the ideal contestability benchmark or
whether barriers to entry lead to a suboptimal (i.e., inefficient) outcome. Once it
arrives at the latter conclusion a policy has to be devised with even greater care
due to the immanent risk of creating new obstacles to the frictionless working
of markets.

Concerning industrial policy, the approach holds that the first task has to be the
dismantling of legislative impediments to market access. Deregulation has to
stand high on the political agenda. At the same time it has to be made sure that
exit from the market is a palpable option. Artificial barriers to entry set up by
incumbent firms are another important policy target. Finally, natural obstacles
to market entry call for direct government intervention. This is, however, a delicate task since these barriers first have to be isolated and then tackled with sur-
gical precision.

At the heart of the contestable market theory stand barriers to market entry.
Some of these are the direct consequence of past government activity (i.e.,
regulation), some stem from incumbent firms and others are natural.

Criteria	Position
Image of the state	Judicious guardian over the proper functioning of markets
Can state interven-tion be justified?	Basically yes, but interventions have to be designed and imple-mented with great sensitivity so as not to errect new barriers to entry
Justification for or reasons against state intervention?	Barriers to market entry and exit; public goods; externalities
(In-) ability of state to intervene	Interventions are very information intensive; require high level of analytical skills
Industrial policy	Deregulation; secure contestability of markets; removal of natural barriers to entry
Central argument	Artificial and natural barriers to market entry

Table 3.2: Contestable markets

3.1.2 Neoliberalism

The neoliberal position, although being less of a closed theory than an ideology[114], is discussed here for two reasons: first, it seems important to draw the line between neoclassical welfare economics and neoliberalism. Second, it is introduced because of its dominant influence on public policy in the 1980s and in the early 1990s. When towards the end of that decade the 'iron curtain' fell and the Eastern European countries set sail to economic transition, Western neoliberal advisers were quick to sell their message to the newly elected governments in the East. They uniformly put the case for fast liberalisation and "government by the market".[115]

Neoliberal ideas gained further influence in Eastern Europe since they were (and continue to be) promoted by the World Bank and the International Monetary Fund through the conditionality of their loans. The Bretton Woods institutions designed in reaction to the Latin American debt crisis towards the end of the 1970s the so called *Structural Adjustment Programme* (SAP) empitomising the 'Washington consensus'.[116] In a nutshell the basic idea behind this programme holds that macroeconomic stability and structural reforms are the two key preconditions for sustainable long-term economic growth.

The SAPs put macroeconomic stabilisation on top of the reform agenda. Sweeping liberalisation, both external (i.e., regarding the exchange rate and the trade regime) and internal (i.e., freeing prices so as to let them reflect market realities) and deregulation combined with restrictive monetary, expenditure and income policies should be adopted both immediately and vigorously. Only in this way it is held can inflationary pressures, public finances and the terms of trade be brought under control.

Once these primarily demand-oriented policy measures take hold the focus is shifted to structural issues, the second pillar of the SAPs. The overall goal of structural reforms is to role back the state's influence on the economy. Thus the

---

[114] Buchanan speaks of the economists of the 1980s as "ideological eunuchs" who are "illiterate in basic principles of their own discipline". Buchanan (1986), pp. 14f.

[115] Self (1993), p. ix

[116] On the 'Washington Consensus' see Williamson (1990), pp. 7ff.

privatisation of SOEs, the closure of the remaining state firms that are not viable, radically cutting subsidies and reducing the size of the bureaucracy are the cornerstones of structural adjustment.

Ultimately it is hoped that by 'getting the prices right' the ensuing change in an economy's incentive structure will unleash the market forces that in turn foster sustainable long-term economic growth. The essential role of the state according to the SAPs is to guarantee a stable macroeconomic and institutional framework. To direct policy interventions should only be resorted exceptionally in cases of clearly identifiable market failures, such as public goods (e.g., infrastructure and human capital formation).[117]

Standing at the heart of the 'Washington consensus' and the Structural Adjustment Programmes respectively the neoliberal position dominated the political agenda of transitional countries in the early 1990s:

> The local [i.e. in Eastern Europe] true believers in the market were fortified by advisers from Western universities, the World Bank, and the International Monetary Fund. They pushed the reforms in predictable directions, minimizing the role of the state and postulating that uncontrolled markets are an infallible guarantee for robust output growth. These ideas follow from a fundamentalist reading of mainstream, neoclassical economic theory, which flourished during the administrations of Presidents Reagan and Bush. By the late 1980s this approach had become the "Washington consensus".[118]

The neoliberal position draws a number of arguments from three intellectual pillars: contractarian political philosophy, the Austrian School, and the New Political Economy.[119] The *contractarian model of politics* stands for a highly individualist society.[120] The most extensive state that is morally acceptable from this perspective is the minimal night-watchman state. The latter is the result of a unanimous agreement (i.e., in the form of a voluntary multipartite contract) by

---

[117] Kappel and Landmann (1997), pp. 215ff.; See also Baumer (1994), pp. 3ff. and Fuster (1998), pp. 28ff. and pp. 41ff.

[118] Amsden, Kochanowicz, and Taylor (1994), p. 18

[119] Chang separates analytically very well the different sources of the neoliberal body of thought. See Chang (1994b), pp. 295ff.

[120] On Contractarianism see Nozik (1974) and Buchanan (1986).

all individuals to forfeit some of their individual rights to the state as in Hobbes' 'Leviathan'.[121]

Exponents of the *Austrian School*[122] share a deeply rooted trust in the self-organisational capacity of markets. The fundamental credo of the liberal position holds that a society should rely as much as possible on its spontaneous forces and resort as little as possible to constraint.[123] Markets are the superior economic order. Hayek goes a step further and argues that without economic freedom, personal and political freedom will not exist.[124] Government intervention in the economy is above all an interference with economic evolution. Natural selection turns into 'unnatural' selection potentially jeopardising economic progress.[125]

New Political Economy[126], as the third pillar of the neoliberal position, rejects the neoclassical notion of welfare economics which perceives government as a "benign and omnipotent social guardian which maximizes social welfare."[127] It sets the idea of market failure against one of governmental-political failure.[128] The 'politics-as-exchange' paradigm[129] claims that in the political market self-seeking bureaucrats will create rent-seeking opportunities.[130] This ultimately leads to the political decision making process being captured by particularist

---

[121] Hobbes (1651), pp. 227ff.

[122] The term 'Austrian School' circumscribes here the ideas put forward by Ludwig von Mises and Friedrich A. Hayek and is thus associated primarily with "libertarian ideology in political and social discussion". [Kirzner (1987), p. 149]

[123] Hayek (1944), p. 13

[124] Hayek (1944), p. 10

[125] Wassell, introductory chapter to Burton (1983), p. 9

[126] Although the New Political Economy has different strands, the interest is basically centred on the *public choice approach*.

[127] Chang (1994b), p. 295

[128] The New Political Economy theory is therefore also referred to as the "government failure" literature. Such government failures take the form of, for example, internalities caused by budget-maximizing bureaucrats, too high costs resulting from x-inefficiencies due to non-market production, and additional market failures caused by government legislation attempting to remedy already existing market failures. [Cullis and Jones (1987), p. 58]

[129] Buchanan (1986), pp. 25ff.

[130] See Buchanan, Tollison and Tullock (1980), Krueger (1974) and Tullock (1987).

interests. Rent-seeking activities entail that markets cannot function properly any more: the "invisible foot is stomping on invisible hands".[131]

Taken together the neoliberal state has only minimal functions. The ideal is the night-watchman state which leaves maximum space for the development of the individual citizen. Thus there is *prima facie* no justification for government intervention. From a contractarian perspective such interventions would be immoral since they clash with the rights of the individuals. The Austrian School claims that any active (i.e., constructivist) policy has to be seen as an interference with the spontaneous forces of economic evolution. Turning natural selection into a man-made selection, government interventions potentially put economic progress at risk. Since evolutionary processes are characterised by a high degree of uncertainty, policy makers cannot possess the necessary information to be successful. New Political Economy, finally, rejects an active role of government, arguing that any policy would fail because the political process is all too easily captured by particularist ideas.[132]

From a neoliberal position industrial policy cannot be justified. The only task remaining for government is to create an environment that is conducive to economic evolution (e.g., modest taxation, liberal commercial law, no direct state intervention, etc.). The 'market ideology' consequently wants to trim state functions in order to liberate market forces. Neoliberals try to achieve their goals by a variety of measures, such as liberalisation, deregulation and privatisation. Their belief in 'government by the market' means that:

> governments should in general do less; that they should reduce or relinquish their previous responsibilities for maintaining full employment and a comprehensive system of state welfare; that they should privatise public services or their delivery wherever practicable; and that they should reform their own operations in accordance with market concepts of competition and efficiency.[133]

---

[131] Colander (1984), p. 2

[132] See, for example, Krueger (1990).

[133] Self (1993), p. ix

Criteria	Position
Image of the state	Minimal night-watchman state
Can state intervention be justified?	No
Justification for or reasons against state intervention?	Rights of individual citizen; interference with spontaneous forces of economic evolution; political process is captured by particularist interests
(In-) ability of state to intervene	Government does not have necessary information to intervene; self-seeking bureaucrats and rent-seeking interest groups lead inevitably to government failure
Industrial policy	Rules of the game only; hands-off
Central argument	Government by the market

Table 3.3: Neoliberalism

3.2 Heterodox Approaches

Criticism of economic orthodoxy is based on various arguments. This section treats three objections which seem to be of particular relevance to the issue of industrial policy in transition economies: our reading of the infant industry argument challenges the orthodox line of thought due to its disregarding the phenomenon of learning. Information economics next rejects the neoclassical assumption of perfect information. The third heterodox approach, new evolutionary economics, finally objects to the basically static framework of neoclassical economics and tries to explain the process of economic change.

3.2.1 Infant Industry Argument

At the core of the infant industry concept stand dynamic learning effects (i.e., learning effects that accrue over time as opposed to static effects that accrue at a single moment in time).[134] As a consequence of these learning effects an economy's transformation curve shifts outward over time. The idea is that, after a limited period of protection (i.e., the infancy or maturation phase), the infant industry will eventually become internationally competitive by achieving comparative advantage (i.e., the infant reaches maturity).[135] Without government intervention it is held that international competition might obliterate a new entrant or, at best, compel it to scale down its technological effort and to rely more on foreign technology.[136] Thus the period of protection is supposed to help an infant industry firm to overcome the costs associated with learning.

As to the learning process, the 'capabilities' approach to industrial policy[137] emphasises the importance of acquiring technological capabilities. The latter comprise "the entire complex of human skills (entrepreneurial, managerial and technical) needed to set up and operate industries efficiently over time."[138] Since technological capabilities are responsible for sustained increases in productivity

---

[134] Meier (1987), p. 830

[135] Bell, Ross-Larson and Westphal (1984), p. 107

[136] Lall (1990), p. 23

[137] Lall (1994); also Dasgupta and Stiglitz (1988) and Tomer (1993).

[138] Lall (1990), p. 17

they are crucial to maturation and hence to attain and maintain international competitiveness. The acquisition and deepening of technological capabilities thus stand at the heart of technological development and are therefore the key to successful industrialisation.

In the context of policy interventions it is necessary to look at what elements determine the acquisition of capabilities. Stochastic factors (e.g., historic circumstances, luck, etc.) left aside, there are a number of common determinants that are affecting all firms: (1) incentives (or stimuli); (2) capabilities of the firms to respond to incentives; (3) institutions. Incentives arise from the macroeconomic environment and from product and factor markets, international competition playing an important role. The ability of the firm to react to these stimuli impinging on them from their environment arises from physical investment, the infrastructure, human capital development and their technological effort (i.e., the "conscious exertion to use technological information and to accumulate technological knowledge to choose, assimilate, adapt, or create technology"[139]). Institutions of various kinds finally facilitate capability formation. They provide information, standards, basic research and other services with public good character relevant to the acquisition of capabilities. The interaction of these three determinants leads to technological development. One factor by itself will not lead to sustained productivity growth and thus to industrial success.[140]

It emerges that for successful maturation costless learning-by-doing is only of limited relevance. Successful industrialisation requires a conscious effort to progressively accumulate technological capabilities, a strategy for technological change and continuous responses to incentives from a firm's environment. What has been said here for learning equally holds for relearning, the process of industrial reform. The efforts to be undertaken by existing industries "to become efficient to shed the legacy of inherited attitudes, outdated skills and inappropriate technologies"[141] also entail the acquisition and deepening of new and existing technological capabilities.

---

[139] Bell, Ross-Larson and Westphal (1984), pp. 107f.

[140] Lall (1992)

[141] Lall (1994), p. 86

Turning to policy interventions, the first-best policy instrument – according to the normative theory of international trade – available for infant industry protection, would be a production subsidy specifically designed to remedy the prevalent distortions. Next to subsidies come tariffs. Although they would lead to equality between the marginal rate of domestic transformation and that of transformation through foreign trade, they would at the same time involve consumption distortions as a by-product. Least preferable are quantitative restrictions because instead of customs revenue they produce higher profits and, if coupled with import licenses, they are likely to give rise to rent-seeking activities.[142]

Having emphasised the complexity and the importance of the acquisition and deepening of technological capabilities, the promotion of capability development moves to the centre of attention. Especially in the context of technological learning, both product and factor markets are prone to a number of market failures which result in distorted signals that do not conduce to technological development and industrial upgrading. They may lead to the building up of suboptimal capabilities, inadequate investment in learning and thus ultimately to an equilibrium with little technological change and low growth rates.

From the fact that the best framework in product markets is one that exposes enterprises to constant competition arises an apparent contradiction to the infant industry argument. On one hand international competition bears the risk of wiping out infant-industrial activities. Hence learning needs temporary protection. Protection on the other hand can deprive capability development from one of its most important stimuli, competition, and thus be counterproductive. How can this be reconciled? The experience of the newly industrialising economies (NIEs) suggests the importance of export promotion.[143] Protected industries have to be pushed into export markets and gradually be exposed to world competition. Export orientation disciplines infant industry activities and speeds up the process of technological upgrading of the economy:

> The higher rates of economic growth enjoyed by many countries that have promoted exports suggest that it is possible that the infant-industry proponents are correct in their basic argument that there is a period of learning and of

---

[142] Meier (1987), p. 829

[143] See Chapter 4.2 for an analysis of the East Asian NIEs' approach to industrial policy.

relatively high costs, and that an export-promotion strategy is a more efficient
way of developing an efficient, low-cost industrial structure.[144]

Failures in factor markets affect the development of capabilities through their
effects on skill formation. They may result in under-investment in skill upgrading with respect to formal education as well as to employee training on the firm
level. The interventions necessary to promote human capital formation have to
be both horizontal (e.g., schooling and non-technical higher education) and selective (e.g., more industry-specific specialised forms of tertiary education and
vocational training). Another area for government interventions concerns technical effort. On one side this has to do with domestic technological efforts. The
public good characteristics of many activities in this field may result in a
suboptimal science and technology infrastructure and a general lack of support
institutions. An intervening government could either set up these institutions by
itself or try to co-ordinate technological efforts of different firms. As with the
interventions in skill formation it is essential that interventions trying to encourage technological effort have to be integrated with product market interventions. Finally, failures in capital markets mean that funds needed for
investment in capability development may not be available. A possible remedy
in this situation would be the granting of government loans on concessionary
terms.[145]

Many of the government interventions necessary regarding capability development are selective. This type of intervention bears a higher risk of failure than
do horizontal interventions. Hence they demand a higher degree of administrative capabilities and have to be designed with great care. Thus learning on the
part of government is also crucial.

The image the infant industry argument portrays of government is both one of
a prudent protector of newly emerging industries and of a foresighted, cautious
mobiliser of capabilities. The approach approves government interventions
which give companies the chance to become viable under temporary protection
as well as those which speed up the process of capability formation (i.e., learning). Without protective interventions, it is argued, infant industries do not have

---

[144] Meier (1987), p. 829

[145] Lall (1994)

the chance to reach a state of maturity since they would be wiped out by international competition. To become internationally competitive they have to be able to overcome the initially high costs and achieve efficient production under protection. With regard to this learning process, the state must moreover eliminate market failures which hamper technological development and industrial upgrading by means of horizontal and selective policies.

The notion of industrial policy stands at the heart of the infant industry argument. The state has a catalytic function: aiming at strategic objectives and taking dynamic effects into account, it tries to coherently influence the determinants of technological capabilities, thereby fostering technological development and industrial upgrading. The latter are seen as the key to successful industrialisation.

Selective interventions which favour specific industries are legitimate as long as there are clear-cut 'rules of the game' and protection is strictly limited in time. In addition, infant industries should be pushed at an early stage into exports and gradually be exposed to world competition. The overall goal of policy must be to create an efficient, low-cost industrial structure.

The central argument of this approach, therefore, is that infant industries in an economy which is exposed to world markets need temporary protection and that market failures related to learning justify further government intervention.

Criteria	Position
Image of the state	Prudent protector and foresighted, cautious mobiliser of capabilities
Can state intervention be justified?	Yes, but has to be designed and applied carefully
Justification for or reasons against state intervention?	Without government intervention infant industries will not reach international competitiveness; market failures relating to learning require government action
(In-) ability of state to intervene	High level of administrative capabilities necessary; policies should be institutionalised
Industrial policy	Long-term objectives; functional and selective interventions; rules of the game; protection limited in time
Central argument	*Protection of infant industries and learning process (i.e., capability formation)*

Table 3.4: The infant industry argument

3.2.2 Information Economics

Joseph E. Stiglitz founds his critique of orthodox economics upon the findings of information economics (or the information paradigm).[146] The Greenwald-Stiglitz theorem or the 'nondecentralisability theorem' holds that given an incomplete set of markets or imperfect information a market does not generally yield a Pareto-efficient allocation without some government interventions.[147] Taken by itself this finding might not seem to be pertinent. However, if one recognises that in reality incomplete markets and informational imperfections

---

[146] See Stiglitz (1994). Information economics is a relatively young strand of economics and has been developed during the past fifteen years. It has grown out of a fundamental critique of the neoclassical model based on the latter's assumption of perfect information. The information paradigm has led to a number of important new insights in microeconomic and macroeconomic issues. For an overview see Laffont (1989) and Milgrom and Roberts (1992).

[147] Stiglitz (1994), p. 62

are the rule and not the exception, it becomes clear that "the first welfare theorem that provides the intellectual foundations of our belief in market economies"[148] is of little relevance to the discussion of modern economies, let alone to the discussion of transformation. For markets to be complete there not only would have to be a market for every single product in the present but for all future periods and all possible contingencies. The assumption of a complete set of markets is evidently unrealistic.

The phenomenon of *incomplete markets* can be traced back to the existence of transaction costs, an important element of which are information costs: in other words, a significant amount of transaction costs is incurred by individual actors in an attempt to reduce uncertainty.[149] The volume of exchange is a function of the costs of transactions. Confronted with increasingly costly transactions individuals will economise transactions. If these costs reach a certain maximum level, no trade will occur at all: "In a multimarket framework, therefore, transactions costs can explain why certain potential markets, either for present or future goods, do not exist."[150]

Incomplete markets can be explained by the fact that information is often imperfect. If, as an example, a transaction is to take place between two parties contingent upon specific stipulations (e.g., the delivery of a certain product of specified qualities, at a defined place, date and time), the latter have to be observable to both. In addition, for such a contract to be legally enforceable a third party must be able to verify it. If these conditions are not met the transaction may not occur and consequently the market is thin or even closed. This result is further exacerbated once the effects of *asymmetric information* and the concomitant problems of adverse selection and moral hazard are taken into account.

Unlike market failures of neoclassical economics *information related market failures* are endemic to all market situations. This implies that competitive markets left to themselves will not lead to a Pareto efficient outcome, as suggested by the first theorem of welfare economics, since in reality they are generally incomplete and information is neither perfect nor costless.

---

[148] Stiglitz (1994), p. 28

[149] On 'transaction costs' see Niehans (1987), pp. 676ff.

[150] Niehans (1987), p. 677

The analysis of information economics, thus far, provides for an increased potential role for government intervention. Compared to the second fundamental theorem of welfare economics[151], there are more categories of market failures and the latter are rather the rule than the exception. The scope of market failures associated with imperfect information is such that the majority of commodities would benefit from government intervention. However, since the information available to government is limited and information costs are high such a broad approach is not tenable:

> [F]ull corrective policy would entail taxes and subsidies on virtually all commodities, based on estimated demand and supply elasticities for all commodities (including all cross elasticities). The *practical* information required to implement the corrective taxation is well beyond that available at the present time, and the costs of administering such corrective taxation [...] might well exceed the benefits when the market's distortion is small. Thus it seems reasonable that the government should focus its attention on those instances where there are large and important market failures [...].[152]

Moreover, given limitations on the government's information policy interventions are in general distortionary and thus require corrective action in turn. The state, in other words, cannot remedy market failures and undesirable distributions of wealth simply and neatly by either imposing linear taxes or engaging in some initial lump-sum transfers. Without further government intervention the decentralised price mechanism will not lead to Pareto efficient allocations, i.e., the decentralisability theorem of welfare economics does not hold.

Further results in information economics fortify the notion of the nondecentralisability of the economy. First, Arnott and Stiglitz show that in the presence of imperfect information competitive equilibrium are not Pareto efficient since welfare could be enhanced through cross-subsidisation between industries af-

---

[151] The *second theorem of welfare economics* deals with the distributional aspects of the Pareto optimal equilibrium. It maintains that if a Pareto optimal outcome leads to an undesirable income distribution or an undesirable resource allocation then this second-best optimum can be turned into a first-best solution simply by either redistributing wealth (i.e., by a non-distortionary lump-sum transfer) in the former case or by influencing the price vector (i.e., by means of taxation) in the latter. The decentralised market mechanism will itself then lead to the first best Pareto optimum.

[152] Stiglitz (1994), p. 43

fected by moral hazard problems and those where they do not occur.[153] Second, interpreting information as fixed cost, Stiglitz shows with a simple example of the insurance market that whenever problems of moral hazard or adverse selection are present pervasive nonconvexities[154] emerge, i.e., the law of diminishing returns and diminishing marginal rates of substitution do not prevail.[155] Finally, under imperfect information and given incomplete markets the action of one individual has externality-like effects on others, which they fail to take into account.[156] Taken together, these arguments underline the assertion that the decentralised allocation via the price mechanism of competitive markets will not lead to Pareto efficient equilibrium and that it will not suffice for the government to intervene through linear taxes or the redistribution of wealth respectively.

We thus arrive at a seeming paradox: on the one hand information economics casts serious doubts on the decentralisability of the market economy. On the other hand it reveals that government interventions may be much more information intensive than portrayed by neoclassical economics. Yet, since the information available to the government is limited, interventions tend to be distortionary. How can this be reconciled? The answer lies somewhere in the middle between the neoliberal idea of unrestricted free markets (i.e., complete decentralisation) and a planned economy system (i.e., completely centralised allocation): "Effiency requires not the complete decentralization suggested by the neoclassical paradigm but partial decentralization."[157] Based on the arguments of information economics the state has to play a crucial *complementary role* to the market. Government interventions, however, should focus on the most important and gravest instances of market failures.

What implications does information economics have for industrial policy? Hellmann, Murdock and Stiglitz suggest a policy of *financial restraint* which may be made instrumental to achieve industrial development goals.[158] The proposed set of financial policies is aimed at the creation of rents in the financial

---

[153] See Arnott and Stiglitz (1989).

[154] On the origin and effects of nonconvexities see Mas-Colell (1987), pp. 653ff.

[155] See Stiglitz (1994), pp. 52ff. and Arnott and Stiglitz (1988).

[156] Stiglitz (1994), pp. 29ff.

[157] Stiglitz (1994), p. 60

[158] Hellmann, Murdock, and Stiglitz (1996), pp. 163 ff.

and production sectors.[159] In essence the idea of financial restraint means that if a number of preconditions are met (i.e., a stable macroeconomic environment, moderate taxation of the financial sector, and positive real interest rates) the state sets the deposit rate below the competitive equilibrium level. To preserve rents in the financial sector, it must regulate entry and sometimes direct competition. In order to affect the distribution of rents between the financial and production sectors deposit rate controls may be complemented by a set of controls on lending rates to different sectors. In this way financial restraint may be used to improve access of small- and medium-sized enterprises to long-term credit and, thus, to reduce their dependence on retained earnings as the primary source for investment.

The creation of rent opportunities by government intervention may help to reduce information-related problems that hamper perfectly competitive markets. The rents create incentives for banks to expand their deposit base and increase the extent of formal intermediation. Hence they may contribute to the deepening of the financial sector in cases where in the absence of rent opportunities private incentives would be too weak to provide the socially efficient level of financial services. Rents may also be used to promote specific bank activities to compensate for market deficiencies, such as the lack of long-term lending.

Against the background of our analysis of financial intermediation in transition economies[160] and from what has been just said, the notion emerges that financial restraint is highly relevant to the discussion of industrial policy in the process of transition. This is all the more so since financial restraint is not a static policy instrument. At an early stage of development, when financial intermediation in the economy is highly deficient, the full set of proposed policies (i.e., deposit- and lending-rate controls, restrictions on entry, and limitations on competition) may be feasibly implemented. As the economy matures and financial depth increases, particularly as the capital base of the financial sector strengthens, these interventions may be progressively relaxed: "[F]inancial restraint should be a

---

[159] The term 'rents' in this context does not mean the income that accrues to an inelastically supplied factor of production but rather returns in excess of those generated by a competitive market.

[160] See Section 2.2.1.

dynamic policy regime, adjusting as the economy develops and moving in the general direction of freer and more competitive financial markets."[161]

Criteria	Position
Image of the state	Complementary role to the market
Can state intervention be justified?	Yes
Justification for or reasons against state intervention?	Decentralised allocation in competitive markets will not lead to Pareto efficient equilibrium
(In-) ability of state to intervene	Limits on the information available to the government
Industrial policy	Financial restraint
Central argument	*Information related market failures*

Table 3.5: Information economics

3.2.3 New Evolutionary Economics

The genealogy of evolutionary economics can be traced back to Joseph Schumpeter, Thorstein Veblen, Alfred Marshall and Karl Marx.[162] They were all influenced by Charles Darwin and Robert Spencer and tried to incorporate in their respective theories the notion that economics is in some sense evolutionary.[163] Recent contributions to evolutionary economics[164] reveal a multiplicity of ap-

---

[161] Hellmann, Murdock, and Stiglitz (1996), p. 198; emphasis added.

[162] Hodgson (1993), p. 218, Hodgson (1991a) and Spiegel (1991).

[163] Generally speaking, *evolution* means the "transformation of a system over time through endogenously generated change". [Witt (1991), p. 87] At the core of evolutionary processes stands the creation of novelty. In contrast to the mechanistic system of the neoclassical world where regularities, the repetition of paths, structure and association prevail, evolutionary models deny the existence of repetitive phenomena since all processes are irreversible and cannot be repeated. [Andersen (1994), pp. 13f.]

[164] In order to distinguish the authors of these papers from the 19th century evolutionary economists they are called 'new' evolutionary economists.

proaches which can partially be explained by the different intellectual traditions from which they are drawn.[165,166]

  Bearing in mind the multitude of approaches in evolutionary economics, what then are the 'typical' assumptions and characteristics of evolutionary models?[167] First, the evolutionary approach to economics recognises that processes are irreversible, continuing in time and non-deterministic, i.e., they represent historically unique development trajectories.[168] This concerns transformation in structure as well as the acquisition of knowledge. Second, the long-run development stands at the centre, the grand course of evolution rather than numerous marginal adjustments. Third, it can deal with quantitative as well as with qualitative change in the sense that it tries not only to explain parametric change but includes structural development as well. Fourth, whereas neoclassical models are based on stereotypical individuals and their stylised behaviour, their evolutionary counterpart can handle variation and diversity of phenotypes, all the more so, since this is the "fuel of all evolutionary processes".[169] Fifth, equilibrium situations, being the rule in orthodox models, are rather an exception. Evolutionary theory applies to open systems which are seldom in equilibrium[170], in contrast to neoclassical models with their underlying closed system perspective.[171]

  Although there seems to exist "much confusion about the policy relevance of evolutionary economics"[172] one can, however, derive from the approach a number of interesting ideas for industrial policy. On the basis of a Spencerian inter-

---

[165] These are the Austrian School, the Schumpeterian tradition, Institutionalism and, to a lesser extent, the Marxist school.

[166] For an introduction see Dosi and Nelson (1994), Dopfer (1990), Witt (1993) and Hodgson (1991).

[167] Hodgson (1994), p. 223; see also Andersen (1994), p. 15

[168] This stands in sharp contrast to the mechanistic neoclassical world firmly founded on classical physics with its Newtonian metaphor. See Clark (1988), p. 516 and Witt (1991), p. 86.

[169] Hodgson (1993), p. 223

[170] Evolutionary economics speaks about punctuated equilibria as opposed to the general equilibrium in neoclassical models. [Boudling (1991), p. 13]

[171] Clark (1988), p. 513 and pp. 518ff.

[172] Andersen (1994), p. xi

pretation of evolution (i.e., survival of the fittest) and on Hayek's trust in the spontaneous self-organisation capabilities of market forces, one could presumably make the case for complete laissez-faire. Evolutionary economics, however, does not support the idea that evolutionary processes necessarily lead to optimal outcomes. On the contrary, "an evolutionary process cannot be an optimizing one, at least in the strict sense, because for evolution to work there must always be a variety of forms from which to select."[173] Once this has been understood there is indeed room for policy intervention which turns out to be also desirable, since "spontaneous self-organization by itself, without at least occasional intervention by enlightened policy, may lead far from a happy end."[174]

From an evolutionary perspective, policy making is perceived as a "continuing evolutionary process".[175] As such it becomes an adaptive learning process involving trial-and-error. Superior knowledge on the side of policy makers is no longer assumed. They have to operate as much as private firms under the constraints of localised, imperfect knowledge and uncertainty. Consequently their policy strategies are bound to fail as much as business strategies of private firms.[176] This behaviourist perception of policy making and makers has important institutional implications: a primary task for policy making is then to find "an organizational structure capable of learning and of adjusting behavior to what is learned."[177]

The evolutionary approach also leaves its mark on the parameters of industrial policy. The significance of ready-made policy recipes becomes less important against the background of a synthetic interpretative policy framework. The latter is strongly context-dependent and accounts for the specific circumstances of a particular economy or issue in question. In addition to market structure and institutional variables, it recognises factors such as the fund of experience with similar problems, a society's cultural heritage, its historical background, prevail-

---

[173] Hodgson (1991a), p. 522

[174] Pelikan (1992), p. 49; see also Hodgson (1991a), pp. 520f.

[175] Nelson and Winter (1982), p. 384

[176] Metcalfe (1994), p. 933

[177] Nelson and Winter (1982), p. 384

ing ideologies and beliefs. For a policy analysis understood in this way, an assessment on the surface no longer suffices:

> [It] requires detailed understanding of the institutions, mechanisms, interests, and values at stake. [...] Simple (and simple-minded) arguments about the optimality of private enterprise, or simple pointing to market failures, does not carry the analysis very far. Serious analysis of a particular policy problem inevitably means immersion in a set of relatively unique attributes of that context.[178]

So the question can no longer be simply about how to reach a Pareto-optimal equilibrium point or how to optimise with respect to some objective function. The evolutionary approach could lead to a new type of industrial policy.[179] Here constructivist rationalism does not prevail any longer in an assumption of superior (or even full) knowledge on the part of policy makers about what solutions should be implemented. Rather the latter have a moderating and catalytic function. Policy makers moderate in the sense that they gather and process information at an early stage about movements and developments in the economy (e.g., international political issues such as integration into the European Union, technological innovations, social developments, or such as an increase in the percentage of old people combined with a stagnating birth rate, etc.). They collect information about the opportunity-set of choices, and the claims and activities of the key decision makers. On the basis of this information a strategy is then developed. By bringing together agents who are involved in a certain problem in order to find a solution for it together, policy makers function as endogenised co-ordinators and "political entrepreneurs".[180] In this way they not only co-ordinate the problem-solving process but also speed it up by combining efforts to find new solutions (i.e., the catalytic function).

This framework is undoubtedly demanding. In the first place targets have to be defined unambiguously and agreed upon between the agents including policy makers. Only in this way can efforts be focused effectively on a specific area in question. To reduce the complexity of the problem to be solved, the process

---

[178] Nelson and Winter (1982), p. 385

[179] For the following see Gerybadze (1992).

[180] Gerybadze (1992), p. 170

may be subdivided into smaller tasks and steps, facilitating at the same time the attainment of an agreement between the different agents involved.

The second important task of the 'political entrepreneur' is to assess the political choice set. He should also examine whether a combination of policies which so far have not been co-ordinated could be used to enhance the problem's solution (e.g., the support of a networking policy by complementary financial incentives). In other words, the task is to evaluate whether there exist any synergies and interdependencies between different policies which could potentially be exploited.

Thirdly, the political co-ordinator must make sure that his agency does not become a "bottleneck in information processing".[181] Since this framework is very information intense, its functioning depends to a large extent on whether an organisational form is found that can handle information efficiently and thus lower transaction costs. It is therefore, e.g., crucial that the political intermediary has close communication links with all agents involved.

Central to this joint problem-solving process is the spontaneous organisation of firms and their creation of novelty. Policy makers merely bundle information and co-ordinate activities with respect to the solution of specific problems. Their principal aim must be to facilitate the emergence and the dissemination of change. This may be achieved by institutions such as public consulting services for small and medium enterprises or subsidies for research and development activities.

In sum, what are the central insights for the design of an industrial policy strategy from an evolutionary perspective? The approach dissolves to a certain extent the dichotomy between the economy on the one hand and government on the other. The new role of the government in the proposed joint problem-solving process is one of *primus inter pares*. As an endogenised co-ordinator, it mediates information between the different agents involved. Due to the democratically legitimised power of government and the size and degree of organisation of its agencies, the state is predestined to hold the central node of an information-gathering and joint problem-solving network in the economy. It mediates between different interests in society and tries to incorporate them into

---

[181] Gerybadze (1992), p. 168

a common strategy. In so doing it has to act as a neutral agent. The primary task of industrial policy is to facilitate the emergence of and the adaptation to change. Its design is seen as a continuing evolutionary process implying adaptive learning and subject to trial-and-error. The unique historicity of development trajectories, the central element to the evolutionary position, calls for tailor-made policy strategies.

Criteria	Position
Image of the state	Endogenous co-ordinator and political entrepreneur
Can state intervention be justified?	Yes, but government is only *primus inter pares*
Justification for or reasons against state intervention?	Democratic legitimisation; degree of organisation of government agencies
(In-) ability of state to intervene	State has no superior knowledge; organisational form must be found that can handle information efficiently
Industrial policy	Joint problem-solving process; facilitate change and adaptation to it; integral evolutionary approach to policy making
Central argument	Evolutionary process and uniqueness of development paths

Table 3.6: New-evolutionary economics

3.3 Critical Assessment

After having outlined the basic arguments of the orthodox and heterodox approaches and discussed their respective implications for industrial policy, this section assesses the plausibility of the different theoretical arguments put forward and their applicability to Eastern European transition.

3.3.1 Orthodox Approaches

3.3.1.1 Neoclassical Theory

Two of the major characteristics of the neoclassical model are its clear message in favour of market economy and its simplicity. Although welfare economics is fundamentally pro-interventionist in tone, neoclassical economics with its invisible hand paradigm clearly makes the case for unrestrained markets as the first best optimum. In Eastern European countries, which set out to throw off the yoke of a planned economy, this message was very welcome. The attractiveness of the model, at least at a political level, stems from its neat elegance: "Especially during large systemic changes, when vast complexity requires great simplifications, theoretical refinements tend to be lost in the struggles between overarching visions."[182]

Should the market solution yield suboptimal results, welfare economics furnishes industrial policy with a kit of instruments to tackle market failures and to correct undesired income distributions. The straightforward, recipe-like instructions the approach gives to policy makers (e.g., if externalities prevail use either a tax solution or legal entitlements) is another benefit of the approach.

The model's simplicity, however, is at the same time one of its biggest limitations. Despite later modifications of the basic neoclassical model it is a static framework. The process of economic transition is dominated and characterised by radical and fundamental systemic change. In this world of constant flux the model reveals its shortcomings. Assessing the question of whether neoclassical economics can be applied to the reform of centrally planned economies, Murrell

---

[182] Murrell (1991), p. 73

comes to the central conclusion "that economists must look outside the standard models of competition, the focus on Pareto-efficient resource allocation, and the welfare theorems to build a theory of reform."[183]

The critique of the Austrian School especially holds in the context of economic transition: uncertainty, being a salient feature of evolutionary processes in general, is dominating to an even larger extent in a period of basic structural change. Hence policy makers may lack the necessary information to correctly diagnose market failures. But "if the fundamental uncertainties pervading the market process do not allow us to identify the ideal against which market failures are to be identified, namely, the neoclassical competitive equilibrium, the whole exercise in welfare economics becomes pointless."[184]

The neoclassical optimism about a government's ability to correct market failures is challenged by the New Political Economy government failure argument. During a period of structural change, when entire sectors of the economy are shut down and new industries gradually emerge, pressures from particularist interests can expected to be substantial (e.g., employees of a vast steel mill which has to lay off a large fraction of its work-force will try to exert their influence on the political process to secure their jobs). Hence a more interventionist industrial policy might easily be captured by interest groups and lead to suboptimal outcomes.

So while the neoclassical model for its simplicity may be used in political discussions its usefulness in the context of the transition from a command to a market economy is limited.

As to the contestable market approach, its merit is it to have revealed the significance of barriers to market entry. Since in periods of radical economic change a high entry and exit activity can be expected, the contestable market theory can also be applied to Eastern Europe: in the course of continuing structural change industries are shut down and new businesses and firms emerge. Numerous artificial and natural barriers to entry prevent potential competition from exerting its efficiency increasing effects on incumbent firms. The importance of the proper working of competitive pressures cannot be overstated:

---

[183] Murrell (1991), p. 60

[184] Chang (1994b), p. 295

given that no significant barriers to entry exist, incumbent firms would tend to zero economic profits and would be employing the most efficient production technologies. Thus policy makers in Eastern Europe in the first place should meticulously screen legislation for artificial obstacles to entry and plead for deregulation where necessary. A second area where barriers to market entry play a crucial role are small- and medium-sized enterprises (SMEs). As our analysis of financial intermediation in transition economies in Chapter two has revealed, it is very difficult for small- and medium-sized enterprises to gain access to credit. Thirdly, anti-trust commissions must vigorously watch over the economy given monopolistic market structures particularly at transition's inception. Lastly, natural barriers to entry should be assessed and tackled where possible.

Since the contestable market theory is an extension of the neoclassical model the critique brought forward there holds here as well. The informational argument applies even more to this approach: whereas in the neoclassical framework a monopolistic or oligopolistic market structure can be taken as an *a priori* indicator for imperfect competition, from the contestable market perspective this is not necessarily the case. In order to come to the same conclusion policy makers would have to analyse very carefully whether entry and exit to the particular market is possible. The analysis is by far more information intensive. Against this background, it can be argued that government activity should be limited to deregulation and the production of public goods.

The New Political Economy argument leads to the same conclusion: incumbent firms might try to win political support and get preferential treatment vis-à-vis potential entrants. Government impartiality between the two groups is no longer guaranteed and the notion of contestable markets loses its point.

3.3.1.2 Neoliberalism

The neoliberal critique of welfare economics provides valuable insights in the process of policy making and leads to necessary corrections in the way government interventions are to be perceived. The latter entail their own costs which may actually outweigh the costs of having to live with market imperfections. The basic policy question is which is thus the lesser evil, market failures or government failures?[185] Another important insight is that the political process must be isolated from the influence of particularist interests as much as possible. Prevailing uncertainty, moreover, makes the design of a more activist policy a tricky if not futile task. Finally, the IMF's and IBRD's Structural Adjustment Programmes underline the vital importance of a stable macroeconomic, institutional and political framework for long-term economic growth.

Yet the critical account Self gives on public choice theory (i.e., an element of the neoliberal position) can easily be extended to criticise neoliberalism as a whole:

> The main thrust of public choice writing, and still more of its political influence, have been to discredit democratic government and to extol the market system. [...] By the end of the 1990s it can be seen that the outcome of all these activities has been not so much to slim government itself as to alter quite drastically its economic and social responsibilities as well as its distribution of favours and sacrifices among the members of society.[186]

Neoliberal ideology as an answer to Keynesian statism went too far: the pendulum swung too much to the right. Basically right in their criticism of too much government interference with market forces, Neoliberals accomplished their "demolition job on the role of government"[187] properly and made the case for government by the market instead. The application of SAPs in PSEs lead to the slogan of 'no industrial policy is the best industrial policy', i.e., to the substitution of "intellectual bumper stickers for thought".[188] If this message is promoted in Eastern European countries in transition then at least two important points are all too easily forgotten: first, neoliberal ideas grew under very specific political and economic circumstances, namely in the 1970s and the early 1980s mainly in the Anglo-Saxon world. The situation which Eastern European countries were facing in the late 1980s and at the beginning of the next decade were completely different and had never been experienced in capitalist economies before. Secondly, historically seen governments played an important role in the

---

[185] Cullis and Jones (1987), p. 37

[186] Self (1993), p. xi

[187] Self (1993), p. 56

[188] McCloskey (1994), p. 9

emergence of the capitalist system in Western economies.[189] Why should this be different in Eastern Europe today, all the more as it is a matter there of radical rather than gradual change as in the West?

Thus, the lessons to be learnt from the neoliberal position are: firstly, under the prevailing uncertainty and given that governments do not possess superior knowledge activist industrial policy bears a high risk of failure. Secondly, industrial policy must be isolated from interest groups and is therefore best institutionalised. Thirdly, a stable macroeconomic and institutional framework is vital both for economic recovery and long-term growth.

3.3.2 Heterodox Approaches

3.3.2.1 Infant Industry Argument

The major advantage of the infant industry argument over the neoclassical framework is its dynamic character. Arguing for temporary protection to allow a process of capability formation in emerging industries and stressing the importance of learning for successful industrialisation, the approach directly challenges calls for shock therapies. Sweeping liberalisation inherently runs the risk of wiping out industrial structures. Since the notion of infant industry protection can be applied to newly emerging industries as well as to the reform of existing industries it has interesting implications for industrial policy in Eastern Europe. The price that has to be paid in terms of forgone opportunities for an unreflected adherence to some sort of government by the market may be very high. Another benefit of this approach is that it requires a long-term perspective and commitment by the state. Short-termist corrections of market failures give way to a development strategy.

On the negative side, the infant industry argument entails all the problems of strategic trade policy. In the first place, the promotion of particular industries by means of subsidies runs the risk of retaliatory measures by the country's trade partners and becomes increasingly difficult in the presence of international trade agreements (e.g., WTO, association agreements of the European Union). Trade

---

[189] See, for example, Armstrong, Glyn and Harrison (1991).

conflicts might easily result in a spiral of subsidies. Another problematic feature of the approach is that, given limited financial resources for subsidies at some point, someone has to make a decision which industries are going to be promoted for how long a period. This immediately raises the question as to who is legitimated to make this decision and on what criteria it is going to be based.[190]

The public choice critique applies here again: interest groups will fiercely compete to obtain government funding and thus try to influence the decision process in their favour. Once an infant industry scheme is installed pressure will arise from the subsidy recipients trying to extend the period of protection. This would inevitably lead to high economic and social costs because these infants would quite likely never reach a state of maturity.

Infant industry promotion, in addition, demands a high level of administrative capabilities. Bearing in mind that in Eastern Europe bureaucracies had to be completely reorganised or even newly created, it may be doubted if the expertise necessary for such delicate policies could be found there. Since the costs of ill-advised policies or picking losers are potentially very high and can jeopardise economic growth, the infant industry strategy can hardly be recommended in the context of transition.

Thus the advantages of this approach are that it reveals the importance of learning for successful economic development, that it shows the potential risks of sweeping liberalisation and that it finally calls for a long-term perspective.

3.3.2.2 Information Economics

Information economics has successfully questioned the fundamental decentralisability theorem of welfare economics based on the notion of incomplete markets and imperfect information. By showing that (industrial) policy may have to play an important complementary role given information-related market failures, a theoretically founded case has been presented for the mixed economy. The state and the market are no antipodes. Rather the question must be to find the right balance between the two of them. This finding holds in particular for market economies at an early stage of development: where markets are just

---

[190] For a fundamental critique of the infant industry argument see Baldwin (1969).

beginning to emerge, their functioning is at best deficient and the state has to intervene as a catalyst.

Financial intermediation is a key area in transition economies where information-related market failures critically hamper a faster process of creative destruction. As a result, the financial sector is generally very thin and SMEs find it very difficult to get access to credit. The suggested policy of financial restraint by creating a set of incentives for financial intermediaries may help to overcome these market failures and spur economic development. When combined with lending-rate controls this policy may be used to support selected enterprise sectors thus opening the door to industrial policy.

Albeit these important contributions to the discussion of how to co-ordinate economic activity information economics does suffer from a number of shortcomings. First, the approach does not offer a coherent theoretical framework. Rather, starting from a fundamental critique of welfare economics' assumption of perfect information, it develops a number of results that run counter to the orthodox notion of decentralised allocation via the market price mechanism.

Second, information-related market failures are rampant when economic systems go through a process of fundamental transformation, such as the transition from a planned to a market economy. Yet at early stages of economic development the state administration may not be in the position to effectively diagnose such market failures, let alone design remedial interventions which go well beyond the simplistic correction of classical market deficiencies. Thus, despite the extensive scope of information-related market failures, government action should focus on only a few important cases.

Third, as to the proposed policy of financial restraint, it might turn out to be very difficult to find the optimal level. Too far-reaching interventions in the financial sector may require both extensive capital account controls to prevent capital flight as well as largely restricting competition. Hence allocational distortions may easily outweigh the benefits of the policy regime. Moreover, large interventions in transition economies may simply not be feasible as these countries get more and more integrated into the framework of international trade agreements. Thus financial restraint may have a positive effect on economic growth and financial sector deepening, as long as the interventions are mild.

Fourth, administering a system of regulated deposit and lending rates may be a delicate task. Not only do intervening authorities require a lot of information (e.g., equilibrium market rates, elasticity of deposit funds supply and credit demand, etc.) but rent-seeking activities may interfere with the effective functioning of financial restraint. There are two aspects to be considered: (1) whenever state interventions are selective, i.e., when one industry or sector is favoured over another competition for accruing rents may be expected with the ensuing waste of economic resources.[191] (2) For the government, the timing of and a binding commitment to the phasing out of financial restraint as the economy acquires financial depth may be an intricate problem to solve. Self-seeking bureaucrats in conjunction with rent-seeking business representatives may effectively stall the gradual reduction and eventual abolishment of financial sector interventions. This risk may to some extent be defused by gradually increasing competition in the financial sector by allowing both new domestic and particularly foreign banks to enter the market.

Information economics have contributed two major insights to our discussion: firstly, markets are generally incomplete and information is imperfect. Secondly, the state may have to intervene, especially at early stages of economic development, so as to compensate for acute market deficiencies in key areas.

3.3.2.3 New Evolutionary Economics

Here the integral evolutionary approach to policy making has to be regarded as the primary advantage. It asks for a perception of reality in its entirety. Trying to incorporate historic, cultural, social, and economic determinants of a specific policy context, this approach is definitely more promising than ready-made policy recipes such as 'get prices right'. *In concreto* with regard to privatisation, for example, it would consider the previous socialist ownership structures and design a policy accordingly (e.g., in the case of Slovenia worker ownership). A policy based on evolutionary principles will quite likely be more successful because it can pay attention to the specificity of a particular development path.

---

[191] The East Asian NIEs' industrial policy approach is a successful example of how to diverge inefficient rent-seeking activities into efficiency-enhancing contest for preferential treatment by the state. See Chapter 4.2 for an in-depth analysis.

In the evolutionary framework, government no longer possesses superior knowledge. Policy makers are an endogenous element of a joint problem-solving process. The dichotomy that exists between government and the market in the models standing in the neoclassical tradition is resolved here. The government gathers information and elaborates together with industry a long-term strategy. This strategy, being the result of mediated interests, provides a common focal point. As such it also forms the basis for policy design.

The greatest disadvantage of new evolutionary economics is its vagueness. It does not give clear-cut instructions to policy makers. Another argument regards the joint problem-solving process: how can firms which are quite likely to be direct competitors be convinced so as to fully co-operate in this institution? Free-rider and moral hazard problems arising can expect to be quite substantial. One can even go a step further and ask, if there exists a real need for such a corporate approach to problem solving, why does it not evolve spontaneously without state support? If the answer is a rejection of the joint problem-solving process then the neoliberal position of government by the market is virtually within reach.

The two useful insights one can derive from new evolutionary economics are the holistic approach to policy making and the elaboration of a common vision or strategy for the future.

3.4 Synthesis II

Our analysis of economic theory has, as suspected, not revealed a single unifying theory of government intervention. There is little guidance that economics
has to offer for the justification of industrial policy, let alone for its design and
institutional arrangements. As the following Chapters four and five reveal, there
is a basic dichotomy between what policy may be justified based on economic
theory on the one hand and real life policy making or 'Realpolitik' on the other:
industrial policy, as operated by many governments both in developing countries as well as in advanced industrial economies, does not rest on a coherent
firm theoretical basis.

Against this background, in what follows we eclectically derive from the discussed theoretical approaches some pointers with regard to the justification, the
policy areas and institutional aspects of industrial policy.

3.4.1 Justification

- *Lesson 1*: Adhering to the primacy of markets with regard to allocative efficiency a case nevertheless can be made for the *mixed economy*. This applies
  in particular to the circumstances of systemic transformation when markets
  emerge and uncertainty is rampant. Government intervention may be justified
  based on:
    - classical market failures (public goods, non-convexities in production and
      externalities);
    - information-related market failures and incomplete markets;
    - the democratic legitimisation of the government.
- *Lesson 2*: The state's ability to intervene is, however, determined by a
  number of factors:
    - macroeconomic stability;
    - the information available to the government;
    - the existence of adequate policy instruments;
    - the ability of particularist interests to capture the political process.

Taken together, these factors argue for selective policy interventions only in those cases where key areas – such as financial intermediation – are affected by substantial market deficiencies.

3.4.2 Policy Areas

- *Lesson 3* : The ultimate goal of systemic transformation in Central and Eastern European countries (CEECs) being some type of market economy *competition policy* should be made a priority area of industrial policy in transition economies. Competition policy should focus on:

  - a stable legal framework allowing markets to emerge;

  - barriers to market entry erected both by incumbent firms as well as by regulation;

  - natural barriers to market entry;

  - a body of legislation allowing for market exit, i.e., a bankruptcy law which is enforced;

  - an anti-monopoly office that monitors the proper functioning of markets and intervenes where necessary.

- *Lesson 4*: A policy of mild *financial restraint* when carefully administered may help to overcome information-related market failures and have a catalytic effect on the deepening of the financial sector. When combined with selective lending-rate interventions, financial restraint may be made instrumental for industrial policy purposes. Since financial restraint is a dynamic policy concept, financial sector interventions should be phased out as higher stages of economic development are achieved.

  It should, however, be underlined that such policy is very demanding with regard to the information and administrative capabilities it requires. This casts considerable doubt on the applicability of financial restraint to the context of CEE transition.

- *Lesson 5*: Given the public good character of education and training, the *formation of capabilities* must be made a cornerstone of every policy strategy aimed at industrial upgrading and ultimately successful catching-up with advanced economies. Education and training policies should be geared towards long-term development objectives. Particular emphasis must be put on the formation of administrative capabilities. Since successful learning may require a period of temporary protection, foreign trade should not fully be liberalised from transition's inception.

- *Lesson 6*:   *Technology policy* should be aimed at the acquisition of technological capabilities to speed up the process of technological change. Successful industrial reforms call for continuous efforts to upgrade the science and technology infrastructure. Beyond institutional factors, technology policy should also offer incentives for firms to step up their own technological efforts.

3.4.3 Institutional Aspects

- *Lesson 7* :   The design of industrial policy should be understood as a *joint-problem solving process* involving government, employer and labour representatives. In this process the state acts as a co-ordinating and information-gathering *primus inter pares* thus helping to substantially reduce transaction costs.

- *Lesson 8*:   The jointly elaborated vision of socio-economic development serves as the basis for an industrial policy strategy and provides a *focal point* around which concerted efforts can be organised.

- *Lesson 9*:   The operation of industrial policies should be interpreted as an *adaptive learning process* involving trial-and-error. Against this background ready-made policy recipes are only of limited use.

- *Lesson 10*:   An *integral policy approach* has to account for the specific historical, social, economic, and institutional circumstances of a particular economy. Such an approach, moreover, requires that potential synergies stemming from the combination of different policy areas are exploited.

- *Lesson 11*:   The implementation of industrial policy should as far as possible be insulated from *interest groups* attempting to capture the political process.

* * *

The analysis in this concluding section shows that from economic theory only a few hints and patchy propositions for the design of industrial policy can be derived:

> The transformation of the centrally planned economies into market economies is an immensely complicated task for which economic theories can only provide loose metaphors, rather than precise lessons. Economists are not so fortunate as engineers assigned to build a bridge, armed with a simple goal and with hard and fast, and tested, scientific principles. Rather, economists must rely upon sets of theoretical propositions known to be true only under highly stylized circumstances and empirical results often connected to the basic theories by tenuous extra assumptions. Thus, in deliberating on economy-wide economic reforms, economists should remind themselves that their theories are incomplete metaphors, rather than precise instruction manuals laying out the path to progress in a clear and definite way.[192]

To develop guidelines for an industrial policy in the process of transition one consequently has to turn to practical experiences with such policies. In what follows we first look at advanced industrial economies before we analyse the early experiences of leading transition economies.

---

[192] Murrell (1992), pp. 35f.

4 Western Industrial Policies

The aim of this chapter is to examine the industrial policy experience of the European Union and the East Asian Newly Industrialising Economies (NIEs) with a view to extracting a number of lessons for the industrial policy design in the process of transition. The chapter is structured as follows: first, we discuss the European approach to industrial policy. In this context, the European Phare programme needs to be touched upon since it is a major channel of influence of the Union on the policy design in Central and Eastern European countries (CEECs). Since the East Asian NIEs' 'model' of industrial policy offers various interesting insights we next assess this approach. The chapter ends with Synthesis III where a number of lessons for transition economies are derived.

4.1 The European Union

For at least two reasons the European Union's (EU's) approach to industrial policy ought to be assessed in the context of industrial policies in the process of transition: first, post-socialist economies (PSEs) endeavouring to integrate into the EU have to align their policies with the Community's *acquis communautaire* in order to comply with the criteria for accession set at the European Council meeting in Copenhagen in 1993. As one element of this body of EU legislation, regulation and directives, the Union's industrial policy whose guidelines are set out in the White Paper on growth, competitiveness and employment[193] serves as a reference to Central and Eastern European (CEE) governments designing industrial policy strategies. Second, the European Union launched as early as 1989 various programmes to assist countries in transition. These initiatives developed within a short time into the single largest source of donor financing for know-how transfer to the CEECs. As will be shown below, the Union's influence on a number of industrial policy areas is far-reaching. This influence is to intensify significantly as the EU reorients its aid programmes towards acces-

---

[193] CEC (1993)

sion-driven objectives and strategies. As assistance programmes become less demand-driven and policy-taking, and more accession-driven and policy-making, the Union's *acquis communautaire* and thus its approach to industrial policy will gain in importance.

4.1.1 The Phare Programme

For the leading countries in transition the rapprochement with the European Union and eventual membership have become the principal government policy objectives. The motives behind this striving to 'return to Europe' are various. Governments in PSEs certainly do expect from the closer integration into the EU a catalytic effect on the speed of their respective transformation process and thus on the time needed to catch up with the West. Security policy considerations further intensify the wish to be irrevocably tied into both the Union's and Nato's framework as soon as possible. Finally the cultural and historical proximity and the knock-on effect of higher living standards confirm CEE governments in their intention to take up the places their countries had in Europe before World War II. The significance of the European Union for the countries in transition is underlined when trade relations are considered. For most CEECs the EU has become the foremost important trading partner with both exports to and imports from member countries accruing to over 60 per cent of total trade. Against this background, accession to the European Union has become the focal point of CEECs development strategies. They have already made substantial efforts to approximate both their legal and regulatory framework as well as their economic policies to the *acquis communautaire*.

The European Union responded very swiftly to the momentous changes in Eastern Europe. As early as 1989 the Community established its Phare programme, an initiative designed to assist the PSEs in their transition process that initially only covered Hungary and Poland.[194] Yet, since transition's inception, the programme has been extended in terms of both countries and budget. By 1997, 13 PSEs became eligible for Phare support and, by the end of 1996, cu-

---

[194] Phare stands for Poland and Hungary Aid for the Reconstruction of the Economy, since it originally covered only Hungary and Poland. [CEC, DG 1A (1997b)]

mulative commitments amounted to ECU 6,6 billion, all in the form of non-reimbursable grants.

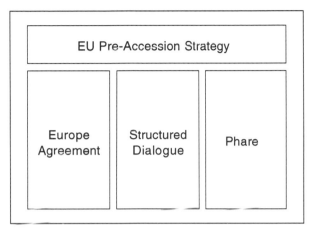

*Figure 4.1. The pillars of the European Union's
pre-accession strategy*

At the Copenhagen summit in 1993 the European Union agreed "that the associated countries of central Europe that so desire shall become members of the European Union, as soon as they are able to assume the obligations of membership."[195] In the consecutive year the Essen summit confirmed that the CEECs with Europe Agreements could become members of the Union. It further outlined a comprehensive *pre-accession strategy* to prepare the associated countries of Central Europe for membership. The strategy's goal is to support these countries in their endeavour by providing a route plan which should guide them and the European Union towards integration. The main tools of the pre-accession strategy are (see Figure 4.1): (1) the Europe Agreements, (2) the so-called structured dialogue, and finally (3) the Phare programme.

---

[195] CEC, DG 1A (1997a), p. 2; The *conditions for membership* then defined require: (1) that the candidate country has achieved stability of institutions guaranteeing democracy, the rule of law, human rights and respect for the protection of minorities; (2) the existence of a functioning market economy, as well as the capacity to cope with the competitive pressure and market forces within the Union; (3) the ability to take on the obligations of membership, including adherence to the aims of political, economic and monetary union. (ibid.)

The *Europe Agreements* are the framework for bilateral relations between the European Communities and their member states on the one hand, and the partner countries on the other.[196] The agreements cover a huge array of subjects, including trade-related issues, political, economic and cultural co-operation. They prepare the way for progressive convergence in a wide range of areas and have become the framework within which partner countries prepare for membership. Under the Europe Agreements, the associated PSEs commit themselves to approximating their legislation, particularly in the areas relevant to the internal markets, to that of the European Community. The agreements, moreover, provide the means whereby the European Union offers associated countries trade concessions and other benefits that are normally associated with full membership of the European Union.

The second instrument, the *structured dialogue*, is a multilateral framework of regular meetings at ministerial level between the Union and the partner countries. It enables the discussion of issues of common concern in areas where solutions require action at European level. The areas of policy range from cultural co-operation to the Common Foreign and Security Policy. The structured dialogue, moreover, allows prospective member countries to become more familiar with the Union's activities and institutions before accession negotiations. As a result, this instrument enhances the close working relationship essential to the European integration process.[197]

The third, and in our context the most important instrument, is the *Phare programme*. This was initially developed in 1989 as an immediate response to the challenges then facing countries in transition. As such it emphasised critical aid, but rapidly moved towards support for institutional reform. As the reforms began taking hold, Phare adapted to the changing economic and social needs of PSEs. Emphasis of the programme shifted to support for restructuring the economy, physical and human capital investment, and changing the role and impact of government through public administration reform. During this second stage of the Phare programme, activities concentrated on the consolidation of re-

---

[196] Europe Agreements have been signed with Bulgaria (1993), the Czech Republic (1993), Estonia (1995), Hungary (1991), Latvia (1995), Lithuania (1995), Poland (1991), Romania (1993), Slovakia (1993), and with Slovenia (1996) (source: CEC, DG 1A (1996), p. 4).

[197] CEC, DG 1A (1996), p. 4

forms, institutional development and investment operations. Aid took the form of policy advice, advisory and consultancy services and investment support.

Particularly in the area of *investment support* Phare has played a pivotal role. It successfully unlocked funds for important investment projects from other donors by providing pre-investment and feasibility studies and direct financing for projects that lacked start-up capital. The collaboration with international financial institutions, *inter alia*, extends to infrastructure, the banking sector and enterprise restructuring, company privatisation transactions, and credit lines to the private sector. The co-ordination and co-financing with international donors has been an integrated part of Phare and increased the leverage of the programme. The fact that the Commission has been given the responsibility for the overall aid co-ordination within the G-24 and the formal arrangement in this field with the EBRD (referred to as the 'Bangkok facility'[198]) illustrates the key position of Phare vis-à-vis transition economies.

How far the influence of Phare goes becomes evident once the priority sectors it extends to are taken into consideration. From Table A.1 in the Appendix it emerges that the programme covers the central aspects of systemic transformation in Eastern Europe. The examples of support given in each sector, moreover, elucidate the multifaceted nature of Phare. The table also reveals that Phare assistance touches on many industrial policy areas. It thus may be considered a major channel of, at least potential, influence of the European Union on the design and operation of industrial policies in transition economies. This influence, however, had not been exerted in a coherent way until the EU outlined the pre-accession strategy and made Phare its main financial instrument. Until 1995 Phare acted as a policy-taker largely accepting policies and programmes as proposed by governments in partner countries.

With the adoption of the pre-accession strategy the focus of Phare has changed fundamentally. The introduction of multi-annual indicative programmes in 1995 means that they will be increasingly set by the accession agenda, and the Commission's influence on policy formulation in the candidate states will

---

[198] Under the 1991 Bangkok facility, Phare provides grant financing to the EBRD to support the technical assistance requirements of its operations. Up to 1996 the facility has helped the EBRD and its partner countries in a crucial way to build up a portfolio of successful investments worth 1.2 billion ECU. [Mergos and Tsantis (1997), p. 18]

gradually intensify. This change of focus was reiterated and reinforced by the European Union's 'Agenda 2000': in the context of industrial policy, the Union expects candidate countries to take over the Internal Market acquis before accession.[199] The Phare approach will thus become increasingly accession-driven and *policy-making*.[200]

* * *

The declared goal of associated transition economies to join the European Union entails a far-reaching adaptation of their legislation and policies. The adoption of the *acquis communautaire* also requires that industrial policies of these countries are brought in line with EU policies. In this respect Phare, which "may be seen to reflect a microcosm of EU/western views on industrial policy"[201], is the most important channel of EU influence. This has become even more the case since the programme was designated the main financial instrument of the pre-accession strategies. With the Phare programme the European Union has a powerful leverage on the industrial policy design in transition economies. For the medium and long term it can therefore be expected that the transition economies will develop industrial policies similar to and compatible with EU policies. This development will be reinforced and accelerated by the PSEs' endeavour to achieve policy alignment ahead of schedule in order to be considered for the first round of EU enlargement.

Hence the Union's views on industrial policy will have a great signalling effect and serve as a yardstick for PSE governments. It is against this background that the next section assesses the European approach to industrial policy.

---

[199] CEC (1997c), p. 55

[200] The European Commission's 1997 communication 'Agenda 2000' outlines the broad outlook for the development of the European Union and its policies beyond the turn of the century, the impact of enlargement on the Union as a whole, and the future financial framework beyond 2000. Aiming at reinforcing the pre-accession strategy, the 'Agenda 2000' introduces two new features: (1) the *Accession Partnerships* intended to bring together within a single framework all the resources and forms of assistance available for facilitating the adoption of the Community acquis; and (2) the extended participation of applicant countries to Community programmes and mechanisms to apply the acquis. See CEC (1997b) and CEC (1997a), pp. 72 ff.

[201] Hughes (1996), p. 14

4.1.2 The Union's Industrial Policy Approach

In 1991 the European Commission published a communication wherein it presented a new approach to industrial policy in a competitive environment.[202,203] This paper, which came to be known as the 'Bangemann proposal'[204], laid out the principles of the European approach to industrial policy. The approach was new in the sense that it aspired to create an environment conducive to the growth of firms without direct public support, only allowing for *horizontal industrial policy measures*. The previous European industrial policies, by contrast, had targeted smoke-stack industries, controlled national subsidies by permitting only those intended to offset the cost of rationalisation and reduction of excess capacity, controlled imports so as to give domestic producers breathing space for adjustment and, in the case of steel, also controlled prices and output with a view to reducing overproduction. In essence, the old policy aimed to help EU firms respond to the competitive challenges from abroad by protecting them from more efficient third-country producers.[205]

The industrial policy of the 1990s, however, is outward oriented. It stresses the importance of 'fair' trade and unrestricted access to foreign markets. Although its publication at the beginning of the decade was prompted by a relative decline in European industry, the focus of the new approach is very much on those industries which are considered to lie at the heart of the future high-tech economy. The emphasis, moreover, is on horizontal schemes that are open to all industries and firms qualifying for support. These measures are intended to improve the ability of firms to adapt to market changes and undertake market-oriented research and development. In addition, they aim to encourage early adoption of new technologies and create an environment that is conducive to the growth of business. The European industrial policy concept, thus, rests on three *principles*: firstly, its main concern is the creation and maintenance of fa-

---

[202] Kommission der Europäischen Gemeinschaften (1991): An Industrial Policy in an Open and Competitive Environment: a Blueprint for a Community Concept (our translation).

[203] For an analysis see Cowling (1990) and Bianchi, Cowling and Sudgen (1995).

[204] The proposal was named after Martin Bangemann, then Commissioner responsible for Internal Market Affairs. See also Bangemann (1992).

[205] Nicolaides (1993), p. 1

vourable private sector conditions. The state may interfere to support firms that
are confronted with the need to structurally adjust. However, it must not replace
entrepreneurial initiative and industry's own responsibility to master the challenges of structural adjustment. Secondly, the Union does not operate a 'defen-
sive' protectionist industrial policy that ultimately retards or precludes
prerequisite adjustment altogether. Instead, it actively promotes and supports
industrial change. The European industrial policy approach, thirdly, is committed to open markets and fair trade.

The industrial policy of the Union is focused at the *process of structural
change*. It aims at facilitating the necessary structural adjustments by strengthening the competitiveness of European industry on world markets. The *role of
the state* is that of a catalyst and a innovative forerunner. As such, it should find
a reasonable balance between stable long-term framework conditions for an effective functioning of the market, developing the main catalysts for the required
structural adjustment and finally the instruments to accelerate this process.

According to the 'industrial policy in an open and competitive environment',
the first *precondition* necessary for structural adjustment to occur is to preserve
a stable economic framework. This requires macroeconomic stability and fiscal
policies that allow firms to generate capital from retained earnings. Second, for
an effective functioning of markets a competitive environment is indispensable.
Competition policy, thus, must prevent anti-competitive practises, and government subsidies should be controlled so as to make sure that they are only used
to support rather than to retard the adjustment process. Third, to compete on
future high-tech markets continued efforts must secure high skill levels. Fourth,
for a frictionless mastering of the adjustment process in European industry regional and social policy measures should promote the economic and social cohesion in the Community. Finally, high environmental standards should secure
sustainable long-term growth.

The Bangemann proposal names two central factors that should have a catalytic effect on industrial change. The first and foremost such *catalyst*, is the
European Union's single market. Here, *inter alia*, the harmonisation of technical
standards, the opening of domestic markets to international competitive pressures, and the emergence of a coherent legal framework are all expected to have
a positive impact on European firms' adaptive capabilities. With regard to the

I Preconditions	II Catalysts	III Accelerators
• Macroeconomic stability	• Single market	• R&D, innovation, technology
• Competition	• Trade policy	
• High skill levels		• SMEs
• Economic and social cohesion		• Training and education
• Environmental protection		• Business services

Source: Kommission der Europäischen Gemeinschaften (1991), p.25

Table 4.1: Key elements of the European industrial policy

internal market the EU, moreover, stresses the importance of developing trans-European infrastructure networks. The removal of existing bottlenecks and interlacing different means of transport (particularly road and rail networks) are given priority. The second catalyst is seen in an open trade regime. However, this must clearly be based on rigorously enforcing the rules of multilateral trade agreements (i.e., GATT, WTO).

So-called *accelerators* are policy instruments to speed up the process of industrial adjustment. The first such instrument is the promotion of technological capabilities and capacities of industry. This calls for a closer co-operation between business, the state and research institutes to improve the framework for research and development (R&D). An active innovation policy, moreover, ought to accelerate the dissemination of research results and of state-of-the-art technologies. In this respect the Commission expects positive demand effects from high-technical standards, the establishment of technologically advanced infrastructure networks, and a public procurement that fosters advanced technologies. The second accelerator is a dynamic small- and medium-sized enterprise (SME) policy. Due to their high flexibility small and medium enterprises play a pivotal role in the structural adjustment process. A labour market policy that focuses on improved employment of human resources, the facilitated introduction of new working methods, and adequate training and re-training schemes is the fourth accelerator. Finally, industrial policy should improve the conditions for the development of business services, particularly financial services. Table 4.1 summarises the key elements of the European industrial policy.

In its proposal the Commission calls for a *coherent industrial policy approach*, i.e., that the various EU policies which have an influence on industrial activities should be co-ordinated. A better coherence is to be achieved, first, by subjecting the Community's industrial policy to the principle of subsidiarity. The Community only takes on those tasks that can better be dealt with at the Community level (e.g., big research and infrastructure projects where the bundling of national resources may attain better results). The policy coherence may be further improved by better integrating the remaining sectoral industrial policies into the general industrial policy framework. Although the paper acknowledges that interventionist sectoral policies as operated by the Union in the 1970s and 1980s are inadequate instruments to promote structural adjustment, it deviates in two instances from the principle of horizontal policies: the first area concerns those sectors where the Commission expects promising future markets, namely information technologies and biotechnology. The second exception to the rule are those sectors which are still deemed to be politically too sensitive to be left without special assistance. Into the latter category fall aviation, steel, textiles and shipbuilding industries. A better coherence of the Union's industrial policy, finally, may be attained by frequent consultations with industry representatives. These consultations serve both to strengthen the social consensus and to make sure that industrial policies are oriented towards actual problems. To achieve these ends it is also of particular importance to involve both SME and labour representatives at an early stage of the policy formulation process. This social dialogue is considered a distinctive characteristic of the European social system, prerequisite to master the structural and social changes.

In November 1993 the Treaty on European Union came into force. It defines the basic task of the Community's industrial policy as ensuring that the conditions necessary for the competitiveness of European industry exist. The Treaty sets out four *objectives*: one, speeding up industry's adjustment to structural changes; two, encouraging an environment in which initiative can thrive and in which undertakings, particularly of SMEs can develop; three, encouraging an environment favourable to co-operation between undertakings; four, fostering a better exploitation of the results of innovation and of research and technological development which are of potential value to industry.[206]

---

[206] CEC (1997d)

Based on these goals the European Commission in its White Paper on growth, competitiveness and employment proposed in very general terms the *guidelines* for the implementation of the Community's industrial policy.[207] Their declared goal is to achieve dynamic, job-creating growth based on the competitiveness of European industry. Leaving the priorities of the Union's industrial policy basically unaltered, the White Paper does however slightly shift the focus towards labour market policies. Against the background of high and rising structural unemployment throughout the EU, the paper places special emphasis on employment policies that focus on the development of human resources and the creation of new jobs.

Based on these principles and guidelines, the communication of the European Commission on the policy for industrial competitiveness[208] puts the Union's industrial policy into more concrete terms by proposing a number of key *policy measures* in the following four areas:

- promotion of intangible investment;

- development of industrial co-operation;

- strengthening of competition;

- modernisation of the industrial role of public administrations.

Given the growth in information-based competition, *investment in intangible factors* such as training and R&D have been made a priority. Thus R&D policies should focus on the promotion of quality norms and standards as well as on the creation of a favourable legal framework for research (e.g., the protection of intellectual property, etc.). It should, moreover, intensify and co-ordinate efforts in the area of ecologically harmless technologies and develop economic incentives to accelerate their diffusion. Professional training should be revamped and geared to the changing needs of industry. The Commission recognises that it is vital to integrate education and training policies into the overall policy for industrial competitiveness.

A second key area regards the *development of industrial co-operation*. By removing legal and fiscal obstacles the EU attempts to pave the way to increased

---

[207] Kommission der Europäischen Gemeinschaften (1993)
[208] Kommission der Europäischen Union (1994)

co-operation among European firms. To this end, it also organises round tables that serve as consultation fora to all interested parties. In this context the EU initiates programmes tailored to the specific needs of SMEs. Efforts are, however, not limited to bringing together European actors. International fora are intended to enable industrialists from inside and outside the Union to exchange experiences and to discuss solutions to common problems (e.g., the EU-Japan consumer electronics programme and the EU-American Transatlantic Business Dialogue).

Among the factors expected to *strengthen competition* the completion of the internal market plays a pivotal role. Despite major progress there remain various deficits in a number of areas, including company law, public procurement and fiscal harmonisation that continue to distort competition. With the establishment of the internal market competition policy has become even more crucial. It has to secure a level playing-field for all firms by preventing single companies from achieving dominant positions in the market. As to international competition, the Commission's role is to seek to analyse the barriers to trade that exist in certain world markets and to take the lead on negotiations aimed at their removal. The EU is only willing to grant producers from third countries access to its market on a *quid pro quo* basis, i.e., given a reciprocal removal of trade barriers and a strict adherence to GATT and WTO rules respectively.

The fourth key policy area relates to the *modernisation of the industrial role of the state*. The Commission ascribes priority to the continued process of deregulation, the goal being to decrease the regulatory burden on economic agents. The application of cost-effectiveness and cost-benefit analysis to regulatory proposals is to further improve the Union's regulatory body. The institutional reforms should also entail a better co-ordination of the various policies that impinge on industry. The necessary reforms should comprise both an institutional consolidation of industrial policy measures as well as the development of a common vision, so to say a common denominator on which the various policies would be based. Finally, the Commission intends to develop closer contacts with industry and other major stakeholders to ensure that current and future structural changes are understood in time and co-operative solutions can be found.

* * *

Despite the vagueness of the official documents, an overall picture of the Union's industrial policy emerges from our discussion (see Figure 4.2 on the following page for an overview). In the 1990s, in contrast with the experiences of the previous two decades, the European Union puts the major thrust on *horizontal policy measures*. Giving priority to private sector initiatives it attempts to create an environment conducive to industrial growth. Yet, despite its framework orientation, the European industrial policy is however not to be confounded with a policy of laissez-faire. The approach is supportive since its goal is to strengthen the competitiveness of European industry on world markets by accelerating the process of structural adjustment. The Commission's role in this policy framework is that of a catalyst and innovative forerunner since it tries, in co-operation with industry, to anticipate in advance changes to the industrial structure. Once such change is immanent it develops corresponding policy responses.

Regardless of the emphasis on horizontal policy measures the European industrial policy still has strong *sectoral or vertical elements*. The two proactive branches of the Union's industrial policy each centre on the adjustment to structural change. In the case of so-called 'sunset industries' (i.e., steel, textiles, etc.), its role is it to retard the speed of adjustment. These industries are considered to be politically too sensitive to leave their development entirely to the market. Industrial policy measures are used to stretch the process of structural change and thus to cushion its negative (social) effects. Regarding so-called 'sunrise industries' (i.e., information technologies and biotechnology), the EU try, on the other hand, to pave their way by actively supporting their development. In these industries policy measures are targeted at accelerating the process of structural change.

As to the *institutional aspects* of the Union's industrial policy, the creation and completion of the internal market stand out clearly. Priority is attributed to legal harmonisation and continued deregulation. Another key element is the institutionalised social dialogue which the Commission regards as vital to secure the social consensus. The latter is an important precondition for the process of structural change to occur at all. The European industrial policy finally helps to facilitate industrial co-operation.

«**Industrial Policy in an Open and Competitive Environment**»: *strengthen competitiveness of European industry on world markets by facilitating structural adjustment*		
Horizontal policy measures	**Vertical / sectoral policy measures**	
• Competition policy	*Accelerative*	*Decelerative*
• Trade policy	• Information technologies	• Aviation
• Regional policy	• Biotechnology	• Steel
• Labour market and social policies		• Textiles
• Training and education policies		• Shipbuilding
• Infrastructure policy		
• R&D and technology policies		
• SME policies		
• Environmental policies		
Institutional aspects		
• Single Market		
• Deregulation		
• Social dialogue		
• Institutional consolidation of industrial policies		
• Industrial co-operation		

Figure 4.2: The European Union's approach to industrial policy

4.2 The East Asian NIEs

The countries of East and Southeast Asia showed the greatest dynamism after 1960 and by 1980, East Asia had become a new industrial centre in the world economy. Their stellar-growth performance was accompanied by significant structural changes both in their economies toward manufacturing (more than one quarter of GDP comes from manufacturing) and within the manufacturing sector itself. Here industrial production was successfully upgraded from simple labour-intensive activities to more complex and skill-intensive ones. These restructuring efforts were so successful that only two decades after their take-off in the mid 1960s the East Asian NIEs[209] were able to join the dozen or so states in the 'world club of innovators'. By the end of the 1980s Korean and Taiwanese firms were sought out by US, European and Japanese multinationals not only as second-tier suppliers but as equal partners in strategic alliances to develop new products at the technological frontier.[210]

Yet what makes the East Asian success story even more spectacular is the fact that the historically unprecedented growth rates were complemented by an impressive general improvement of living standards. The *principle of shared growth* led to a dramatic increase in per capita incomes, a more equitable distribution of income, and meant that social development indicators (e.g., infant mortality, life expectancy at birth, and adult literacy rate) came very close to those of the developed world.

---

[209] The term *East Asian NIEs* in what follows refers to Hong Kong, South Korea, Singapore, and Taiwan. Our discussion focuses primarily on the last three countries. A newly industrialising economy is seen as an event in historical time and demarcates the phenomenon of industrialisation between pre and post Second World War. This comparative-static view of NIEs holds that countries which have been able to transform themselves in the post-war era into industrial economies where manufacturing plays an important role qualify as NIEs. The more dynamic and global definition of NIEs sees their emergence as a result of a changing world production structure and corresponding shifts in the international division of labour. Additional Asian states such as Indonesia and Malaysia as well as some Latin American countries would therefore also fall into the NIEs category. [Chowdhury and Islam (1993), p. 2]

[210] Wade (1990), p. 4

Given this phenomenal catching-up process, recurrent reference is made to the East Asian NIEs in the debate on the appropriate role of the state in the Eastern European transition process.[211] However the question of what policy prescriptions can be derived from the NIEs' experience is heavily debated among (development) economists.[212] There exist basically two differing and competing views on the East Asian miracle: in the first group some neoliberal observers go so far as to outright deny the existence of any government interference. To them the East Asian NIEs are a textbook example of successful development policies along the lines of the 'Washington consensus'.[213] A less radical and better informed variant of the neoclassical view acknowledges the existence of widespread state intervention in East Asia but holds that it was at best irrelevant and at worst harmful but somehow neutralised.[214]

Conventional orthodox wisdom of dogmatic approaches in development theory has been challenged on different grounds by exponents of the second group.[215] They hold that government interventions and industrial policy in particular have been a hallmark of the East Asian development strategies. This position, however, does not claim that industrial policies have been the single factor responsible for the NIEs' success. State actions, however, have been one key component in the successful catching-up process and thus cannot be ignored.

The debate on whether or not government interventions have been of importance in the context of the East Asian NIEs has not yet been decided. Methodological problems hitherto have precluded a conclusive proof based on empirical data of the causality between government interventions and actual economic development or the contrary thereof. In this situation one is left to rely on the plausibility of arguments used in this controversy which often tends to give way

---

[211] See Amsden, Kochanowicz and Taylor (1994), Amsden (1994), Brabant (1993), Chang and Nolan (1994), Jovanovic (1995), and Scholtès (1996b).

[212] For an overview of the controversial arguments see Rodrik (1993), pp. 21ff.

[213] On the 'Washington consensus' see Williamson (1990), pp. 7ff. and Chapter 3.1.2 on Neo-liberalism.

[214] Balassa (1988), Lal (1983), Little (1982), and World Bank (1987).

[215] Chowdhury and Islam (1993), p. 103. Among the supporters of the East Asian development state are: Amsden (1989), Chang (1995), Deyo (1987), Roumasset and Barr (1992), Wade (1990) and White (1988).

to ideology and fixed-point ideas. To us, the case of the proponents of the 'capitalist developmental state' or the 'governed market economy' is by far more conclusive than the contentions made by the neoclassical free market position. That government policies played a role in East Asian development is even acknowledged by a number of orthodox economists. To claim that the effects of these interventions neutralised each other and thus on balance did not contribute to the NIEs' growth performance does not seem realistic. The conclusion of Robert Wade in his in-depth analysis of the NIEs phenomenon is therefore far more to the point:

> [T]he balance of presumption must be that government industrial policies, including sectoral ones, helped more than they hindered. To argue otherwise is to suggest that economic performance would have been still more exceptional with less intervention, which is simply less plausible than the converse.[216]

In contrast to its earlier reports the World Bank relates in the 'East Asian Miracle Study'[217] the economic success story of these countries in part to carefully administered government policies. However, since it concludes that "industrial policy [...] was generally not successful"[218], the Bank still leans more to the neoclassical side. Meanwhile a more recent IBRD discussion paper goes a step further by conceding a role for industrial policy: "[T]he fact that the economies of Japan, South Korea, and Taiwan [...] have exhibited the most rapid economic change over the last thirty years suggests that the whole idea of industrial policy cannot be simply dismissed."[219]

Against this background it thus seems legitimate to hold that *industrial policy was one element in the East Asian NIEs' successful catching-up process*. Before we now proceed to analyse the NIEs phenomenon and go on to ask what lessons may be derived from this experience for the East European transition, two caveats ought to be mentioned. First, talking about an East Asian 'model' is somewhat misleading for two reasons: firstly, the countries under scrutiny used a diversity of different policy mixes at different times. Secondly, Singapore, South Korea and Taiwan are far from uniform economies. They differ with re-

---

[216] Wade (1990), pp. 305ff.

[217] World Bank (1993) and Rodrik (1994).

[218] World Bank (1993), p. 354

[219] Harrold, Jayawickrama and Bhattasali (1996), p. 52

spect to country size, historical experience, cultural heritage, and their respective political regimes. Yet, despite these differences, we hold that there do exist common threads among NIEs and that it is possible to derive a *pattern of East Asian industrial policies*. Using the newly industrialising economies of East Asia as a point of reference for our discussion, we are primarily interested in these common characteristics. In what follows we will therefore only refer to particular country experiences to illustrate our arguments.

Second, in the discussion of East Asian development strategies the objection of their uniqueness is often raised. It is argued that the idiosyncratic cultural, social, historical and political circumstances would make the emulation of the NIEs' development path *a priori* a futile undertaking. There are two points to set against this argument of 'East Asian-ness': first of all it goes without saying that the specific circumstances (i.e., the Confucian heritage, social cohesion, legacies of Japanese colonialism, dictatorship, etc.) are an integral part of the NIEs' experience and contributed in one way or another to their success. It is therefore clear that an attempt to learn from their success cannot mean to indiscriminately copy their policies and institutional arrangements.

However, and this is the second point, neither can accepting these special factors mean dismissal of their experience out of hand. The East Asian experience reveals the key importance of 'learning' in successfully overcoming backwardness.[220] To catch up with neighbouring Japan and with other advanced economies, the NIEs closely studied economic policies applied in these countries as they embarked on the road to industrialisation and structural change. They did so, despite the dramatic differences in initial conditions of their own countries and the countries they tried to learn from. It seems that the openness and the determination to learn from others is one of the success factors that made the East Asian miracle. Adapted to the context of Eastern Europe, this means that the NIEs' experience ought to be considered as *one* source for the design of successful economic and industrial policies.

The World Bank's East Asian Miracle study holds that the NIEs' outstanding performance was based on three fundamentals, namely macroeconomic stabil-

---

[220] On economic backwardness and catching-up see Abramovitz (1986). On the role of learning in 'late' industrialisation see Amsden (1991), pp. 283ff., Chang (1994a), pp. 385ff. and Stiglitz (1987).

ity, outward orientation, and investment in human capital. The following section broaches these basics that built the foundations on which the East Asian miracle rests. The next section elucidates the nature and extent of industrial policies pursued in the countries under scrutiny. Next we discuss the institutional arrangements that are prerequisite for NIEs type government interventions. The final section of this chapter then draws a number of lessons that may be derived from the NIEs' experience for the post-socialist transition in Eastern Europe.

4.2.1 Fundamentals

The East Asian Miracle study identifies three pillars on which rests the economic success story of the newly industrialising economies. The first of these fundamentals necessary for their rapid growth performance is *macroeconomic stability*. The governments in East Asia successfully contained inflation by exercising prudent monetary and fiscal control and thus checking inflationary expectations. The NIEs, moreover, reacted rapidly and effectively to imported or domestic price shocks.[221]

Sustainable fiscal positions were achieved by an early focus on improved revenue effort and curbs on government consumption. Budget rules and legislation requiring that sovereign debt be used for development expenditures helped to ensure that borrowing rather than consumption funded investment. Where considerable foreign debt was acquired, debt-export ratios lower than in other developing countries made sure that creditors never lost faith and meant that these countries never faced a serious debt crisis requiring rescheduling.

A key element in the export-driven growth strategy was a remarkably stable and competitive real exchange rate over the years. Exchange-rate movements were kept aligned with changing structures of trade protection and inflation differentials with trading partners. Exchange-rate adjustments were supported by fiscal measures reducing expenditures, while macroeconomic stabilisation

---

[221] On the fundamentals of the East Asian NIEs development strategy see World Bank (1993) and Harrold, Jayawickrama and Bhattasali (1996).

strategies emphasising the role of the exchange rate to break inflationary expectations were avoided.

Pro-savings policies are another hallmark of East Asian economic development strategies. Low inflation, positive real interest rates, high forced savings, savings instruments available to all segments of the population at low transaction costs, stringent controls and high interest rates on loans for consumer items, stiff taxes on so-called luxury consumption, unusually high public savings, and a gradual liberalisation of capital account transactions induced savings to steadily rise as a proportion of total income and meant that a larger proportion of total savings was held in the domestic financial system. These savings financed investment rates exceeding 20 per cent of GDP on average between 1960 and 1990 which was one of the principle engines of growth.

The *outward orientation* of newly industrialising economies is the second cornerstone of their economic success.[222] Their trade regimes coupled export promotion with import protection. Whereas nascent industries were pushed into exports by a variety of means, imports were liberalised only gradually and selectively.[223] Another central element of the NIEs' outward orientation is technology policy. East Asian governments relied heavily on foreign sources of technology in their effort to build up indigenous technological capabilities. During their rapid growth periods all these countries absorbed foreign technology through licensing, imports of machinery, and reverse engineering. In addition they promoted foreign direct investment that came bundled with technical, managerial, and sometimes labour force skills. In this way East Asian NIEs managed to overcome their initial technological backwardness and successfully upgraded their industries. The ensuing productivity increases fed into economic growth.

Finally, the third fundamental that built the foundations of the NIEs' success was *investment in human capital*. Governments of East Asian NIEs fostered education in general and basic education in particular. As a consequence, universal primary education was attained early, literacy was high and cognitive

---

[222] On the importance of exports in the context of East Asian NIEs' economic development in the case of Korea see Westphal (1990).

[223] For a more detailed account of the NIEs' export push cum import protection strategy, refer to the next section.

skills lay substantially above those in other developing countries. Whereas basic education is highly oriented toward the acquisition of general academic skills, post-secondary training has a strong bias towards vocational skills. The emphasis on professionally and technologically sophisticated disciplines complemented by enterprise-level training, much of which was subsidised, was a key precondition for the absorption of foreign technologies and the creation of indigenous technological capabilities.

In short, by getting these basics right, East Asian NIEs created a stable incentive framework for business, achieved an above average accumulation of physical and human capital, and were able to technologically catch up with advanced industrialised countries in only a short period of time.

4.2.2 Interventionist Policies

The policy interventions in East Asian NIEs went beyond 'market conforming'[224] (i.e., horizontal) industrial policies. Thus, except for Hong Kong, these countries have followed activist industrial policies. However, do exist *major differences* in approaches and outcomes of their industrial policies. First, the governments differed in their treatment of foreign direct investment (FDI). Since Korea and to some extent Taiwan stipulated a certain level of domestic ownership, joint ventures and minority ownership are the prevailing pattern of FDI in these two economies. Singapore, on the other hand, showed a far more liberal attitude towards foreign investors which is mirrored by its dominant form of FDI, namely wholly or majority foreign ownership.

The second difference regards government's direct engagement in industrial production. The governments of Taiwan and Singapore at an early stage of their respective development process invested heavily in industry.[225] They started many industries including shipbuilding, oil refineries and iron-steel which they deemed 'strategic' but where private investment was limited. Hence the govern-

---

[224] See World Bank (1993), p. 355.

[225] In the 1950s, the Taiwanese state-owned enterprises (SOEs) accounted for over 50 per cent of total manufacturing output. In the 1980s they still contributed 15 per cent to industrial production and the Taiwanese government still owned seven of the country's ten largest industrial enterprises. [Chowdhury and Islam (1993), p. 98]

ments of Taiwan and Singapore used public enterprises or public laboratories to initiate big pushes in new fields, while Korea and Japan steered private firms by sometimes aggressively orchestrating their activities.

The third major difference among the East Asian NIEs – this holds in particular for Taiwan and Korea – concerns the size of the enterprises. Taiwan's industrial policy assigned greater importance to the emergence of a SME sector. As a consequence of these political priorities the industrial sector is dominated by small and equity-based companies. The selective credit and low interest rate policy of Korea, on the other hand, was focused on big and debt-based enterprises.

Yet despite these differences there exists a *common pattern* of industrial policy among the East Asian NIEs. To varying extents the governments of these countries took the lead in the structural transformation of their economies. They identified and selectively promoted those industrial activities where they assumed growth potentials and where they expected substantial sectoral spill-over effects. These policies, however, are not to be confused with 'picking winners', which would imply that out of existing potentially competitive industries those are chosen and supported that most closely fit a country's given comparative advantage. This static conception means to passively respond to a comparative advantage determined by a country's initial set of endowments. The East Asian NIEs, however, rather *made* than picked winners. They did so by creating an environment that was conducive to new industries and by controlling the key parameters on investment decisions.[226]

East Asian governments exercised a very strong influence on the process and direction of industrialisation through four major channels: trade policy, competition policy, financial sector interventions, and finally through state-owned enterprises. The cornerstone of the NIEs' success is a *trade regime* which is based on the combination of import restrictions with a strong export orientation. Hence "'inward'- and 'outward'-oriented development were not mutually exclusive and proceeded pari passu."[227] Not only were exports put on the very top of the policy-makers' agenda but they became above all an attitude. East

---

[226] Wade (1990), p. 334

[227] Amsden (1994), p. 84

Asian NIEs created a veritable national export culture that entirely dominated the process of industrial transformation. Confronted with limited home markets and an unsophisticated domestic demand structure at the beginning of their take-off, East Asian NIEs realised that for industrial upgrading and thus for productivity growth the penetration of world markets and in particular access to the markets of advanced industrialised economies was indispensable.

To foster export development priority industries and producers of intermediate goods for exports were granted a series of incentives. These encompassed *inter alia* a reform of the exchange rate, domestic content requirements, the use of public procurement rules to steer demand toward domestically made products, a wide range of fiscal investment incentives, and assistance to companies to negotiate technology transfer deals with multinationals. Yet one of the most important spurs to export activities stemmed from the modulation of international competition. Export producers were shielded from foreign competitors and thus allowed to mature under an umbrella of temporary *import restrictions*.[228] A hallmark of this 'inward' orientation has been, however, that the NIEs assured an equal footing with foreign competitors in access to inputs at world market prices. Inputs for export industries, particularly capital goods, were exempted from the protection system. The NIEs' protective import regimes thus allowed exporters to acquire state-of-the-art production technologies. Imports were only very gradually liberalised over the years. Both Korean and Taiwan maintained import restrictions until the mid-1980s, while they were encouraging at the same time strong export growth.

Beyond the modulation of international competition some East Asian governments also intervened to protect industries from new domestic entrants. By restricting entry of new producers *competition policy* has been used so as not to endanger economies of scale of established enterprises. Korea, as an example, during the 1970s promoted the growth of giant conglomerates (so-called *chaebols*) imitating Japan's *keiretsus*. The rationale was to concentrate resources on entrepreneurs with proven track records, and to encourage technological and organisational economies of scale. By 1984 the combined sales of the ten largest chaebols totalled two-thirds of Korea's GNP, up from one-third one year be-

---

[228] Recall in passing that this is the infant industry argument. See Chapter 3.2.1.

fore.[229] Wade pertains that the Korean auto industry may owe much of its success in becoming a major world producer to such state intervention.[230]

The most important interventions occurred in the *financial sector*. It is here where East Asian governments have exerted the strongest leverage on the industrial transformation. *Credit allocation* has been the main channel through which NIEs guided markets. Financial repression meant that deposit and lending rates were kept below market-clearing levels. The ensuing excess demand for credit resulted in credit rationing. In this situation governments were able to use directed-credit programmes to channel investment funds to priority industries. Concessionary credits were targeted through a contest-based allocation mechanism where enterprises had to compete for available funds. The funds were distributed in so-called deliberation councils, institutional platforms where both government and business representatives meet.[231] Beyond the actual allocation of financial means the directed-credit programmes primarily served to signal commercial banks and private investors, which sectors enjoyed government support. Banks and private investors then selected projects within those sectors and offered them additional funding at commercial rates. Targeted credits thus gave the industrial catching-up process a *general sense of direction* which was readily discernible to economic actors.

NIEs were able to use directed-credit programmes for two reasons. First, interest repression of the kind practised in East Asia requires a *bank-based financial system* on which the state has far-reaching control. This was achieved in several ways. To begin with, strong prudential regulations to improve banks' project selection were enforced and their activities were closely supervised. At the same time, competition in the banking sector was limited through restrictions on new entry. State control was further secured by the creation of public financial institutions, especially long-term credit (development) banks. In some economies the government offered explicit credit guarantees or implicitly guaranteed the financial viability of promoted projects. Relationship banking by a variety of public and private banking institutions involved the banking sector in the management of troubled enterprises, thus increasing the likelihood of creditor

---

[229] Wade (1990), p. 309 and Amsden (1989), p. 116

[230] Wade (1990), p. 311

[231] For further details on deliberation councils refer to the next section.

workouts. Through these measures a bank-based system was created in which enterprises depend heavily on banks for finance and the long-term growth preferences of government officials have more weight.

The second prerequisite for directed-credit programmes to work is that the economy is cut off from international capital markets. *Capital account restrictions* are necessary for two reasons: first, it has to be ensured that accumulated savings do not flow out of the country and that profits earned are reinvested in the domestic industry. Second, liberalised capital flows would deprive the state of its most important instrument to lead the market. Without capital account restrictions the entire idea of targeted credits would be invalidated since enterprise in need of investment finance would simply turn to foreign financial institutions.

Inherent to directed-credit programmes is a trade-off between high social returns, particularly where credit is allocated to export activities, and the potential risk that capital will be misallocated due to wrongly set government priorities. Whether or not centralised credit allocation leads to superior social outcomes crucially depends on whether investment projects competing for scarce credit are technologically complementary or substitutes. If they are complementary, information and expectation assimilation through deliberation councils will lead to a collective choice of a mutually consistent investment configuration. Co-ordination of expectations among independent agents improves the outcome, even if the expectation turns out to be inaccurate *ex post*, by minimising costs of co-ordination failure. If, however, projects are substitutes decentralised investment decisions based on differentiated expectations will attain a better social outcome. In this case, if the expectation was inaccurate *ex post*, assimilated expectations would only ensure that all agents uniformly chose an inappropriate level of investment.[232]

Yet, despite the apparent risks of co-ordinated investment decisions, the directed-credit policies of East Asian NIEs were successful. This was also conceded by the World Bank's East Asian Miracle study:

> Recent assessments of the directed-credit programs in Japan and Korea provide microeconomic evidence that directed-credit programs in these economies

---

[232] Aoki, Murdock and Okuno-Fujiwara (1996), pp. 6ff.

increased investment, promoted new activities and borrowers, and were directed at firms with high potential for technological spillovers. *Thus these performance-based directed-credit meachanisms appear to have improved credit allocation, especially during the early stages of rapid growth.*[233]

Finally the fourth major channel through which some East Asian governments exercised their influence on the structural change in manufacturing were *state-owned enterprises*. Where governments directly took the initiative and launched industrial activities this served above all two functions: one, the state got directly involved in industrial production in cases where private investment failed to materialise in designated priority areas. Thus state-owned enterprises (SOEs) signalled the state's development preferences, and were hoped via spill-over effects to spark off a self-perpetuating and self-reinforcing process of dynamic structural change. Two, state ownership of major banks, particularly of long-term lending institutes, increased the government's bargaining leverage with the big firms in the credit allocation mechanism and hence strengthened the state's ability to influence the direction of structural change.

Which then are the factors that contributed to the success of interventionist policies in East Asian NIEs? Beyond institutional arrangements which we discuss below two factors stand out: first, government assistance to specific industries was based on *stringent conditions*. These comprised the use of international prices and demanding export performance criteria to assess the efficiency and the economic performance of enterprises that wished to get access to preferential tax treatment and concessionary credits as well as to have their imported inputs exempted from tariff protection. The extreme *selectivity* with regard to the amount, duration, and the form in which assistance was extended to firms stood at the heart of the contest-based credit allocation. Enterprises competing for scarce investment funds had to constantly try to outperform their competitors in terms of export growth and efficiency. The use of exports as a yard-stick led to a clear understanding between firms, the general public, and the government about the objectives of industrial strategies and performance requirements. Since non-compliance with these standards was sanctioned by the revocation of government support it was warranted that enterprises that were protected from international competition would mature.

---

[233] World Bank (1993), p. 20, emphasis added.

Second, successful state interventions were based on a *pragmatic and flexible approach to industrial policy making*. This approach was not so much one of deliberate long-range planning, but more one of getting started, observing results, and modifying or reversing policies when they resulted in adverse economy-wide effects or macroeconomic disequilibria. This flexible trial-and-error method of experimenting with varying policy mixes allowed both to swiftly react to shifts in anticipated comparative advantage as well as to external shocks. Government assistance to firms that faced a contracting world demand for their products or world-wide overcapacities was gradually phased out, while at the same time they were pushed into new activities. Their approach to policy making also meant that the East Asian NIEs recovered faster than other developing economies and some OECD countries from oil-price shocks.

4.2.3 Institutional Arrangements

A key factor determining the success of East Asian NIEs was the institutional backbone of their economic policies. The organisational arrangements for formulating and implementing industrial policies were such as to make plausible the claim that the government led the market in a coherent rather than an *ad hoc* way. The first institutional prerequisite relates to a *stable macroeconomic framework*. The East Asian experience confirms that for the proper conduct of (targeted) industrial policies a stable macroeconomic environment is paramount. These countries used prudent macroeconomic management to prevent inefficiencies that could arise from interventionist policies getting out of hand. Some countries built *institutional constraints* that kept deficits and inflation within narrowly defined limits. Such constraints effectively acted as an early warning system for the government. Korea's retrenchment and redirection of its Heavy and Chemical Industry Drive in the late 1970s occurred in response to burgeoning macroeconomic imbalances.[234] Institutional constraints that confined inflation and fiscal imbalances were thus a constituent element in the flexible industrial policy framework of the NIEs. It allowed for an early modification or even a complete reversal of interventions that ultimately turned out to be a burden for the economy.

---

[234] Harrold, Jayawickrama and Bhattasali (1996), pp. 54ff.

The selective industrial policy of the East Asian NIEs places high demands on the *economic bureaucracy*. The identification of priority industries based on anticipated shifts in future comparative advantages, the formulation and the implementation of industrial policies, 'getting prices *wrong*' in order to achieve set policy goals, monitoring policies, and revising strategies where they turn out to fail is a highly complex and difficult task. It calls for two conditions to be met: first, a high-quality civil service must be established capable of administering these policies, and second, the economic bureaucracy must be insulated from day-to-day policy interference. Two factors helped to set up such competent and technocratic state agencies in East Asian NIEs: first, state employment was made attractive vis-à-vis private sector occupation with regard to remuneration and other benefits and second, civil service careers enjoyed a high reputation due to tough entry examinations. The ensuing competition among applicants ensured a continuing flow of the brightest students. The institution of meritocratic recruitment combined with life-time career paths, moreover, helped to support the corporate identity and internal coherence of the bureaucracy. This coherence was further fortified by dense informal networks between officials of different bureaux and ranks primarily based on the membership of elite universities.

At the same time, the interior cohesion led to a relative insulation from outside influences, the second necessary condition. The corporate identity of an elite bureaucracy, combined with life-time employment, made civil servants fairly immune to attempts to politically interfere with the management of industrial policies. The monopolisation of interest representation in deliberation councils, moreover, ensured that the economic bureaucracy was shielded from all but the most powerful interest groups. In this way it was successfully precluded that particular interests could capture the process of industrial policy making and thus influence it according to their preferences.

Deliberation councils are the third decisive factor that has contributed to the success of East Asian industrial policies.[235] These councils serve as consultation fora between the public and the private sector and are made up of high-ranking government officials, representatives of the business community and, in some

---

[235] On the institutional set-up of government-industry relations in East Asian NIEs, refer also to Scholtès (1996a).

cases, representatives of academia, consumer groups and labour. This collaborative arrangement has fulfilled several functions: first, deliberation councils have facilitated the interaction both between government officials and private sector groups as well as between major economic interest groups. The repeated interaction between them and the government has permitted an effective management of conflicts and thus contributed to the conciliation of interests. At the same time these consultation fora helped to nurture trust between the parties involved and were a basis for developing co-operative relations among them. The ensuing corporatist structure involved the co-operation and close collaboration between business and government. As such it facilitated the directed-credit policies:

> [The] fusion of interests between government and large private firms helps to sustain a relatively well-developed policy network between the economic bureaucracy and these firms. In this context long-term exchange relationships can develop, in which the government makes help available in return for specified performance on the firms' part.[236]

Second, the close and repeated contact between private and public sector agents meant an intensive *exchange of information* from which both sides benefited. It helped reduce the uncertainty that the business community normally associates with respect to the policy environment and thus encouraged private investment in long-term economic activities. The frequent interaction with business representatives, on the other side, allowed members of the economic bureaucracy to collect and sift information that they needed to formulate policies that would enhance the performance of the private sector and the economy as a whole. Thus deliberation councils ameliorated the informational problem inherent to all market economies due to various imperfections. These problems are particularly acute at early stages of development as prices do not capture all the necessary information. In such situations deliberation councils may complement the function of the price mechanism as a transmitter of information.[237]

Third, deliberation councils have helped to minimise the deleterious effects of *rent-seeking*. Since the rules for allocating rents through directed-credit pro-

---

[236] Wade (1990), p. 322

[237] On information economics see Chapter 3.2.2.

grammes were clear to all the groups and firms involved, 'under-the-table' favour seeking or lobbying was successfully converted into a more transparent process in which private sector actors openly contended with each other for government support: "In contrast to lobbying, where rules are murky and groups seek secret advantage over one another, the deliberation councils are intended to make allocation rules clear to all participants."[238] The contest for government assistance, moreover, ensured that interventions attempting to guide resource allocation were relatively successful despite the lack of competition *via* the market due to import restrictions. Deliberation councils, thus, have both reduced resources devoted to rent-seeking activities and created competitive pressures among interest groups and firms wishing to receive assistance from the state.

Fourth, the consultation fora add *legitimacy* to policies as the consent is sought from private parties. Since the most important interest groups are involved in the formulation and implementation of economic policies these are based on a broad social consensus. The resulting concerted activities of economic actors have meant that resources were effectively focused on a common economy-wide development strategy.

Fifth, deliberation councils increased the *flexibility* of policy makers and business to react to a changing environment. Due to the improved communication between the government and the private sector, changes have been anticipated at an earlier stage and policies that led to unintended outcomes could be reversed earlier. The institutional arrangement itself, moreover, has been subject to modifications. In Korea and Japan they changed over time to a more indicative and consensus-building role as industrial policies became increasingly horizontal.

In short, institutional factors have played a pivotal role in building the 'East Asian miracle'. Institutionalised constraints ensuring a stable macroeconomic environment, an elite civil service and deliberation councils have been the institutional basis for the success of state interventions in East Asian NIEs.

---

[238] World Bank (1993), p. 14

* * *

Our reading of the East Asian NIEs' development relates their economic success to a combination of getting the fundamentals right and of tying highly selective policy interventions through the credit market to strict performance criteria. These policies and the concomitant institutional arrangements helped to make credible the government's long-term commitment to set development objectives (see Figure 4.3 on the following page for a summary of our analysis of the East Asian NIEs' approach to industrial policy). By identifying priority industries the state created focal points for the process of structural change. The ensuing *long-term perspective* meant that the short-termism inherent to early stages of the industrialisation process was successfully overcome: "In this environment lumpy and long-term investment projects were undertaken which would probably not have been undertaken in an economy with free trade and capital movements, because they would not have been consistent with short-term profit maximization."[239]

The East Asian NIEs' experience epitomises a successful application of an infant industry development strategy as we have interpreted in Chapter 3.2.1 (i.e., the capabilities approach to industrial policy). At the core of the NIEs' successful catching-up process stand consistent efforts to build up indigenous technological capabilities and to take advantage of dynamic learning effects. The trade regime enabled nascent industries to grow under an umbrella of temporary import protection. Shielded from international competitive pressures, firms were given a breathing-space which they used both to adopt and acquaint themselves with foreign technologies as well as to build up economies of scale.

That, in contrast to the experience of many other developing countries, infant industry protection was successfully applied in East Asian NIEs may be ascribed to two factors: one, state protection and assistance were only granted to firms that complied with stringent export performance and efficiency criteria. Firms that did not meet these performance requirements were sanctioned by the immediate revocation of public support. Two, East Asian NIEs created a technocratic elite bureaucracy that possessed the prerequisite expertise to successfully manage these interventionist industrial policy measures. Thus the strict

---

[239] Wade (1990), p. 334

conditionality of government assistance and administrative capabilities were both crucial for nascent industries to become internationally competitive.

«Making Winners»: *dynamic conception of comparative advantage*		
Policy interventions		**Institutions**

• Trade policy
  – Modulation of international competition
  – Export promotion
• Financial sector interventions
  – Contest-based credit allocation
  – Bank regulation and supervision
  – Capital account restrictions
• Competition policy
  – Protection of economies of scale
• SOEs
	Strict efficiency
	
	and
	
	performance criteria
		• Institutional constraints to secure macroeconomic stability
		• Elite civil service
		• Deliberation councils

Fundamentals		
• Macroeconomic stability • Outward orientation • Human capital investment		

Figure 4.3: The East Asian NIEs' approach to industrial policy

4.3 Synthesis III

The goal of this section being to forge a link between the analysed industrial policies and the process of transition, the attempt is made to derive a number of lessons for the design of industrial policies in CEECs. In what follows, we first examine the European Union's industrial policy approach for pointers that may serve as a reference for transition economies before we come to the experience of East Asian NIEs.

4.3.1 The Rapprochement with the European Union

This section presents a number of lessons for transition economies that may be derived from the industrial policy approach of the European Union. The lessons are structured as follows: first, we examine general insights that our analysis offers for industrial policies in the process of transition. Then we turn to more detailed policy lessons before we finally turn to pointers relating to the institutional set-up of industrial policies.

4.3.1.1 General Lessons

- *Lesson 1*: From the progressing integration of transition economies into the European Union a *convergence of industrial policies* may be expected. PSEs will bring their respective policies in line with the EU's approach to industrial policy which entails the adoption of primarily horizontal, i.e., framework oriented policy measures.

  This tendency is reinforced from two sides: the Union expects prospective member states to take over its *acquis communautaire*, i.e., its body of regulations, directives and standards. The Commission, moreover, disposes with the Phare programme over a powerful leverage on the policy design in transition economies. The latter, on the other hand, in their attempt to fulfil accession conditions ahead of time are eager to adapt their industrial policies to those of the European Union.

- *Lesson 2*: The current European approach to industrial policy is a reaction to the interventionist policies of the previous two decades and is tailored to the current situation of European industry faced with the challenges of globalisation. The European approach to industrial policy, thus, roots in the western European historical experience and corresponds to the specific needs of EU member states.

From our analysis of the socio-economic transition process in Chapter 2.2 it emerged, however, that PSEs for some time to come may have quite different industrial policy needs. The sheer amount of structural change that these economies are experiencing, coupled with weak financial intermediation, suggests that the PSE governments may have to play a greater role in managing the direction of industrial change than the European approach to industrial policy would allow for.

Therefore an indiscriminate adoption of the European industrial policy conception that does not account for the specific problems transition economies are confronted with has to be rejected.

- *Lesson 3*:   Yet despite the different policy needs of advanced western European industrial economies and transition economies respectively the Union's industrial policy approach does address a *problem common to both worlds*. Its goal to strengthen the competitiveness of the industrial sector by targeting and accelerating adjustment to structural change is also of great relevance for industrial policies of PSEs. Both Western European as well as transition economies are faced with the challenge of successfully mastering the process of 'creative destruction'. They differ, however, with regard to the scope, depth and direction of necessary changes.

- *Lesson 4*:   Since the European industrial policy is only vaguely defined it leaves *ample scope for different emphasis on appropriate types of policies*. This means that, although PSEs will have to adapt their industrial policy concepts to that of the EU, this does not save them from having to develop industrial policy frameworks of their own. As the comparison of Germany (coherent framework; focus on regional aspects and SMEs) and the UK (range of ad hoc measures; emphasis on competitiveness) reveals, the industrial policy approach of the Community does leave enough room both to incorporate idiosyncratic systemic features as well as to account for the specific policy needs of a given economy.[240]

- *Lesson 5*: Within specific policy areas there is also *substantial scope for more or less active policies* – as well as choices about how and whether to fit industrial policies into a general framework, and how to relate industrial policies to other policy areas.

4.3.1.2 Industrial Policy Areas

- *Lesson 6*: An industrial policy approach as broad as that of the European would by far exceed the budgetary scope of transition economies. PSEs adapting the EU's industrial policy will, thus, have to *prioritise on certain key areas*. The Commission's industrial policy approach does indicate these priorities. They are: a stable economic framework, competition policy, SME promotion, education and labour market policies and, infrastructure policies.

- *Lesson 7*: The European approach to industrial policy emphasises the importance of getting right the *preconditions for structural change*. Those that are particularly relevant to the context of transition are: macroeconomic stability, high skill levels and, economic and social cohesion. The last factor confirms our conclusion derived earlier from the analysis of political-economy aspects of transition, that for industrial policies to be sustainable a *social consensus* is indispensable. The required economic cohesion, moreover, calls for regional policy measures to be an integral element of industrial policies in the process of transition.

Another important precondition are *high skill levels* which largely determine the extent to which an economy may adjust to industrial change. Yet a highly trained labour force does not suffice. Professional qualifications, in addition, must match the needs of industry.

- *Lesson 8*: The European experience reveals that, with increasing deregulation of economic activities and the integration into the Single Market, *com-*

---

[240] Although the Commission sees no need to modify the objectives of the European industrial policies it acknowledges the necessity to adapt them to the specific needs of both the acceding states and the resulting broader integration process. [CEC (1997c), p. 12]

petition policy becomes vital for the proper functioning of markets. This applies in particular to the emerging market economies of Central and Eastern Europe where competition is under constant threat due to dominating positions of (former) SOEs.

- *Lesson 9*:   The Commission of the European Union has made *small and medium enterprises* the centre of gravity of its industrial policies. This is based on the insight that SMEs form the flexible backbone of an advanced industrialised economy. Against this background various EU industrial policy initiatives (e.g., R&D programmes, regional policy, etc.) provide for the promotion of SMEs. For PSEs it may, therefore, be concluded that SME policies should stand at the heart of their industrial policies. This is even more so given that this company sector is particularly disadvantaged by the dysfunctional financial intermediation.

- *Lesson 10*:   A central area of the European industrial policy approach are *education and labour market policies*. They are aimed at the changing skill requirements of industry and increasing the responsiveness of labour supply to industrial change. As such, these policies attempt to facilitate and at the same time accelerate the necessary transition of skill profiles. They, thus, significantly contribute to social cohesion. Adapted to PSEs this implies that education and manpower training policies should focus on the needs of industry. Labour market policies, on the other hand, should be geared toward re-training.

- *Lesson 11*:   *Infrastructure projects* have a prominent place within the EU's industrial policy framework. Efforts extend to transport, energy and telecommunication networks. The significance that the EU attributes to infrastructure for competitiveness and economic integration is reflected by its corresponding efforts within the Phare programme. A major fraction of total resources goes to infrastructure support in PSEs. From the latter this requires, in turn, substantial efforts. These should be co-ordinated by a coherent infrastructure policy that is integrated in the overall industrial policy framework.

4.3.1.3 Institutional Aspects

- *Lesson 12*:   The European Commission recognises that the effectiveness of its industrial policy measures suffers from a lack of co-ordination and institutional dispersal. Against the background of scarce public finance an *overall co-ordination and institutional consolidation of industrial policy* should be given priority by PSE governments.

4.3.2 The East Asian Experience

After having extracted lessons from the industrial policy concept of the European Union we now turn to the East Asian NIEs and attempt to derive from their approach to industrial policy pointers for PSE strategies. The section is structured as follows: first, we focus on guidelines concerning the general nature of industrial policy. Next, we turn to specific policy areas and try to find an answer to the question of what lessons can be learnt from the NIEs' experience for the transition process in Eastern Europe. The final part then deals with institutional aspects. It is here where the East Asian NIEs offer the most elucidating insights.

4.3.2.1 General Lessons

- *Lesson 1:* Industrial policy strategies ought to provide a *long-term vision* of economic development to give the process of structural change a general sense of direction. East Asian NIEs successfully created such a long-term perspective and set out with determination to design and implement policies to realise their vision. Like this they managed to bundle economy-wide efforts to achieve development objectives.

- *Lesson 2:* The success of East Asian NIEs indicates that the catching-up with advanced industrial economies demands a *flexible and pragmatic approach* to industrial policy making. Rather than ready-made policy recipes and holding on to ideologically biased fixed-point ideas a trial-and-error approach is required in order to swiftly react to fast-changing circumstances. This applies specifically to the context of East European transition where policy makers are often confronted with historically unprecedented challenges. Hence a consistent and co-ordinated attentiveness to the problems and opportunities of designated industries, and a close watch on external markets are needed to anticipate at an early stage developments that call for policy modifications.

- *Lesson 3*:   The NIEs' experience corroborates the importance of getting the *fundamentals* right. They constitute the foundation on which industrial policies have to be based. The three pillars of industrial policy are:
  - maintenance of macroeconomic stability
  - outward orientation of the economy
  - investment in human capital

- *Lesson 4*:   Following the East Asian NIEs' principle of shared growth PSEs in order to secure political stability as the *conditio sine qua non* for a successful transition should make sure that the costs of adjustment are shared by all social groups. A highly unbalanced distribution of transition sacrifices bears the inherent risk of social instability. So the *principle of shared adjustment costs* and – once these economies take off – of *shared growth* add to the government's legitimacy and may help to win the support of the society at large.

- *Lesson 5*:   The experience of the East Asian NIEs reveals that their *national learning culture* is a decisive success factor. This holds both for the level of policy-making as well as for the industry or firm level:

  a) East Asian governments showed no reluctance to carefully analyse, adopt, and adjust where deemed necessary policies of advanced economies that proved worthwhile. East Asian NIEs, however, not only show a great interest in industrial policy strategies of advanced industrial countries but also keep a close watch on each other. They monitor markets in which the other is successful (e.g., Taiwan went into Eastern Europe after observing Korea's earlier success[241]), and also copy policies in meticulous detail.

  With a view to Eastern Europe, one might therefore conclude that the willingness and openness to learn from others will be paramount for rapid industrial restructuring and thus ultimately for the success or else catching-up with the advanced industrial economies. It also means that PSE governments should widen their horizons when consulting other countries' experiences for policy advice. This may *inter alia* include the industrial policies of neighbouring transition economies and the experience of East

---

[241] Wade (1990), p. 334

Asian NIEs. The yard-stick ought not to be ideological policy prescriptions but rather the success of policy instruments applied elsewhere.

b) Firms were encouraged and assisted by the state to access the latest technologies, whether this be through joint-ventures with foreign partners or via licensing agreements. Once production in a new industry was started firms were granted temporary protection from domestic and international competition to move up the learning curve.

Education policies with a thrust on vocational training and with strong orientation toward engineering ensured that firms had access to human capital that was prerequisite first to absorb imported technologies and then to build up indigenous technological capabilities. For Eastern Europe this implies that education policies must be a cornerstone of industrial policies. The necessary structural change requires a highly trained work force and constant efforts to accumulate human capital. Firms, moreover, should be assisted to acquire the know-how needed for a market economy environment.

4.3.2.2 Industrial Policy Areas

● *Lesson 6*: For PSEs the *ability to govern markets* in a similar way to East Asian NIEs is greatly *limited* due to several reasons:

a) The modulation of international competition is next to impossible because of: (1) the early liberalisation of foreign trade at the beginning of the transition process; (2) the obligations arising both from the Europe Agreements and; (3) from WTO membership; (4) the negative repercussions that retaliatory measures of trade partners in response to PSEs' import restrictions would have on their growth performance.

b) The instrument of directed-credit allocation as operated in East Asia in transition economies would be largely ineffective, if not counterproductive, since: (1) state banks are privatised and governments thus lose an important leverage on the financial sector; (2) capital account transactions have been largely liberalised; (3) such a credit allocation mechanism would most seriously hit SMEs which already find it difficult to get access to scarce capital. By contrast, larger firms could simply turn to foreign sources of finance and thus bypass efforts of local governments to influence the direction of structural change.

c) Given the slack growth of the world economy for PSEs today, it is much more difficult to harness exports as the primary engine of growth than it was for the NIEs during the 1960s and 1970s.

- *Lesson 7*:   The East Asian export push strategy shows that an unconditional outward orientation is a key to overcoming economic backwardness. Eastern European transition economies should create a *national export culture* along the lines of the NIEs, i.e., focus long-term policy strategies on the penetration of sophisticated export markets of advanced economies. Only in this way will the Eastern European industrial production become efficient and competitive on world markets.

The integration of PSEs with multilateral trade agreements and the rapprochement with the EU, however, precludes interventionist versions of the export-push model. Hence priority should be given to export-promotion policies that encompass measures such as marketing, transmission of information and quality control.

- *Lesson 8*:   PSE governments should attempt to attract *foreign direct investment* that produces for export markets and from which significant spill-over effects can be expected. This finding, however, is qualified by the weak bargaining position of PSEs vis-à-vis multinationals due to the intense global competition for FDI.

- *Lesson 9*:   The experience of the high-performing East Asian NIEs divulges that *investment promotion* is a key to overcoming capital market imperfections, particularly at early stages of development. These market imperfections above all affect SMEs which find it difficult to raise the needed investment funds. It is crucial that PSE governments by offering concessionary credits or credit guarantees substitute for malfunctioning capital markets. Yet our analysis of the East Asian NIEs underlines the importance of *quid-pro-quo* conditions, i.e., the strict conditionality of state assistance. Industrial investment promotion cannot mean an indiscriminate all-round distribution of subsidies. Instead, state assistance ought to be granted only when based on selective performance criteria. The necessity to discriminate among firms applying for state support at the same time enables governments to influence the direction of structural change. Thus, in accordance with the goals set down in an overall development strategy, state support might be targeted on those SMEs that build ancillary industries in designated priority sectors.

- *Lesson 10*: Similar to East Asian NIEs, Central and East European governments should promote a *bank-based financial system* that has several advantages over a capital-market based system:

a) It permits higher investment than would be possible if investment depended on the growth of retained profits alone or on the inevitably slow development of capital markets.

b) Particularly with regard to the SME sector, a bank-based financial system may help to instil a long-term perspective of co-ordinated investment decisions. Relationship banking involves a long-term commitment by the creditor (either the state and/or private banks) to the borrowing company. The former needs the latter to do well so as to enable him to repay his loans over the long term. The lender has a genuine interest in the performance of debtor companies and will allocate capital accordingly. From a bank-based financial intermediation, thus, an improvement of corporate governance problems in PSEs may finally be expected.

c) A financial intermediation along these lines puts banks due to their engagement across sectors and industries ultimately in the position to better co-ordinate investment decisions and to encourage a more rapid sectoral mobility in anticipation of structural changes.

However, such a system contains certain *imperatives*:

1) The banks' balance sheets must be cleaned of non-performing bad loans that have accumulated between them and SOEs. This requires the state to socialise some risk so as to counter the danger of financial instability in the economy.

2) Suppliers of credit must get involved with the company management. Only in this way will they be able to effectively co-ordinate investment decisions in the economy and ameliorate corporate governance of firms.

3) Institutional capacities are to be developed that allow banks and/or the state to discriminate between responsible and irresponsible borrowing. The

required expertise compounds *inter alia* the evaluation of investment projects and the capacity to effectively monitor business performance.

4) A strict bank regulation and supervision of their operations is needed to
ensure the stability of the financial system.

- *Lesson 11*: PSEs need to develop *R&D policies* that complement private
sector initiatives or substitute them where necessary. These policies should
be developed in close co-operation with industry and given limited public
funds and above all be focused on applied research. The East Asian experience elucidates that R&D policies ought to be a centrepiece of industrial
policy and thus should be closely tied in with other policy areas.

4.3.2.3 Institutional Aspects

- *Lesson 12*: From the East Asian experience the lesson may be extracted that
for an industrial policy to be effective the institutional responsibility for the
formulation and implementation of these policies should be concentrated in
one or two state agencies. The policy heartland of this *'pilot agency'* or 'economic general staff'[242] within the central bureaucracy is the industrial and
trade profile of the economy and its future growth path. It should be assigned
the paramount task of co-ordinating the work of the different ministries involved in the implementation of industrial policies and hence ensure that the
various policy areas are complementary. The technocratic staff of this central
industrial policy agency should be highly competent and protected from day-
to-day political interference.

- *Lesson 13*: At the heart of the East Asian 'model' stand *deliberation councils*. These consultation fora serve as an interface between government on
one side and business representatives on the other. They assure the exchange
of information between the parties involved. The councils allow the government to formulate better policies inasmuch as state officials are better informed. Deliberation councils may also entail a greater acceptance of
industrial policies since these are the outcome of negotiations between the

---

[242] Wade (1990), p. 371

private and the public sector. For private business there is the advantage of a greater transparency of public policies and thus reduced uncertainty.

In Eastern Europe the corporatist structure of deliberation councils representing a limited number of major economic interest groups may help to mediate the uneasy tensions between unrestricted market forces and social peace. They may be harnessed to buffering the costs of the socio-economic transformation while at the same time allowing adjustments to occur. Deliberation councils thus may play a prominent role in the creation and preservation of a social consensus.

Where deliberation councils are created they should initially be charged with more straightforward tasks (e.g., FDI promotion strategies, removal of legal and bureaucratic obstacles) before moving on to more complex (e.g., sector strategies) or more sensitive (e.g., privatisation approaches, tariff reforms) issues. The gradual building-up of the role of these councils can be justified by the danger that initial failure from being over-ambitious could undermine the confidence of both sides in such mechanisms.[243]

- *Lesson 14*: Making a *council system* work has several *requisites*:

a) The council members must have mutual respect for each other. Unless economic bureaucrats have the skills and the authority to formulate and implement good industrial policies, business representatives are unlikely to take the deliberations seriously since government officials have nothing much to offer in negotiations. Conversely, if private sector representatives were incompetent and not sufficiently authorised to represent their interest groups the consultations would be futile for the government. For deliberation councils to work, therefore, well organised major interest groups are important.

b) Moreover, both bureaucrat and private sector members of councils must enjoy a high degree of respect among their peers to be able to deliver on the commitments made at the bargaining table.

c) For the continuity of these consultation fora some reasonable degree of longevity of the political regime is important. If private sector agents ex-

---

[243] Harrold, Jayawickrama and Bhattasali (1996), p. 111

pect the regime to be replaced in the near term, they are likely to discount
the value of collaboration with the councils quite heavily. They will consequently be much less willing to participate seriously in any deliberative
process. This implies that for deliberation councils to make sense a certain
degree of political stability is prerequisite.

d) A minimum level of trust between the government and the private sector is
indispensable. Co-operation will not emerge where government officials
and private sector agents are mutually suspicious of each other and suspect
the other of dubious motives. In such an atmosphere it would be next to
impossible to enter a constructive dialogue. The nature of trust between the
parties involved for the most part depends on historical factors. One
benefit of deliberation councils is that they may help to engender mutual
confidence in the participants. This seems particularly relevant to the circumstances of Eastern European transition where the image of government
officials in the public is still strongly associated with the pre-1989 bureaucracy.

* * *

Our analysis of the industrial policies of the European Union and the East Asian
NIEs respectively has turned out to be much more fruitful in terms of concrete
insights for the design of industrial policies in transition economies than the
previous theoretical chapter. Based on the two approaches to industrial policy,
we have been able to derive a whole list of lessons for the process of transition.
It is, moreover, noteworthy that both the European as well as the East Asian industrial policies run counter to orthodox policy prescriptions in that the role of
government transgresses the narrow boundaries defined by these theories. In
other words, there exists, in advanced market economies a wide hiatus between
economic theory on the one hand and industrial 'Realpolitik' on the other:

> That mainstream economists warn, with what at times seems virtual unanimity,
> against the inefficiencies and distortions that allegedly derive from state
> interventions, whereas governments in the First and Third Worlds, not to
> mention the Second, proceed almost without exception against that advice, is
> not an accidental absurdity. It is but the ongoing manifestation of the normative

antinomies and the contradictions of analysis and prescription that have the modern state accompanied throughout its history.[244]

It might, thus, be concluded that policy recommendations for transition economies should not so much be based on economic theory but on concrete experiences. The question should be about which policies worked under what circumstances successfully and which turned out to be a failure. It is against this background that we will draw particularly on the present chapter's findings when we outline an industrial policy framework for transition economies in Chapter 6. Yet, before we join together our findings, we first want to analyse the industrial policy experiences of the leading transition economies and see what can be learnt from them.

---

[244] Evans, Rueschemeyer and Skocpol (1985), p. 364

5 Early Experiences – The Leading Countries in Transition

The leading post-socialist economies (PSEs) in transition, i.e., the Czech Republic, Hungary, Poland and Slovenia are already well advanced on their path to a market economic system.[245] They have all quite successfully stabilised their macroeconomy and are well into the second phase of the transition process, that is, economic restructuring. In that they may learn from these forerunner experiences, countries lagging behind in their systemic transformation have a distinct late-comer advantage. PSEs are faced with comparable problems and hurdles in their respective transition process. Bearing in mind the idiosyncratic nature of historic, economic, social and cultural development paths, it is argued that generalisations can be made and thus lessons can be derived from these early experiences.

Against this backdrop the purpose of this chapter is to analyse the industrial policy experiences of advanced transition countries. In what follows the industrial policies of the Czech Republic, Hungary, Poland and Slovenia are discussed in turn. First we analyse the policies pursued in each of these countries. Next we look at institutional aspects and examine how the industrial policy formulation and co-ordination is carried out. The concluding section finally gives an overview of the different industrial policy approaches and derives a number of lessons for the general industrial policy framework in transition economies.

---

[245] Recall at this stage that the present paper does consider developments in Central and Eastern European transition economies from the inception of the transition process in the region in 1989 until 1997.

5.1 The Czech Republic

The Czech Prime Minister Vaclav Klaus and his party were the self-styled model pupils among Central and Eastern European reforming countries.[246] Government rhetoric has propagated time and again a 'market economy without adjectives'. Since this officially uncompromising freemarket stance leaves next to no room for an industrial policy it is not surprising that the Czechs have not yet formulated a comprehensive policy vis-à-vis the industrial sector. The focus of economic policy has been on macroeconomic rather than on microeconomic issues related to economic restructuring. The three pillars of the Czech economic policy are: first, a restrictive monetary and fiscal policy, second, wage controls, and finally, low exchange rates. Taken together, the last two elements lead to labour costs in the Czech Republic which are below OECD countries and even lower than in Hungary and Poland.[247]

Besides the ideological complexion of the ruling party the absence of a general approach to industrial policy in part may also reflect that no need was felt for an active role of the state with regard to industrial restructuring. The Czech record of economic reforms was a remarkable success story until 1995 when both trade and current account got into deficits. The transition started under favourable conditions[248] and the government managed quite rapidly both to liberalise and stabilise the economy and to balance the budget (see Table A.2 in the Appendix.). The two waves of voucher privatisation brought a swift denationalisation of state-owned enterprises (SOEs) and secured public support. The nonexistence of an industrial policy strategy may further be related to the break-up of former Czechoslovakia and the location of some hard-hit sectors (above all the armaments industry) in Slovakia rather than the Czech Republic.[249]

---

[246] Neue Zürcher Zeitung (1997c) and (1997f)

[247] OECD(1994), p. 100. In future, the control of the exchange rate will be more difficult since the Czech National Bank was forced by capital markets to change to a regime of managed floating of the Koruna. Wage controls, in contrast, have been reinforced by the latest macroeconomic stabilisation programme. See Neue Zürcher Zeitung (1997b).

[248] I.e., the industrial tradition of the pre-communist era, the vicinity to European markets, relatively small monetary disequilibria, small foreign debt, and finally the chance to learn from the experiences of the two transition forerunners, namely Hungary and Poland.

[249] Hughes (1996), p. 5

5.1.1 Policy Areas and Instruments

A closer look at the actual policy measures implemented by the Czech government, however, reveals a whole range of industrial policy interventions. Firstly, this can be related to a compromise that was struck at the beginning of the transition process between the Prague Spring reformers and the 'new' liberals headed by Vaclav Klaus.[250] The latter, the nominal winners of this debate, agreed as a concession to tripartite negotiations (government - trade unions - employers) and gradually included some industrial policy elements into their economic policy. Moreover, it seems that despite its radical free market ideology the Czech government is rather pragmatic when it comes to everyday policy making.[251]

Small- and medium-sized enterprise (SME) policy, export promotion, large-scale privatisation and competition policy build the *four main pillars* of the Czech *de facto* industrial policy. To begin with, the Czech government has an active and comprehensive *SME policy*.[252] Several policy areas which in OECD countries have various addressees across different firm sizes and sectors are almost exclusively focused on the development of a strong, small, and medium enterprise sector. They are, thus, a subset of the country's SME policy. *Industrial investment* is promoted by various tax concessions and an accelerated depreciation of fixed assets. To foster the diffusion of modern technologies in the SME sector science and technology parks have been established. Beyond the primary goal of enabling SMEs to access advanced technologies these institutions assist the development and use of technologies related to energy savings, environmental protection and the informatisation of the economy. These programmes are financed through state subsidies and borrowing on conditional

---

[250] The debate was about the future course of the reform process. The Prague Spring Reformers gave priority to systemic reforms. They argued above all for an improvement of SOE management and for the adoption of a structural industrial policy. The 'new' liberals, however, favoured a complete transformation of the economic system and an unconditional transition to a market economy. Privatisation and systemic changes were given top priority. [Bohata and Mladek (1996)]

[251] Bohata and Mladek (1996), p. 42

[252] For a description of the Czech industrial policy see Bohata and Mladek (1996) and OECD (1994).

terms. In addition, the state funds centres conducting fundamental research. It is, however, noteworthy that the Czech Republic does not have a general *research and development (R&D) policy*. This "may in fact be one of the most distinctive features of the Czech position not only in comparison to the other CEE countries but also in comparison to western countries."[253]

What has just been said about the R&D policy equally holds for the Czech *regional development policy*: a homogenous and genuine policy does not exist. Rather, regional policy instruments are used to encourage and support the development of SMEs in underdeveloped regions. Additionally, it covers environmental programmes for areas which have been seriously polluted in the course of socialist industrialisation and infrastructure projects in most disadvantaged regions.

The Czech SME policy in the narrower sense consists of different programmes providing enterprises with less than 500 employees with capital, training, consultancy and information. Financial assistance is provided within the framework of the Czech and Moravian Development Bank. The bank not only gives credit guarantees and financial support but also consults SMEs on state assistance programmes. From what has been said emerges that the area of SME policy is one cornerstone of the Czech industrial policy.

The second salient industrial policy area is *export promotion*. This is the industrial policy most accepted by the Czech government and thus the most elaborated and comprehensive one. Exchange rate and monetary policy have been used to fix the exchange rate of the Koruna well below purchasing power in order to facilitate the re-orientation of trade towards the West. This strategy was successful: macroeconomic stability was attained, exports were growing rapidly and the balance of payments was in surplus. These positive results, however, are qualified once the concomitant negative side effects of an undervalued currency are taken into consideration: on the one hand, the low exchange rate to some extent ossified socialist industrial structures since firms which under an exchange rate based on purchasing power would not have survived in an open economy suddenly found it profitable to export. On the other hand, competition in world markets by means of lower prices tends to lock industrial production in

---

[253] Hughes (1996), p. 12

raw materials, semi-manufactures, and generally products whose quality is easy to judge. That this may be problematic is best illustrated by steel exports: "[E]xport winners in this case are not necessarily determined by long-run comparative advantage vis-à-vis other industries in the Czech Rebpulic, but rather by the ease with which these sorts of goods can penetrate world markets."[254]

The above mentioned recent switch of the Czech National Bank to managed floating means that the leeway for exchange rate policy has been considerably narrowed. Though the ensuing appreciation of the Koruna will lead to a further deterioration of the trade balance in the short and medium term one might expect positive effects on the long-term competitiveness. This will be based on genuine comparative advantages of Czech firms rather than on an undervalued currency.

Czech exporters also benefit from financial support and a variety of information services. The Export Guarantee and Insurance Company (EGAP) is an institution similar to the German HERMES, the French COFACE and the Swiss ERG. EGAP provides firms with export guarantees covering both political and financial risks and offers export consultancy. In 1994 the Czech Export Bank was established as a relatively inexpensive source of export finance. Although the bank was furnished with considerable founding capital its impact has been very limited. This may in part be explained by the Prime Minister's opposition to this institution.[255] Information centres under the aegis of the Ministry of Industry and Trade as well as the Ministry of Foreign Affairs have the task of gathering and disseminating information on foreign markets and promoting Czech products abroad.

Large-scale privatisation is the third centrepiece of the Czech industrial policy. Firms earmarked for privatisation had to submit privatisation projects to the Ministry of Privatisation for approval. The latter, in the course of the pre-privatisation process, conducted a series of restructuring measures such as de-monopolisation by breaking up large SOEs and the transfer of social assets to municipalities. Restructuring even went a step further because, after disman-

---

[254] OECD (1994), p. 102; See also Zeman (1994), pp. 61ff.

[255] Bohata and Mladek (1996), p. 27

tling large conglomerates and stripping them of viable assets, the remaining SOEs which were not scheduled for privatisation were left with a more than proportionate share of debts. In other words, the pre-privatisation procedure has to be interpreted as a form of structural industrial policy.

A large fraction of enterprises was privatised through voucher schemes. This method allowed for a nearly free distribution of company shares and thus a rapid transfer of ownership to the private sector. State influence on the economy, however, has remained extensive for two reasons: first, the institutional set-up of the privatisation programme included investment funds which were to hold shares in privatised enterprises. These funds in turn are owned by the main banks in which the state, through the National Property Fund (NPF), has retained a substantial minority ownership. The ensuing rather diffuse ownership structure has negative repercussions on the corporate governance of privatised companies.[256] It, moreover, created an atmosphere prone to illegal practices and contributed to the dominance of debt over equity finance. In all, mass privatisation has yet no lead to 'real' owners who provide for capital and know-how and effectively control management.

Second, the NPF owns two categories of SOEs: companies which could not be privatised and designated 'strategic' enterprises.[257] The remaining approximately 50 enterprises of the latter category are estimated to account for at least 20 per cent of GDP. These are energy utilities as well as industrial companies in the iron and steel and coal mining sectors and are among the biggest enterprises in the country. Summing up, it emerges that the Czech state can potentially exert a considerable indirect leverage on the economy. However, since the state shows a hands-off approach towards the companies it owns these firms are managed rather on an *ad hoc* than on a systematic basis:

> [G]overnment ownership has not been exercised through normal corporate governance *via* boards of directors, but rather through agreements, directives and contracts between government agencies and the enterprises and managers they supervise. At the same time, important decisions that vitally affect owners' interests, and that would clearly come under the purview of boards of directors

---

[256] For a detailed discussion of corporate governance problems related to mass privatisation schemes refer to Chapter 2.1.2.

[257] See also Charap and Zemplinerova (1993).

of private firms, seem to have escaped the notice of the Government. Thus, issues where managers ought to have freedom of decision are micro-managed by the Government, while in other areas managers have exceptional, and perhaps undesirable, freedom.[258]

Voucher privatisation and the lack of effective SOE management control entail an ossification of old structures since restructuring efforts are curbed or foiled altogether. Sinking competitiveness on international markets and with respect to import competition, the bankruptcy wave failing to materialise, and an unemployment rate well below PSE average despite real wage increases above productivity growth, are all symptomatic of the above outlined state of affairs.

Against this background *foreign direct investment* (FDI) may play an important role due to its potentially catalytic effects on restructuring.[259] The Czech Government in its attempt to attract foreign investors concluded a number of successful deals (e.g., the Volkswagen-Škoda arrangement, the partial sale of the state-owned petrochemical company and of SPT Telecom to consortias of Western companies[260]). However, the Volkswagen-Škoda deal is but one example where government organs on an *ad hoc* basis have negotiated entry conditions for foreign investors. The example is indicative of the Czech approach to industrial policy: without officially abandoning its free-market course the government pragmatically intervenes where it sees it desirable to do so. This by itself does not give cause for concern but, since the policy is *ad hoc*, it is unclear "where pragmatism should end and interventionism begin [...] if some direction and limits for industrial policy are not set."[261] Making government policy in this way less predictable such an approach adds to the already rampant uncertainty in transition economies. This finding is further aggravated if the far-reaching concessions are taken into consideration which the above mentioned deals involved: to attract the German car manufacturer, anti-monopoly provisions were waived and a number of trade barriers against imports of competing cars were erected. In other words, the Czech Government made use of *selective industrial policy measures* to pave the way for this important foreign direct in-

---

[258] OECD (1994), p. 99

[259] See Chapter 2.1.1 for the role of FDI in economic restructuring.

[260] EBRD (1996), p. 146

[261] OECD (1994), p. 101

vestment. What makes this policy undesirable is the fact that the rules of the game are not clear and may be bent according to government's preferences. This lack of transparency is fair game for unfair practises and thus reduces the rule of law.

Competition policy is the fourth building block on which the Czech industrial policy rests. Given the government's "ultra liberal"[262] complexion one would expect the predominant emphasis to be on the establishment and the proper functioning of a competitive economy framework. Anti-trust legislation and fair trading laws, indeed, clearly stand out as a major policy concern and fall into the realm of the Czech Ministry of Economic Competition. However, the Czech government, as noted above, deviated on different occasions from its own principles. This watering down of anti-trust legislation on an *ad hoc* basis opens the door to interest groups trying to negotiate favourable conditions for their respective business with the concomitant negative implications for competition.

The overhaul of vocational training and education in general as a central element of *employment policy* is crucial. Given its rich industrial tradition dating back to the 19th century and the fact that Czechoslovakia was the second industrial power in Eastern Europe after the German Democratic Republic, the Czech Republic has a highly skilled human capital base.[263] Yet at least three major factors contribute to the erosion of the skill base and require urgent countermeasures: first, both government agencies and enterprise managers are under pressure to economise. Due to scarce public funds and other policy priorities, particularly during the first years of the transition process, vocational training and educational concerns were pushed into the background. Firms, on the other hand, having to restructure their business and to adapt to the market environment tend not to invest sufficiently into human capital formation. The reasons for this are twofold: one, because capital allocation in transition economies is still to a large extent inefficient available financial sources are very scarce. Rather than investing in vocational training schemes enterprises use their capital to finance restructuring programmes and to buy new means of production. Two, interconnected with the first reason and reinforcing it stands the public

---

[262] Neue Zürcher Zeitung (1997d)

[263] OECD (1994), pp. 11ff.

good character of vocational training: a company employing apprentices might see that they are appropriated by another firm, as soon as they are fully trained. The second employer, however, did not have to bear any cost of vocational training at all. Under these conditions vocational training schemes will not be sufficiently provided. Thus educational matters continue to be neglected in the face of high youth unemployment typically found in PSEs, and a dramatic erosion of the future skill base is to be expected.

The second factor substantially eroding the Czech skill base are suppressed wages. At the start of the transition process a maximum growth rate of real wages was agreed upon as a result of the aforementioned tripartite negotiations. Real wage growth above this maximum was to be punished by excessive taxation. Although this tight wage regulation was relaxed in time it has just recently been reinstalled as a central element of the Czech officials' renewed efforts to stabilise the macroeconomy.[264] Although this measure is perfectly comprehensible from a stabilisation policy perspective, it may have serious negative consequences for the rate at which the labour force adapts to the needs of a restructured economy. Under conditions of pervasive uncertainty about future job prospects, workers will not invest in human capital acquisition as long as there is no greater upward flexibility in wages and in their distribution across jobs. This may seriously curb the adaptive capability of the entire economy.

Finally the third factor deteriorating the skill base is the slow pace of economic restructuring. A comparatively low unemployment rate is symptomatic for insufficient restructuring efforts if one recalls the chronic overmanning of socialist SOEs. To survive in a market economy environment these enterprises cannot but lay off the major part of their work force. Postponing this unavoidable step means the ossification of old production structures. Workers are locked in non-viable structures and unable to adapt to the changed skill requirements of an open market economy.

Against this background it emerges that the Czech employment policies, i.e., setting up a labour market infrastructure, job creation measures, public works and wage controls do not suffice. Once the bankruptcy wave finally and fully sets in, much more will be needed to efficiently reallocate the labour set free

---

[264] Neue Zürcher Zeitung (1997b)

due to mass redundancies: the emphasis must be on retraining and vocational training programmes. The design of these schemes, together with the reform of university education, has to take account of industry's specific requirements. The Czech economy is thus a good example to illustrate the fact that to successfully master the structural adjustment process it is indispensable that employment policies work towards a more flexible and more mobile industrial work force.

The Czech *environment policies* have been rather selective.[265] The primary focus of these policies are energy programmes (e.g., the reduction of energy-related pollution, the closure of inefficient coal mines) and, as noted above, regional programmes for areas worst affected by ecological problems. As a consequence of the socialist industrialisation strategy ruthlessly exploiting and damaging natural resources, industrial production was one of the main sources of the gravest pollution. Against this background it is a major shortcoming of the current industrial policy that environmental concerns are dealt with in isolation rather than integrating ecological parameters into the decision-making process:[266] the sheer size of the twofold task, namely the cleaning up of existing industries inherited from the previous system on the one hand and the establishment of a progressive environmental legislation on the other require the coordination of environment policies with other industrial policy areas.

Our analysis of the Czech industrial policy is summarised in Table 5.1.

---

[265] Two reasons may help to elucidate this state of affairs: first, since the budget is under much strain during the transition period, financial means available for environmental programmes are very limited. The disposable funds have to be focused on most seriously polluted areas. Second, rising unemployment means that ecological concerns are pushed into the background with regard to public perception.

[266] OECD (1994), p. 81

Policy Area	Measures
• *Promotion of industrial investment*	Tax concessions; accelerated depreciation of fixed assets
• *R&D & technology policy*	Support for science and technology parks; assistance to innovative SMEs
• *Employment measures*	Wage controls; job-creation measures; public works; labour market infrastructure
• *Privatisation*	Voucher privatisation; main industrial policy tool
• *SME policy*	Special credit facilities; consulting and information services; regional development; technology access
• *Regulatory reform & competition policy*	Ministry of Economic Competition; but important concessions to large companies and joint-ventures
• *Regional development policies*	No homogenous policy
• *Environmental & energy policies*	Energy programme including closing inefficient coal mines, reduction of energy related pollution
• *FDI*	Attract FDI through favourable concessions
• *Trade policies & export promotion*	Devaluation; strong export promotion: export insurance and finance, information services
• *Management of state enterprises*	National Property Fund: ad-hoc measures

Table 5.1: The industrial policy of the Czech Republic

5.1.2 Institutional Aspects

In the Czech Republic there does not yet exist an overall industrial policy strategy which would set down strategic goals and define institutional responsibilities for the formulation and implementation of these policies. The Czech industrial policy is rather an uncoordinated patchwork of policies pursued in different areas. Overlapping and ill-defined ministerial assignments result in inefficiencies and waste of resources much needed elsewhere. Moreover, much of the decision making is happening on an *ad hoc* basis rather than on guidelines deducted from policy objectives. This leaves government officials with considerable leeway and thus bears the risk of the political process being captured by specific interest groups exerting their influence on selected civil servants.

The *Meeting of Economic Ministers* chaired by the Prime Minister is the central body determining and co-ordinating to a large extent industrial policy issues. The representatives of the Ministry of Finance, Ministry of Economy, Ministry of Competition and finally the Ministry of Industry and Trade formulate and implement both vertical and horizontal industrial policy measures. The Meeting provides credit guarantees in the case of large loans as well as subsidies, and decides upon enterprise restructuring and major foreign direct investments at the firm level. It is also concerned with broader issues that cut across firms and sectors, i.e., the general improvement of the market framework. What was said above about the general lack of direction of the Czech industrial policy holds for the Meeting of Economic Ministers in particular: "[N]either the participating Ministers nor the Government have formulated general guidelines that define or govern the Meeting's decisions, and thus industrial policy measures are *ad hoc*."[267]

The fact that there is no institutional *primus inter pares*, e.g., a section within the Ministry of Industry and Trade, that would be responsible for the policy co-ordination of the ministries represented at the Meeting of Economic Ministers, has to be seen as a further weakness of this committee. The previous section finally has pointed to the need to integrate environmental parameters into the design of industrial policy. Against this backdrop it would be crucial to involve the Environment Ministry into the Meeting's decision-making process.

Disputes over respective areas of competence are also a hallmark of *export promotion*. There are no clear standards regulating the co-operation between the Ministry of Industry and Trade, the Ministry of Economy and the Ministry of Foreign Affairs which are all involved in promoting exports. Bringing the respective policies of these ministries in line by formulating strategic goals and by assigning clear responsibilities would give the Czech export promotion and trade policy a more general character and thus make it less erratic.

The Ministries involved in export promotion, together with the NPF, build an *informal industrial policy framework*. In this the *National Property Fund* is an important centre of gravity. As a state-holding company, the NPF is controlling semi-privatised firms and the remaining (strategic) SOEs. As noted above, these

---

[267] OECD (1994), p. 91

companies together contribute as much as 20 per cent to GDP. Despite the enormous share in industrial output these companies are not managed on a systematic basis. This can be related to two reasons: first, the Ministry of Industry and Trade and the NPF both in accordance with the Czech Government's free market stance have adopted a hands-off attitude towards the firms they control. Second, neither the Ministry of Industry and Trade nor the NPF have the manpower nor the necessary skills to efficiently supervise and control enterprise management. Together the lack of political will and resources lead to severe corporate governance problems.[268]

Manpower and vocational training policy also play a pivotal role with regard to institutional aspects of industrial policy. The risk inherent to the current Czech macrostabilisation programmes is that civil service may become less attractive due to wage freezing, and therefore the public sector may suffer from brain drain: in particular higher bureaucrats might find it more rewarding to change to the private sector if remuneration there is higher. Besides the financial aspects, efforts must be intensified to improve the quality of the government administration. One possible solution would be to establish higher education schemes (e.g., university degrees) that prepare future civil servants for their jobs.

---

[268] Refer to Chapter 2.1.2 for an in-depth discussion of corporate governance problems.

5.2 Hungary

Hungarian reformers formulated an industrial policy strategy for their country as early as 1991. At this stage of the transition process the development of an industrial policy framework might already reflect both an early effort to learn from and copy Western policies and the fact that systemic reforms had been introduced in the country long before 1989[269], i.e., that a political environment prevailed in which industrial policy issues could be discussed "without these being seen as some form of reversion to central planning."[270] It is also against this background that the decision for a more gradual reform course must be seen: Hungarian reformers did not feel the need to radically break with the past by means of an economic shock therapy.

Yet, despite this comparatively favourable starting position, legacies of the past continue to seriously constrain the leeway of economic policy: as a result of policy misjudgements in the 1970s and then again in the 1980s, Hungary had accumulated the highest per capita external debt in Eastern Europe. Since these obligations, in contrast to other countries in the region, were consistently met macroeconomic policy became very restrictive. The ensuing persistent government deficit, together with the need to deal with continued external disequilibrium (trade and current account deficits since 1993, see Table A.3 in the Appendix), severely limit funds disposable for industrial policy. Thus macroeconomic problems inherited from the past are a binding constraint for the type and range of industrial policy that can be implemented in the transition to a market economy: "In such an environment, there is a risk that industrial policy can do little more than offset some negative effects of the macroeconomic environment rather than serve as a means of creating a vital industry."[271]

What has just been said, together with a dramatic crisis of Hungarian industry between 1988 and 1992, means that the 1991 industrial policy strategy could not be implemented. The economic downturn lead to a loss of 45 per cent of in-

---

[269] During the 1980s, the period of so-called 'Gulash-Communism' Hungary witnessed a wide range of reforms, notably of banking and tax, and the beginnings of price and trade liberalisation.

[270] Hughes (1996), p. 3

[271] OECD (1995), p. 13

dustrial output between 1985 and 1992 and, in 1992, about 20 per cent of state-owned industrial firms declared bankruptcy. Hence instead of *'picking winners'* by directing resource flows to promising products, technologies and enterprises the Hungarian Ministry of Industry and Trade could do little more than try to moderate between enterprise management, banks and the Ministry of Finance.[272] So, although the government's stance would have favoured a rather proactive industrial policy approach, the Ministry of Industry and Trade was forced by the prevailing economic conditions to adopt *reactive* policies with the overall focus being on crisis management.

The industrial policy formulated in 1992 took into account these developments and defined a number of strategic policy objectives that were to be achieved over time. Under the impression of the severe industrial depression crisis management and restructuring efforts were given short-term priority. In the medium term, the process of deindustrialisation should be brought to a halt and Hungarian industry be placed on a growth path. In the long term, the strategy aimed at bridging the gap between Western Europe and Hungary and at the country's international economic integration.

The 1992 industrial policy further distinguished between 'transitional', 'strategic' and regulatory policy instruments. The first category comprised tools helping firms to adjust to the competitive environment of a market economy (e.g., privatisation, reduction of concentration in several industries, adjustment aids, etc.). The 'strategic' tools were to be used in order to achieve the longer-term industrial policy objectives. They included, among a variety of instruments, investment incentives to shortcut the vicious circle of deficient financial intermediation, incentives to entrepreneurs, technology policy, and export promotion measures. It is clear that these tools could be applied selectively and thus open the door to a vertically oriented industrial policy. Yet these proactive policies had hardly any impact due to the lack of funds inhibiting their implementation. The normal functioning of the market, finally, was to be secured with regulatory instruments.[273]

---

[272] Török (1994), p. 39

[273] Török (1994), pp. 44ff.

In short, one can notice a shift of focus from a more proactive industrial policy towards policies primarily aimed at improving the market framework, i.e., horizontal industrial policies. This trend is confirmed by later versions of Hungarian industrial policy documents: swift integration into the European Union (EU) and the compliance with EU regulations stand out as the overall strategic policy goals. "By 1995, the temporary measures were removed from the general industrial policy measures and the main guidelines were taken to be the tasks set by the aim of EU accession."[274] Since Hungary is among the first PSEs with which accession negotiations are to be started in 1998 one can expect the emphasis on horizontal policies to further increase.

5.2.1 Policy Areas and Instruments

One of the key features of the Hungarian industrial policy is *large-scale privatisation*.[275] Instead of opting for a give-away scheme, SOEs have mostly been privatised through direct negotiations with potential buyers, auctions, and management workers buy-outs. Hungarian privatisation must be regarded as a success both in *quantitative* as well as in qualitative terms. Total receipts from privatisation since 1990 have surpassed Ft 1,000 billion, of which Ft 654 billion have come in foreign currency. Until mid-1997 85 per cent of the banking sector were privatised, and by the end of 1997 all of the former five major state-owned banks were expected to be in private hands. The privatisation process is scheduled to end in 1998.[276] Contrasting with the Czech mass privatisation scheme, which is comparable to the Hungarian experience with regard to speed and extent of the transfer of assets from the public to the private sector, the Hungarian large-scale privatisation is, however, above all a *qualitative success*: by consistently stressing the importance of bringing in new management, technology and investment to revitalise privatised firms the state was replaced by 'real' owners and corporate governance could be improved significantly.

That the sale of SOEs through *standard methods at market prices* was such a success in Hungary can be ascribed to two factors: first, the bulk of privatisation

---

[274] Hughes (1996), p. 4

[275] For a description and an assessment of Hungarian industrial policies see OECD (1995).

[276] EBRD (1997a), p. 29

revenues stems from FDI which might partly be explained by fewer xenophobic fears related to the sell-out of assets to foreigners. Second, the Hungarian government showed little inhibition in extending privatisation to sensitive sectors and thus started at an early stage to privatise public utilities and banks.[277]

The State Holding and Privatisation Agency (SHPA) is also responsible for the *management of the remaining SOEs*. Since Hungarian privatisation stands close to its completion, the SHPA's future task above all will be to effectively manage those 109 'strategic' firms (e.g., the power sector, the oil company MOL and telecommunications) in which the state will retain some share in the long term.[278]

Albeit its apparent successes, the Hungarian privatisation programme has been criticised due to its over-emphasis on revenue maximisation. Given deficient financial intermediation and the lack of resources due to the strained situation of the state budget, critics argue that a larger fraction of privatisation revenues should be allocated to the restructuring of privatised firms.[279]

Restructuring assistance and *crisis management* of firms in financial distress fall in the realm of the SHPA[280] and the Hungarian Investment and Development Bank (HIDB) respectively. Crisis management is another central pillar of the Hungarian industrial policy. As a reaction to the 1988-1992 crisis the HIDB initiated a bank and credit consolidation programme with privatisation revenues earmarked for this purpose. Banks were relieved of a proportion of their bad debts to restore their health. At the same time the HIDB took over a fraction of the debt of selected firms in order to break through the vicious circle of accumulated bad debts between banks and (privatised) enterprises symptomatic of PSEs. The Hungarian crisis management programme, however, is controversial due to inherent moral hazard problems. Hence it is important that state interventions in this area should be exceptional and unusual. The criteria for crisis

---

[277] Neue Zürcher Zeitung (1997a)

[278] ibid.

[279] OECD (1995), p. 184

[280] The SHPA resulted from the merger of the former State Property Agency (SPA) and the Hungarian State Holding Company (HSHC) in 1996.

assistance should include stringent conditionality, some degree of risk sharing by the firms involved, and a hard termination date.

Since Hungarian privatisation went as far as to include public utilities, *regulatory reforms and competition policy* are of major importance. Hungary's approach to this issue was the establishment of an Office of Economic Competition, that is, to ensure the proper functioning of competitive markets. As to the regulation of public utilities, it was decided to create separate regulatory bodies for each of the major utilities which have to report to the relevant minister and to the parliament. Regulating prices and other dimensions of the utilities' market behaviour, these bodies have similar responsibilities to regulatory institutions that were created in the course of public utilities privatisation in OECD countries during the 1980s.[281]

The Hungarian economy suffers from a discouraging investment climate: although inflation could be contained below 30 per cent uncertainty about macroeconomic stability remains. This, together with poorly functioning capital markets, leads to high real interest rates and high collateral requirements of lending institutes. Hence private firms have to turn to retained earnings to finance their investment. Yet the onerous tax burden for business which also includes high wage-related costs (e.g., social security contributions) substantially reduce retainable profits.

Against this background *investment promotion* is crucial. However, budgetary pressures heavily constrain the scope for fiscal investment stimulation by the Hungarian state. Tax treatment of depreciation and other allowances against costs are consequently quite unfavourable for investment. The lack of public resources also precludes a significant leverage effect of public investment on the whole economy. The share of public investment in government spending is low by international standards. The ensuing infrastructural backwardness and the low quality of many public services constitute a serious obstacle to private investment. The Investment Incentive Fund managed by the Ministry of Industry and Trade is thus primarily designated to support investment in infrastructure. In addition, it attempts to stimulate projects introducing new or modernised manufacturing facilities.

---

[281] OECD (1995), p. 105

A number of support funds, moreover, provide subsidised loans to stimulate labour-intensive and employment-creating investments. These funds mostly operate at a local level target, above all in SMEs. At the federal level the National Office for the Development of Small Business was established to support SMEs. However, this institution suffers from its weak position within the administration and from insufficient funding. Another source of SME investment finance are the START loans to assist SME start-ups. Despite these initiatives, promoting small and medium-size business *SME policy* has not yet received sufficient attention within the Hungarian industrial policy framework and is not well co-ordinated. Hence, although SMEs have been net creditors to the banking system, they find it difficult to raise necessary investment finance due to high real interest rates and the general lack of venture capital. A vicious circle emerges in which small business is losing out: "Small business development requires financial resources, but the funds made available for these purposes should originate from the development of small business."[282] The resource gap is to some extent eased by Hungary's participation in international programmes (e.g., EU Phare, World Bank, EBRD and EIB projects).

Yet another shortcoming of Hungary's SME policy is the lack of an information and consultancy infrastructure tailored to the specific needs of small business. The importance of such services has already been noted in the previous section on the Czech industrial policy where they form a central element of the country's SME policy.

Not only has *foreign direct investment* played a dominating role in Hungary's large-scale privatisation but foreign investors also substantially contribute to the ongoing restructuring process in the industrial sector through a massive input of capital, technology and know-how. Hungary has been the largest recipient of FDI in the region. Cumulative FDI-inflows per capita between 1989 and 1996 add up to 1,288 US$ as compared to 642 US$ in the Czech Republic, ranking second in Eastern European FDI statistics.[283] Until the end of 1993 Hungary conceded tax concessions to foreign investors and, since then, has continued to promote foreign capital inflows with favourable conditions. However, given

---

[282] OECD (1995), p. 123
[283] EBRD (1997a), p. 12

that Hungarian privatisation has almost come to an end and because of in-creased competition for foreign investment from other countries in the region, a decline in capital inflows from abroad is to be expected. Against this backdrop, Hungarian efforts to attract FDI must be continued. Due to the lack of domestic resources, foreign capital is vital both for the future modernisation of Hungarian industry as well as to gain access to export markets.

Yet, as the discussion of the Czech experience has already shown, FDI promo-tion can become rather problematic if the price for such investment is excessive in terms of import protection and market power. Thus, with regard to economic restructuring, FDI cannot be relied upon alone. Building up supply chains to provide high-quality inputs to incoming firms is just one way in which indus-trial policy can augment the impact of foreign investment. A SME policy that complements existing foreign direct investment by fostering the development of supply clusters around firms under foreign ownership can have a catalytic effect on industrial restructuring.[284] Part of Hungary's SME support has this objective in mind and local content rules of the EU Association Agreements can actually further encourage the development of local suppliers.[285]

Hungary's *science and technology policy* has not yet been subordinated to its industrial policy. Hence the Ministry of Industry and Trade plays only a very limited role in this area. The design and the application of specific micro-level tools are assigned to the National Commission of Technical Development. This office has initiated a number of measures to promote applied R&D (e.g., re-search institutes based on the German Frauenhofer Institutes' model to facilitate co-operation between universities, R&D institutes and industry, a Technology Transfer Office, the Hungarian Innovation Chamber). Yet the significant drop of both public and private R&D expenses causes concern. As in the case of the Czech Republic, there is a risk that Hungary may lose its well-educated scien-tists and engineers, i.e., that the country's R&D skill base erodes.

It is vital for Hungary's future competitiveness that this development is brought to a halt. At this stage of the transition process a science and technol-

---

[284] On the importance of such clusters for the competitiveness of an economy see Porter (1991), pp. 172ff.

[285] Hare (1995), p. 12

ogy policy that focuses on a few selected key areas is not desirable. Rather the R&D infrastructure needs to be revamped and efforts must be increased to build up indigenous technological and research capacities. Such a more general approach requires R&D policy to be integrated into a larger industrial policy framework so as to assure that research and development is linked to the specific needs of industry. In addition, fiscal incentives should be used to stimulate private R&D activities.

Export promotion falls in the realm of the Ministry of International Economic Relations. The instruments applied include export financing, credit guarantees and linear export incentives offered by the Trade Policy Fund. Export promotion, however, is constrained by several factors: first, the devaluation of the exchange rate to foster exports became impossible from January 1996 when Hungary's officials declared the forint convertible for current account transactions and pegged it to a basket of currencies. Second, both the Europe Agreement and Central European Free Trade Agreement (CEFTA) and Hungary's WTO membership (since December 1994) make export promotion measures increasingly difficult. Against this background the focus of Hungary's export promotion should be shifted towards information services that provide consultancy and counselling for firms wishing to enter export markets. Particular emphasis again should be given to SMEs since generally they cannot profit from the experience of foreign investors and neither are they familiar with foreign markets.

What has been said about the constraints on export promotion equally holds for *trade policy*. Trade has already been liberalised to a large extent: in 1995 licensing requirements and quotas for 95 per cent of imports were eliminated. A general import surcharge of 8 per cent introduced in the same year is to be phased out until 1997. A number of 'sensitive' products (i.e., textiles and agriculture) remain substantially protected by import tariffs. These tariffs, however, are phased out both for trade with the EU in compliance with Hungary's Europe Agreement and with CEFTA members.[286] It emerges that trade policy as an industrial policy instrument is losing its importance with increasing trade liberalisation and Hungary's participation in international agreements.

---

[286] EBRD (1996), p. 154

Hungary's increasing internal differentiation with regard to unemployment rates and a number of other social and economic indicators makes *regional development policies* an urgent matter. The Regional Development Fund managed by an inter-ministerial committee devises various employment and infrastructure support schemes which are then implemented by regional development agencies distributed all over the country. For most depressed areas programmes have been designed spanning several years.

Against the background of the increasingly diverging development of regional labour markets related to the decline of uncompetitive heavy industries *employment measures* are a cornerstone of Hungary's regional development policy. Job creation and protection schemes thus focus on underdeveloped areas. Additional steps to improve the overall employment situation require both labour market flexibility and labour mobility to be improved. The former may be achieved by allowing wage-rate differentials between different regions to reflect the differing imbalances on respective labour markets. A more mobile labour force could be facilitated through access to job-related information, relocation financing, and by improving housing market flexibility.

The Ministry of the Environment and Regional Development and the Ministry of Industry and Trade are together in charge of Hungary's *environmental policy*. As the country is approaching the EU its environmental regulation is more and more adapted to European environmental standards. Moreover, programmes have been launched aiming at a more efficient use of energy and waste recovery. Since the command economy industry caused the gravest pollution, a deeper integration of environmental concerns into the industrial policy framework is needed both to remove environmental damages as well as to assure the compliance with environmental norms in current industrial production.

The different policy areas and respective measures of Hungary's industrial policy are summarised in Table 5.2.

Policy Area	Measures
• *Promotion of industrial investment*	Rather limited depreciation allowances
• *R&D & technology policy*	Concentration on a few key areas
• *Employment measures*	Job creation and protection schemes focusing on underdeveloped areas
• *Privatisation*	Key element of industrial policy; mostly based on sales and management workers buy-outs
• *SME policy*	No coherent programme; centres for the development of entrepreneurship; special credit facilities
• *Regulatory reform & competition policy*	Office of Economic Competition; separate regulatory bodies for each of the major public utilities
• *Regional development policies*	Regional development agencies
• *Environmental & energy policies*	Interest-related tax allowances for water saving and environmental protection
• *FDI*	Favourable conditions for FDI; tax preferences for foreign investors until end-1993
• *Trade policies & export promotion*	Export (pre-) financing; export guarantees; liberalisation
• *Management of state enterprises*	State Holding and Privatisation Agency

Table 5.2: The industrial policy of Hungary

5.2.2 Institutional Aspects

That at present no single ministry or agency has the *overall responsibility* for Hungary's industrial policy is a major shortcoming in its institutional arrangement. It bears the risk of potentially costly co-ordination failures and inefficiencies due to institutional overlapping. Given the budget deficits, an institutional consolidation of industrial policy seems all the more important.

A further general weakness is the separation between policy-making responsibility and access to relevant funding: the Ministry of Industry and Trade, although being responsible for the industrial policy design, does not have the prerequisite funds to implement these policies. Funds must be made available by the Ministry of Finance. Such a separation is not desirable. Ideally the Ministry of Industry and Trade should have an annual budget at its disposal to realise industrial policy measures.

 Since Hungarian privatisation is coming to an end, the merger of the former privatisation agency and the state-holding company into the *State Holding and Privatisation Agency* (SHPA) is to be welcomed. However, the government's emphasis on revenue maximisation to reduce its deficits and not properly functioning capital markets have left too little funds for restructuring. Either the SHPA or a new restructuring agency should give those firms access to capital that can be made viable within a reasonable period and at reasonable cost and which cannot profit from capital and know-how of foreign investors. Support should essentially be given based on commercial terms, but with less stringent collateral requirements and lower interest rates. In this way overdue restructuring might be speeded up.

 Given the decentralised implementation of *regional development* initiatives, a better co-ordination and monitoring of these measures could be achieved by establishing intermediate development agencies functioning as the connecting link between central government and regional agencies. Improved co-ordination of Hungary's regional development policies is all the more important due to the shift in orientation of Hungary's industrial policy from primarily sectoral to increasingly horizontal policies and the concomitant growing weight of the regional dimension.

 What has been said about the institutional arrangement of Hungary's industrial policy in general holds for the country's *SME policy* in particular: at present no single organisation has been assigned the overall responsibility of small business promotion. Given the pivotal role this enterprise sector plays in advanced economies, specialised institutions that focus on supporting SMEs are urgently needed.

 Finally, *science and technology policy* needs to be tied in more closely into Hungary's industrial policy. From an institutional perspective it is not desirable that both the National Committee for Technical Development (NCTD) and the Ministry of Industry and Trade are involved in the design of the country's R&D policy. Given the overall importance of technological progress for the modernisation of Hungary's industry, the NCTD should be integrated into the Ministry of Industry and Trade.

5.3 Poland

At the beginning of the country's transition process the Polish government had no comprehensive industrial policy framework. Rather the officially proclaimed attitude was quite similar to the position held by Czech officials, i.e., a free market approach. Against the background of an economy in complete disarray with a huge and fast growing external debt amounting to 40.2 billion US$ and CPI inflation (end year) soaring to 640 per cent in 1989[287], the main thrust of economic policy lay with macroeconomic stabilisation. In January 1990 the first democratically elected government initiated an economic shock therapy which came to be known as the *Balcerowicz programme*, named after its architect the Minister of Finance at the time, Leszek Balcerowicz.[288] Polish reformers seized the window of opportunity at the beginning of the transition process and virtually over night introduced tight fiscal and monetary policies which were accompanied and complemented by the radical liberalisation of both prices and foreign trade.

The stabilisation programme was very successful: inflation was brought down from over 600 per cent in 1989 to double-digit figures as early as 1991 (70 per cent, CPI annual average; see Table A.4 in the Appendix). The extent of the success is all the more remarkable given the country's lack of political stability which has led to frequent changes in government.

The radical break with pre-reform economic policy in part also may account for the fast recovery from recession in the early 1990s as compared to other leading PSEs. As early as 1992 economic contraction had been overcome and GDP began to grow. Yet, despite these impressive successes, the economic downturn provoked a change in the political climate: the electorate blamed the crisis on the liberalism of Poland's first reform government and pressures for a proactive approach to economic restructuring increased.

Most affected by the 1990-1992 economic crisis was the industrial sector. Here output declined by 30 per cent, the rate of investment sunk by 15 per cent, and employment fell by 18 per cent. The resulting decline in productivity of 15 per

---

[287] EBRD (1995), p. 203

[288] See Balcerowicz (1995), pp. 305ff.

cent was twice as high as in the economy at large.[289] Thus, whereas the previous government did not have a coherent industrial policy programme and instead followed a "*strictly selective restructuring policy*"[290] focused on a few key sectors, the Ministry of Industry and Trade under the new government elaborated a *comprehensive industrial policy strategy* for the 1993-1995 period.

With the long-run aims of improving competitiveness and increasing the efficiency and innovative capacity of enterprises, the strategy was based on two different policy approaches: the first was primarily *horizontally* oriented and defined tasks of the state in various industrial policy areas (i.e., industrial restructuring, SME and investment promotion, labour market and regional policies, etc.). The second *sectoral* approach, based on a number of sectoral studies mostly conducted by foreign consulting firms, was to encourage desired structural changes and accelerate the flow of funds to the most efficient areas. It identified four different categories of sectors on which industrial policy would be focused: strategic sectors (defence industry, fuel and energy industries), energy and capital intensive sectors (shipbuilding, iron and steel metallurgy, cement industry), industries satisfying the needs of a 'higher order' (development areas deemed important for the economy: e.g., petrochemistry, electronics, automobile industry), and finally sectors and products of 'greater opportunity' which were already competitive or would become so with minor support.[291]

The 1993-1995 industrial policy programme suffered from a number of major *shortcomings*. First of all against the background of scarce resources there was a general *lack of focus*. The policy strategy was all encompassing and extended to a wide range of industries despite the diverse nature of problems in individual industrial segments. *Financial constraints* precluded the implementation of

---

[289] Socha and Sztanderska (1994), p. 84

[290] Balcerowicz (1995), p. 319. Balcerowicz in his book on the Polish transition process is eager to delimit the reform programme named after him from industrial policy measures: "But some parts of the industrial structure, where the need for quick downsizing was especially great and the informational requirements for the central decision-makers were relatively simple, called for and allowed a *strictly selective restructuring policy*. Such a policy, limited basically to mining, energy and metallurgy, was included in the overall economic programme. It had, however, nothing to do with the typical 'industrial policy' of picking winners or bailing out losers." (ibid.)

[291] Belka and Krajewski (1995), pp. 8ff.

these comprehensive policy measures: double-digit inflation, a strained budgetary situation and high external debts, despite the successful finalisation of debt forgiveness negotiations with both the Paris and the London Club, largely limited public spending. The sectoral approach furthermore meant *far-reaching government interventions.* The planned implementation of industrial restructuring by means of sectoral contracts[292] was seen by critics as an attempt to replace the market allocation mechanism and even as a reversal to methods of central planning.[293] Another shortcoming arose from the introduction of various new institutions which led to *institutional overlapping* and ensuing conflicts of competence particularly between the Ministry of Industry and Trade and the Ministry of Ownership Transformations.

The next industrial policy programme to run from 1995 to 1997, named 'International Competitiveness of Polish Industry', eliminated some of the weaknesses of the previous strategy: the number of priorities was reduced and the financial resources for implementing the policy measures were clearly defined. A further improvement was the closer integration of the programme into the Government's general economic strategy.[294]

5.3.1 Policy Areas and Instruments

Polish *privatisation* has followed many simultaneous tracks, leaving almost no option unexplored. Three main methods were applied: first the direct privatisation or liquidation which covered primarily small and medium-sized enterprises. The second route is capital privatisation that involves open sales of shares and the search for a strategic outside investor. Mass privatisation finally is the third method used for the divestiture of state ownership and control. However, the Polish mass privatisation scheme had been delayed by intense and lengthy po-

---

[292] Sectoral contracts were to be concluded between the government, employers, SOE self-management bodies, supervising boards and trade unions in a given sector. In these contracts, the goal and model of sector restructuring as proposed by the Ministry of Finance and approved by the government were not subject to negotiations. However loans, tax reliefs, subsidies, wage policy and the detailed schedule for restructuring were negotiable.

[293] Socha and Sztanderska (1994), p. 88

[294] Belka and Krajewski (1995), pp. 15ff.

litical struggles and implementation of the National Investment Funds (NIF) programme did not begin until July 1995.[295]

The reasons for privatisation having thus far been a cumbersome and relatively sluggish process are various. Above all, under the 1990 Privatisation Law participation in the national privatisation programme is voluntary, requiring the consent of enterprises and their workers' councils. The *strong position of the work-force*, both within the socio-political system in general and within SOEs in particular is a distinct feature of the Polish transformation process:[296] the country's as many as 245 trade-union organisations (against only three federations of employers) enjoy far-reaching privileges (e.g., the right to organise political and solidarity strikes, activists being paid with public money, trade unions being allowed to participate in parliamentary elections). In self-managed SOEs employees' councils elect enterprise management and have the exclusive right to distribute profits.

Unbalanced industrial relations, together with dominating employees' insider control, work to the detriment of the speed and the depth of both restructuring and privatisation. It also means that the Government's pre-privatisation plans have been thwarted and that the state as *de iure* owner of SOEs has only very limited control over enterprise management. Under SOE self-management safeguarding of jobs and wage maximisation become the prime objectives. Incen-

---

[295] The Polish NIF programme includes 512 medium-sized and mainly industrial companies representing about 8 per cent of the sales of medium- and large-sized Polish enterprises and one tenth of the book value of state enterprises according to 1994 financial data. Each of the 15 NIFs holds shares in every company but one of them holds a majority stake. 51 per cent of the shares are to be converted into share certificates which can then be acquired by the public. 15 per cent of the shares are reserved for employees and 9 per cent are intended as a performance-related remuneration for the NIF managers. The new State Treasury finally will retain 25 per cent of total shares. For details of the Polish mass privatisation programme see OECD (1996b), pp. 159ff.

[296] The strong influence of Polish trade unions on political issues and especially on the course of economic restructuring is related to the country's recent pre-transition historical experience. In 1980 Poland's opposition originated in the form of the 'Solidarnosc' trade union. As a result of the 'Round Table' negotiations in 1989 the organisation was legalised and strongly represented in Parliament where it could directly bring its influence to bear on the design of Poland's reform programme. The agreement reached also involved massive concessions to employees, whose position vis-à-vis SOE management was subsequently enormously strengthened. See Balcerowicz (1995), p. 316

tives for investment and innovation are effectively eradicated. Restructuring and privatisation are stalled since these would be tantamount to depriving workers' councils and trade unions of many of their privileges.

The Law on the Commercialisation and Privatisation of State-Owned Enterprises promulgated in September 1996 is an attempt to cut short excessive insider control.[297] The law still provides for the commercialisation of SOEs scheduled for privatisation. Yet the prior consent of enterprise employees is not any longer required. Commercialisation under the new law involves the abolition of the workers' council as a management body, depriving it of the ability to block privatisation. Another *legislative hurdle* to privatisation which has not yet been dealt with, is that Poland is one of the very few countries in central Europe that up to now has no law on business-property restitution. As long as the issue of expropriation has not been settled and restitution claims have not been dealt with uncertainties related to the ownership status of SOFs will further delay their restructuring and privatisation.

Another major obstacle to a swift divestiture of SOEs is to be seen in Poland's *lack of political stability*. Frequent changes in government have meant that the average life span of a Polish government since 1989 has been one year. During this period the finance portfolio alone has changed six times. Even though political turmoil has not put in question the general direction of the reform process towards a market-economy system, it has nevertheless delayed a number of key reforms, particularly those concerning privatisation and the pension system. That the credibility of the public to the Government's commitment to reforms may have suffered is a further negative effect of these political upheavals.

Slowed-down privatisation and stalled restructuring have damaging implications for the survival prospects of SOEs due to the erosion of their capital and skill base. Regarding the economy wide allocation of scarce financial resources means, moreover, that capital much needed in the SME sector is wasted unproductively since this is being used for securing work-places and wage increases in SOEs. Thus the Polish privatisation experience indicates that in a specific political climate and given unbalanced industrial relations the state may be unable to carry out pre-privatisation restructuring. In such a situation in order to

---

[297] OECD (1996b), p. 68; also EBRD (1997b), p. 189

limit the damaging effects of delayed reforms the only opportunity for enterprise restructuring is to privatise them as quickly as possible. Against this background it is paramount to find the means and ways of speeding up the Polish
privatisation process.

  Among the sectors partly or completely excluded from privatisation plans are
postal services, railways, sea- and air-ports, oil and gas pipelines, and mining.
In the *residual state sector* the role of the state is particularly important in large
enterprises. In 1995, 19 of the largest 100 Polish companies were state-owned,
35 were wholly state-owned joint-stock companies, and 17 were concerns
dominated by state-owned shareholders.[298] Many of these are concentrated in
and around heavy industry which is in dire need of deep restructuring and
where social problems are rampant. A prominent example is coal mining where
productivity fell sharply and prices remain above world-market level. In the
light of the aforementioned hurdles to restructuring, official plans drafted in
1996 calling for an 18 per cent drop in production and a 30 per cent reduction in
employment in this sector merely seem realistic.[299] Except for those SOEs under
self-management the Ministry of Industry and Trade and the Ministry of Ownership Changes, are formally responsible for the *management* of the remaining
commercialised state-owned enterprises. However, given the strong position of
employees and the lack of manpower and expertise by the state to effectively
manage its enterprises, control over SOE management is very limited.

  Corporate governance problems in SOEs of the kind just mentioned all the
more give rise to concern, since 15 of Poland's banks together accounting for
more than 70 per cent of total book value in this sector in 1995 were state
owned. Financial intermediation is thus still dominated by the state. As with
other enterprises, the idea has been to first restructure and consolidate state
banks before they are privatised. The financial restructuring of banks, which
was launched in 1993 in an attempt to deal once and for all with the stock of
large bad loans, seems to have been quite successful.[300] On the whole, however,
the performance of the Polish banking sector remains weak and the economy is
distinctly underbanked. Due to expected inflows of capital and expertise FDI

---

[298] OECD (1996b), p. 71
[299] EBRD (1996), p. 16
[300] OECD (1996b), p. 78

could play an important role in upgrading and reforming Polish financial intermediation. Yet privatisation of banks turned out to be more difficult than originally envisaged.[301]

As a legacy of the socialist strategy of forced growth, Polish heavy industry (e.g., shipbuilding, steelworks, mining, petrochemistry) constitutes a major challenge for industrial policy. These highly vertically integrated enterprises often dominate as the single largest employer, entire regions and cities. As in the case of Hungary, regional and unemployment problems are largely interrelated. Due to large discrepancies regarding unemployment rates between regions (unemployment reaches 27 to 40 per cent in regions worst affected by structural unemployment[302]), a major focus of *regional initiatives* lies with employment measures such as extended unemployment benefit entitlement periods and extra resources for active labour market policies. Other regional measures have included the identification of distressed areas chiefly based on the criterion of registered unemployment which are granted a number of advantages. The latter encompass lower taxes or tax holidays for new investors and infrastructure development subsidies. Also the Ministry of Industry and Trade is considering offering exemptions from social-security contributions.

As a further step to reduce disparities in regional development, special economic zones (SEZ) were created along the lines of similar programmes in Ireland. Investors in these zones are granted total corporate tax relief for ten years, and 50 per cent relief for the following ten years in the case of substantial investments. Other advantages granted include the exemption from the real-estate tax and accelerated depreciation. The Council of Ministers decides on the establishment of SEZs on a case by case basis if deemed necessary for the restructuring of an area. This discretionary decision-making process means, however, that large foreign investors may have the leverage to request SEZs to be created where they suit them best.[303]

---

[301] The transfer of ownership of Powszechny Bank Kredytowy, one of the major state banks, by tender to strategic investors has just been stopped. According to the Ministry of Finance, the bank now is to be privatised through the stock market instead. See Neue Zürcher Zeitung (1997e).

[302] Socha and Sztanderska (1994), p. 99

[303] OECD (1996b), pp. 82ff.

Since labour was strongly represented in the Polish Parliament right from the beginning of the transition process comprehensive *labour market policies* were introduced at an early stage. Active policies *inter alia* include the financing of retraining courses, financial assistance to unemployed willing to start up their own business, and loans to employers for the creation of additional jobs. Such extensive labour market policies, however, do have their price: in Poland expenditures on pensions and labour market policies in 1993 approximately accrued to 20 per cent of GDP.[304] Given the budgetary situation, labour market policies and the pension system urgently need to be overhauled.

Thus far *small and medium-sized business* has received only limited support in the form of minor tax concessions. Hence SMEs to finance their investment primarily depend on retained earnings as commercial banks are still reluctant to give them credit and real interest rates are high due to inflation. The situation of scarce capital is somewhat defused by policy measures aimed at the *promotion of industrial investment*. Provisions broadening the deductibility of investment expenses from income taxes and tariff reductions on capital goods and raw material imports considerably helped private business to increase capital expenditures. Firms exporting more than half of their production are granted further tax allowances. Yet to actually give small firms access to these support schemes, hitherto underdeveloped information services tailored to the specific needs of SMEs need to be improved.

Given the lack of domestic capital and the fact that cumulative per capita *FDI* inflows are low compared to other CEFTA countries[305], the Polish Government has taken a number of measures to ease entry for foreign investors. Among these is the removal of bureaucratic obstacles (e.g., permit requirements for foreign investors in a number of sectors). The State Agency for Foreign Investment, moreover, offers special incentives such as income-tax reductions for companies operating in regions with high structural unemployment or to foreign investors introducing new technologies. The reasons for the reluctance of FDI to enter the Polish market until recently may be related to at least initially pre-

---

[304] Socha and Sztanderska (1994), p. 81

[305] Per capita FDI-inflows in Poland for the 1989-1995 period accumulated to 63 US$ as compared to Hungary with 1,113 US$, the Czech Republic with 532 US$, and Slovenia with 253 US$. See EBRD (1996), p. 116, Table 8.5.

vailing xenophobic fears and to the high uncertainty caused by the country's socio-political situation, unsettled property questions surrounding industrial facilities, and macroeconomic instability.

The restricted financial room to manoeuvre of the Polish Government has meant that *technology policy* has received only very limited funding. The inherent risks for the country's skill and technology base have already been discussed above in the context of the Czech Republic. Tax incentives are granted for industrial R&D and related investments.

The budgetary and the macroeconomic situation also greatly limit the possibilities of *stimulating exports*. Exports are mainly facilitated by the asymmetric gradual phasing out of EU tariffs on Polish industrial exports which started in 1992. Polish export performance up to now has suffered various hurdles. Among these are the insufficient restructuring in the industrial sector, non-tariff export barriers of the EU for Polish goods in sensitive areas such as steel and textiles, increased production costs due to wage growth and rising energy prices, and finally the unavailability of export credits because of high interest rates. Within the framework of its *trade policy* Poland makes use of the restructuring clause as stipulated by the EU Association Agreement which gives enterprises that undergo restructuring temporary protection from imports. Beyond these measures, Poland's trade regime is brought in line with the country's obligations arising from its CEFTA and WTO membership and in accordance to the Europe Agreement regulations.

Under the 1990 Law on Monopolistic Practice the Anti-Monopoly Office (AMO) was established. It closely monitors enterprises with a market share of over 80 per cent. As in the case of the Czech Republic, *competition policy* is potentially conflicting with other industrial policy areas in the transition process: Polish officials in their restructuring efforts of key sectors combined several firms under the roof of one holding company thereby creating huge conglomerates with dominating market shares.[306] The intention behind this concentration was to create players big enough to sustain foreign competition once tariff protection under the restructuring clause was abolished. On these grounds,

---

[306] An example is Nafta Polska SA, a holding company which comprises several enterprises in the refining and distribution of fuels. [EBRD (1997a), p. 31]

anti-monopoly objections by the AMO have been waived on different occasions.

With the government's 1991 National Environmental Plan Poland's ambitious *environmental and energy policies*, the first of its kind developed in Central and Eastern Europe, experienced an early start. Economic incentives play a major role as use is made of a comprehensive system of fees, fines and tax allowances. It thus became possible that already in 1994 about 40 per cent of environmental expenditures were financed by polluters. Needed investment for the environmental clean-up and the introduction of environmentally friendly production technologies was facilitated by financial innovation: in the course of the debt relief negotiations with the Paris Club, several creditors agreed to the first debt-for-environment swap involving public debt. US$ 460 million, to be spent between 1992 and 2010, were earmarked for eco-conversion, i.e., they are to be used to subsidise investments in environment protection.[307] This example shows an interesting way of overcoming the constraint of limited public finance in the transition process.

Table 5.3 gives an overview of Poland's industrial policy.

---

[307] OECD (1996b), pp. 130ff.

Policy Area	Measures
• *Promotion of industrial investment*	Income tax incentives; tariff reduction on capital goods and raw material imports
• *R&D & technology policy*	Poor funding; tax incentives for industrial R&D and related investments
• *Employment measures*	Retraining programmes; public works and support especially in areas of major decline
• *Privatisation*	Relatively sluggish progress particularly with mass privatisation programme; no law on business property restitution
• *SME policy*	Limited support; minor tax concessions
• *Regulatory reform & competition policy*	Anti-Monopoly Office
• *Regional development policies*	List of distressed areas which are granted various advantages; special economic zones
• *Environmental & energy policies*	Economic incentives to promote clean-up efforts; debt-for-environment swap
• *FDI*	Measures to facilitate entry
• *Trade policies & export promotion*	Tariffs in line with EU Association Agreement; import tariffs based on Europe Agreement restructuring clause
• *Management of state enterprises*	New Ministry of Treasury

Table 5.3: The industrial policy of Poland

5.3.2 Institutional Aspects

The Polish experience indicates that a dominating *representation of labour* both at government and at firm levels may effectively slow down economic restructuring and even stall it completely. Against this background there clearly evolves the risk that industrial policy is captured by trade unions who will attempt to keep inefficient capacities in operation in order to secure jobs while at the same time contending for wage increases. The ensuing delay of economic reforms occurs at the expense of the dynamic SME sector where capital is scarce and thus constitutes a major obstacle to faster growth and economic recovery.

However, beyond these considerations based on the criterion of *economic efficiency*, the Polish transition process also illustrates that the country's particular *historical experience* has to be taken into account when designing the institutional set-up of policy making in general and industrial policy in particular. The opposition to the socialist system originated in the workers' movement at the beginning of the 1980s when Solidarnosc strikes in the Gdansk shipyards rang in the decay of the socialist power base.[308] Against this background, industrial workers, particularly those employed in heavy industry, enjoy a high reputation in the population at large. This popular standing further strengthens the position of employees vis-à-vis the government. It requires officials responsible for the design and implementation of economic policies to pay increased heed to the social dimension of the transition process. In such a situation it is paramount to find a pragmatic compromise between allocative efficiency on the one hand and socio-political arguments on the other. This task may easily turn out to be a balancing act between foregone dynamism of economic growth and the risk of social unrest, i.e., political instability.

Due to certain *tensions and overlapping competences* relating to the current organisation of economic administration, the Council of Ministers in 1995 approved a package of laws reforming the ministries in charge of economic and financial affairs. The main goal of these *institutional reform efforts* are to shift the focus away from micro-management to policy and regulatory issues; to limit administrative interventions in business; to improve the co-ordination of medium-term policies; and to increase the quality of the professional civil service. Tensions are particularly rife between the Ministry of Industry and Trade and the Ministry of Ownership Changes, where both are involved in the process of privatisation and the management of SOEs. Against this backdrop the Ministry of Foreign Economic Relations and the Ministry of Industry and Trade will be merged into a new Ministry of Economy. The latter, together with the Ministry of Finance, will be in charge of economic policy. Enterprise management of some 1,300 small and medium-sized SOEs is to be transferred to regional administration organs. The new Ministry of Treasury will become the sole owner and manager of the remaining 150-200 larger SOEs. It will also be responsible for the largest capital privatisation projects and supervise smaller-scale privatisation conducted by the Privatisation Agency.

---

[308] On the Solidarity crisis in Poland see also Crampton (1994), pp. 367ff.

The planned reorganisation of central government, moreover, involves the creation of a *cross-ministerial Integration Committee* which is to co-ordinate work on the rapprochement with the *European Union*. On the whole, the *institutional consolidation* of economic policy implies that the number of ministers would be cut by two and the governmental staff by about five per cent. The reforms were approved by Parliament in 1996 and they were implemented in the same year.[309]

---

[309] OECD (1996b), p. 55

5.4 Slovenia

Slovenia, a former republic of Yugoslavia which became a newly independent
state in 1991, differs quite considerably from other former socialist systems.
Yugoslavia was never an entirely socialist regime of central planning. Instead
the country had deviated in many ways from socialist ideals (e.g., a relatively
high degree of firm independence and of economic relations with Western
countries; Yugoslavia, moreover, was not part of the Council of Mutual
Economic Assistance (CMEA) and was not subjected to the Soviet Union as the
hegemonic power[310]).

   A distinctive feature of Yugoslav socialism was the *'socialist market economy'*.[311] There are four interrelated salient elements of this system: first, instead
of state ownership and control, *social ownership* and control of the means of
production. Social ownership as an economic category is not vested in any
holder, it is a "philosophical concept".[312] No one holds the right of social ownership, not even the state. Second, a fundamental principle of Yugoslav social-

---

[310] In 1948 Tito successfully opposed attempts by the Soviets to extend their sphere of influence to Yugoslavia. With the rejection of a federal agreement with the USSR there ensued
a schism between Yugoslavia and the rest of the socialist camp. Diplomatic relations between the Soviet Union and Yugoslavia were severed on 25 October 1949 and Tito was
tagged as a 'Hitler-Trotskyite agent-enemy'.

This development had far-reaching economic implications. All agreements with the East
European bloc were cancelled and Yugoslavia found itself facing a virtual trade embargo.
Not being part of the Western camp and thus excluded from Marshall Plan aid, and
shunned and rejected by the socialist camp, Yugoslavia was forced into a quasi-autarchic
development programme. Poor, with just a little industry in the north, no natural resources,
and no political sponsor to dispense financial largesse, Yugoslavia had to start from very
difficult conditions after World War II.

It was not until 1955, after Stalin's death, that the dispute between the USSR and Yugoslavia was settled. Tito was rehabilitated by the Soviets and had not even to rejoin the
various East European institutions. Yugoslavia therefore managed to maintain its neutral
position and even received considerable economic assistance from the USSR into the bar-
gain. See Crampton (1994), pp. 259ff. and Gros and Steinherr (1995), pp. 322f.

[311] World Bank (1979), p. 154

[312] World Bank (1979), p. 155

ism is the *workers' self-management*[313]: the worker is vested with the management of the means of production and has the right to dispose of the product. Self-management is regarded as a pre-condition vital to the functioning of socialism since, without it, the worker would not have the disposition of the 'surplus value' created in production. Third, *political and economic decisions are decentralised* from the federal government to republics, communes, and enterprises because workers' management would be meaningless otherwise. Fourth, correlated to decentralised decision making there has to be *greater reliance on markets* as a guide to the allocation of resources. This implies a reduction of centralised planning and control.

As the economic powerhouse and principal trading arm of former Yugoslavia, Slovenia was relatively open to international trade and more familiar with the market mechanism than other Central and Eastern European countries (CEECs). Compared to the latter, Slovenia at the time of independence faced quite *favourable starting conditions* and in terms of its degree of development was much closer to Western European countries. When the country embarked on its transition process in 1991 GDP per capita stood at US\$ 6'331[314], which put the country closer to the EU member states Portugal and Greece than to the Czech Republic, Poland and Hungary.

The *structure of the Slovene economy* at the beginning of the 1990s, moreover, came close to advanced industrial economies with the industrial sector con-

---

[313] In the 'socialist market economy' enterprises enjoy a high degree of economic autonomy. Firms are basically free to determine what to produce, how to produce it, how much of it to produce and, in principle, the price of its product.

The system of *self-management* grants far-reaching rights to the workers of an enterprise. Its management is carried out by a workers' council elected by all the employees (the work collective); a managing board elected by the workers' council; and a director, appointed by the workers' council and approved by the commune. The director has the sole responsibility for implementing the management's decisions and for organising production.

The workers' council adopts economic plans and annual financial reports, and decides on the utilisation of funds and the distribution of the enterprise earnings between personal income and investment. The workers' council also decides on issues such as employment and dismissal of personnel. See World Bank (1979), pp. 170ff. On the Yugoslav system of self-management refer also to Estrin (1983), Lydall (1984), Sacks (1983) and Tyson (1979).

[314] See OECD (1997b), Table 2, p. 18.

tributing 36.9 per cent to GDP and services accounting for 52.8 per cent. With only 5.5 per cent of GDP the agricultural sector was small in comparison to other PSEs.[315] Within the industrial sector small and medium enterprises were dominant. Slovenia was thus to a lesser extent confronted with the problem of having to restructure large-scale SOEs. Due to various sub-contracting relations between Slovene and EU enterprises, production in manufacturing industries, moreover, was rather modern by Central and Eastern European (CEE) standards. In sum, Slovenia had a head start on East European transition economies in terms of the achieved level of development and the familiarity with international trade and the market mechanism.

After the split of former Yugoslavia, Slovenia suffered a large trade shock at the beginning of its transition process due to the collapse of trade caused by the war in the Balkans and the associated international sanctions. Slovenia was forced to drastically reorient its trade from the Yugoslav market to foreign markets. Sales to other former republics of Yugoslavia decreased from US$ 6.7 billion in 1990 to US$ 1.2 billion in 1995, while exports to the rest of the world increased from US$ 4.1 billion to US$ 7.1 billion. Against this background it is a remarkable achievement that the Slovene government managed macroeconomic stabilisation successfully in bringing down retail price inflation from around 300 per cent to just over 20 per cent during 1992 and 1993. In late 1995, the inflation rate moved to single digits for the first time since 1976 (see Table A.5 in the Appendix). Given that the economy was cut off overnight from its former home market, it is also noteworthy that Slovenia, nevertheless, after Poland, was the second PSE where growth started to resume after the transition shock: in 1993 the GDP growth rate reached 2.8 per cent and in 1996 the economy recovered the GDP level of the pre-independence years.

The overall positive image of the Slovene transition process is confirmed by the country's low *foreign indebtedness*. At the end of 1996, gross debt amounted to US$ 4.1 billion (compared with US$ 3 billion in the previous year), or around 22 per cent of GDP. At the same time, foreign currency re-

---

[315] See OECD (1997b), Table 3, p. 28.

serves of the entire banking sector stood at US$ 4.3 billion, of which US$ 2.4 billion were held by the Bank of Slovenia.[316]

Yet, despite considerable progress and the favourable circumstances of the Slovene transition to a market economy, there remain a *number of problems* to be tackled: first, overall growth in real net wages between 1992 and 1996 has been around 35 per cent. Growth has been particularly fast in the public sector, with ensuing pressures on the budget. Second, although the reorientation of trade was successfully accomplished it resulted in a too-strong geographical dependence. In 1995, 45 per cent of the country's exports went to the Italian and German markets. In the same year imports from these countries together amounted to 40 per cent. This leaves the Slovene economy largely exposed to the economic development in these two countries. Third, privatisation in Slovenia has been a relatively slow process. The selected methods of ownership transfer have led to dispersed ownership of privatised enterprises with substantial insider control. The ensuing corporate governance problems have a retarding effect on enterprise restructuring.

The *evolution of Slovenia's industrial policy* until 1995 reveals a pragmatic policy approach which has not made excessive use of vertical policy measures. Until then there did not exist any coherent strategy. Industrial policy focused on trade liberalisation, the privatisation of socially owned enterprises, SMEs and the labour market. In 1995, after lengthy debates, the Slovene parliament finally passed an industrial policy strategy, the so-called 'Strategy for the Economic Development of Slovenia'.[317] The paper covers a broad range of policy areas and is designed *along the lines of the EU's approach to industrial policy*. As such, it proposes primarily horizontal policy measures with the aim of assisting domestic industry in the process of globalisation based on the country's competitive advantages.[318] The strategy, moreover, stands at the heart of Slovenia's industrial policy approach since policies in separate industrial policy areas are derived from it (e.g., the technology policy, the 'Strategy for Increasing the

---

[316] OECD (1997b), pp. 20ff.

[317] Republic of Slovenia (1995)

[318] Republic of Slovenia (1995), p. 142

Competitiveness Capabilities of Slovene Industry'[319], the 'Strategy of Foreign Economic Relations'[320], etc.).

5.4.1 Policy Areas and Instruments

Privatisation of socially owned enterprises is a corner-stone of the Slovene industrial policy.[321] The debate on privatisation methods was fiercely led and resulted in the resignation of the deputy prime minister at the time, Joze Mencinger. His first draft law proposal in 1991 favoured a gradual, commercial and decentralised approach to privatisation. According to this plan, enterprises were expected to themselves initiate the process of transforming into private companies and to autonomously implement privatisation procedures, including the choice of prospective owners or partners. The government's role would have been limited to setting the rules of privatisation and to monitoring the process. A group of politicians and government advisors around Jeffrey Sachs proposed an alternative privatisation method based on a give-away mass privatisation scheme.[322]

The adoption of the 'Law on the Transformation of Social Ownership' in November 1992 meant a political compromise between the two proposals.[323] In es-

---

[319] Republic of Slovenia (1996a)

[320] Republic of Slovenia (1996b)

[321] On the Slovene privatisation process see Bicanic (1992), Mencinger (1993), Mencinger (1994), Pleskovic and Sachs (1994), pp. 210ff, and Stanovik and Milan (1995).

[322] On 2.11.1994 we had the opportunity for a personal interview with Professor Joze Mencinger at the Economic Institute of the Law Faculty, University of Ljubljana. During our conversation Professor Mencinger criticised Jeffrey Sachs' approach to privatisation for not doing justice enough to different starting positions of transition economies and their respective specific historical, economic and social backgrounds.

[323] According to the privatisation law, which excludes banks, insurance companies and public utilities, enterprises may themselves work out their privatisation programmes which they then have to submit to the Privatisation Agency for approval. The social capital left after restitution and debt-equity swaps is to be distributed as follows: 10 per cent are transferred to the Pension Fund, 10 per cent to the Restitution Fund, and 20 per cent to the Privatisation Fund which has to distribute the shares to private investment funds. The remaining 40 per cent are to be sold via management and employee buy-outs, public tenders, public auctions, or the public sale of shares. Ownership certificates which were freely distributed among the population entitle the holder to acquire shares through internal buy-outs or in

sence, the Slovene privatisation scheme is an attempt to incorporate two fundamental ideas: one, it respects the deeply rooted perceived rights of insiders to 'their' firms which the latter derive from the previous system of self-management and social ownership. Two, the distribution of ownership certificates to the public at large is based on the idea of social justice.

With the adoption of the 'Law on Transformation of Social Ownership', the privatisation process in Slovenia gained momentum. By the end of 1996, privatisation plans had been completed or were in implementation for companies that represent over 95 per cent of the total share capital in the trade and industry sectors. As a result of the chosen privatisation approach, 44 per cent of the book value of privatised companies are majority-owned by employees.[324] Above all, this concerns small and medium enterprises since the value of large-scale SOEs exceeds resources available to their management and workers.

The large *concentration of insider ownership* in the SME sector can be traced back to the past self-management system. It appears that dominant insider control has hitherto had a negative impact on the speed of enterprise restructuring. This may be attributed to two interrelated factors: first, since employees are primarily interested in securing jobs, necessary rationalisation and restructuring are retarded. This situation is further aggravated by the fact that workers have a direct influence on wage setting. Judging from available empirical evidence on real wage growth, insiders have pushed through substantial wage increases thereby reducing the means for much needed investment.[325] Second, insiders tend to oppose raising additional equity capital from outside investors since this would be tantamount to weakening their influence on enterprise management. They thus effectively block the inflow of fresh capital and, in the case of potential foreign investors, additionally access to required know-how and expertise. Together these factors result in persistent *corporate governance problems* which remain to be tackled.[326]

---

public sales of enterprises. They may, in addition, be used to buy shares in investment funds. See Stanovik and Milan (1995).

[324] EBRD (1997a), p. 33

[325] See Table A.5 in the Appendix on nominal wage growth.

[326] Neue Zürcher Zeitung (1998)

Hitherto only 27 socially managed enterprises which are mostly non-viable and will have to be restructured or liquidated have not presented privatisation plans. *Crisis management and the restructuring* of socially owned enterprises fall into the realm of the state-owned Development Fund of Slovenia (SKLAD).[327] SKLAD has the legal status of a joint-stock company with 100 per cent shares being owned by the state. Subordination of enterprises to the fund is voluntary and, if accepted, ownership rights have to be transferred to it completely. SKLAD in turn assumes control over the companies by introducing new management. The focus is then on short-term activities (within a two-year time horizon) in terms of organisational, financial and personnel restructuring with the goal of achieving an operational turn-around, resulting in restoring profitability and a positive cash-flow.[328] SKLAD thus assists enterprises with their restructuring and attempts to privatise them thereafter. Neither viable enterprises nor parts thereof are to be liquidated. The Development Fund has been quite successful in down-sizing the labour force of companies in their portfolio and in economic restructuring, both by effectively circumventing the problems associated with dominating insider control and by injecting firms with fresh capital and management know-how.[329]

Although some *banks* have already been privatised the two largest banks both in terms of market share and capitalisation, Ljubljanska Banka and Kreditna Banka Maribor, remain state-owned. Today around 40 per cent of banking sector assets are still under state control. In 1993 the two largest banks were recapitalised by the Agency for Bank Rehabilitation and their balance sheets cleaned from a major share of accumulated bad debts which were swapped with government bonds. As a consequence, banks by now are well-provisioned against non-performing loans and assets. Yet, corporate governance problems

---

[327] Our impression from a personal interview with the then director of SKLAD's Sector for Corporate Restructuring and Rehabilitation, Mr. Valter Nemec, was that of a highly trained staff and professionally run restructuring agency. (Interview held on 25.10.1994 in Ljubljana).

[328] Republic of Slovenia (1993), p. 4

[329] SKLAD is to be restructured and recapitalised into the 'Slovene Development Company'. This will assist any Slovene enterprise in its restructuring efforts as well as dealing with those socially managed enterprises that were not privatised until 1997. [EBRD (1997b), p. 201]

remain rife. They are a legacy of the Yugoslav economic system where social enterprises were the founders and owners of banks. Social control of banks implied that lending behaviour was driven largely by political and ownership interests, with insider lending institutionalised. There appear still to exist important links between private banks and the enterprises that used to fully own them. The situation is expected to improve significantly with continued privatisation of banks. The privatisation of the two largest banks is scheduled to be initiated during 1997.[330]

Slovenia's *competition rules* are laid down in the 'Law on the Protection of Competition' which was adopted in 1993. The law is administered by the Office for the Protection of Competition (OPC) which was established in 1994 and is part of the Ministry of Economic Relations and Development. Whereas the law in many respects follows the conventional standards known from advanced industrial economies, a number of sectors are exempted from it. Public utilities do not fall under the competition law and separate regulations apply to financial services such as banking and insurance. The EBRD comes to the conclusion that "[e]ntry barriers have been completely removed in the manufacturing sector, but not in agriculture and services."[331] It appears that the Slovene government, in certain cases, is prepared to subordinate competition regulation to political considerations. In 1995 a cartel agreement among Slovene banks setting a maximum deposit rate passed before the anti-monopoly commission. As a result competition in the banking sector is currently artificially restrained. A further weak point of Slovenia's competition policy regards its institutional set-up: being a branch of the Ministry of Economic Relations and Development the OPC is not a truly independent institution.

Investment activity in Slovene enterprises is much greater than elsewhere in CEECs. Only around 20 per cent of enterprises report no investment, compared to over 50 per cent in other transition economies.[332] Yet persistently high real interest rates continue to have a depressing effect on investment demand. Against this background the Slovene government offers tax concessions and interest subsidies to promote investment. The major thrust of Slovenia's indus-

---

[330] OECD (1997b), pp. 80ff.

[331] EBRD (1996), p. 175

[332] 1996 Eurostat survey quoted in OECD (1997b), p. 99.

trial policy is, however, on improving the general investment climate. Policy measures focus on a stable macroeconomic environment, a balanced budget, and the legal framework.[333]

In this situation *foreign direct investment* may have a potentially catalytic effect on economic restructuring and upgrading Slovene industry.[334] In 1995 cumulative FDI inflows in Slovenia stood at US$ 505 million. This amount is modest when compared to other transition economies.[335] Although the picture is somewhat more positive with regard to per capita figures the participation of foreign investors in the economy could be more important. In value terms, moreover, FDI is concentrated in a few big projects involving European multinationals (e.g., Renault in the car industry, Reemtsma and Seita in the tobacco industry). This situation may be seen as a result of the latent reluctance to accept foreign investors in the first privatisation round. The 'Strategy of International Economic Relations' endorses the principle that the state should avoid direct intervention in FDI units. The country's FDI policy will be based on stable macroeconomic conditions and transparent regulations, focused on Slovenia's comparative advantages and equal treatment of foreign investors and domestic enterprises. Yet, despite the overall emphasis on horizontal policy measures, the aforementioned strategy does leave room for a more active approach in specific cases: "The industrial policy must enable the government to actively attract FDI for projects vital for the restructuring and development of the Slovenian economy. [...] Slovenia should target specific investors for specific projects."[336]

Another corner-stone of the Slovene industrial policy is the support for *small and medium enterprises.*[337] SME policy initiatives had a very early start and go back to the pre-independence period. Slovenia was, moreover, the only country in transition which had a Ministry of Small Business which was later integrated into the Ministry of Economic Affairs. The main policy focus is on establishing a core of small businesses which will be capable of generating high-quality jobs

---

[333] Republic of Slovenia (1995), pp. 88ff.

[334] On the role of FDI in Slovenia see also Rojec (1992) and Rojec, Jasovic and Kusar (1994).

[335] See EBRD (1996), Table 8.5, p. 116.

[336] Republic of Slovenia (1996b), p. 21

[337] On Slovenia's SME policy see Bartlett and Prašnikar (1995) and Bartlett (1995).

in terms of value added per worker. Since, however, there already exist a large number of SMEs, start-up assistance is not given priority. In 1991 the Fund for the Development of Small- and Medium Enterprises was set up to overcome the problem of SMEs, getting access to financial resources. The fund provides loan guarantees and also subsidises bank loans. In addition the Ministry of Industry organised a consortium of Slovene banks to provide a venture capital fund for small firms.

Beyond these measures SMEs are offered various tax concessions. Small firms are entitled to a basic 20 per cent tax relief on profits over a four-year period. Until 1993 far-reaching exemptions were also granted to newly established enterprises. There exist also fiscal incentives for SMEs to re-invest part of their attained profits. A 30 per cent tax deduction is granted, moreover, to induce small firms to employ additional workers. To fight youth unemployment, firms taking on workers or trainees who are entering employment for the first time can deduce 34 per cent of gross wages against profit tax.

There also exists a large support network for SMEs which is organised by the Small Business Development Centre. The network comprises 600 members from other ministries, local enterprise agencies, consultants, training centres and individuals involved in small business development. It offers to small and medium enterprises a wide range of services, including training, consultancy and access to technology via the Technological Development Fund.

It emerges that Slovenia's SME policy compared to other PSEs is highly developed. To finance the various policy measures and support structures the government *inter alia* tabs privatisation proceeds which are channelled through different funds.

The Slovene *R&D policy* puts emphasis on joint research and innovation projects. Firms are encouraged to enter co-operation or strategic alliances with research institutes and universities. Firms' R&D activities, moreover, are assisted by subsidies and state guarantees for bank credits, the establishment of technology parks and financing the Technological Development Fund.

The economic transition seems to have caused less social hardship in Slovenia than in most CEECs. Several features of the advanced social security system, including the fact that it has not faced insurmountable financing problems during the transition period, have been contributing significantly to this favourable outcome.[338] The labour market infrastructure in Slovenia is already well developed and unemployment benefit rules are more generous than in many other PSEs. In certain respects they are comparable with some of the more generous systems of Western Europe (i.e., France, Germany and the Nordic countries). However, less than one third of the registered unemployed receive such benefits.

Slovenia's active *labour market policy* measures include several types of enterprise subsidy. The dominant subsidy programme managed by the Ministry of Labour, Family and Social Affairs aims at preserving productive jobs. Priority is given to labour-intensive industries that are net exporters. Support is granted on the condition that applicant firms are engaged in restructuring and have a chance of becoming viable. The programme was a temporary measure to cushion the social effects of economic transition. In 1996 funds for these subsidies were cut substantially since they have tended to slow down the pace of restructuring. Other programmes of the National Employment Office (NEO) cover the redundancy costs in SOEs and support for the creation of new jobs in which registered unemployed persons are hired. The NEO also assists unemployed workers who wish to start their own businesses. A system of community works organised by local governments with NEO support is primarily targeted at long-term unemployed.

A major shortcoming of Slovenia's labour market policy is that by international standards vocational training plays a very modest role. Given that primarily individuals in the age groups of under 25 and over 49 are affected by unemployment, the Slovene government should step up its efforts with regard to training and re-training programmes. The need to become more active in this policy area was acknowledged by the 'Strategy for the Economic Development of Slovenia'[339] and special policy measures have already been initiated. A further problem which remains to be tackled is the hitherto excessive real wage growth in the public as in the private sector. Wage negotiations thus far have been settled

---

[338] OECD (1997a), p. 84; On the Slovene labour market see also Vodopivec and Hribar-Milic (1993), Vodopivec (1995) and Verša (1996).

[339] Republic of Slovenia (1995), p. 83

within a tripartite framework between the government, employer associations and trade unions.[340]

To finance *regional development policy* measures a 'Fund for Regional Development' was established. Given both Slovenia's favourable enterprise structure inherited from the previous system (a large number of SMEs and a few large-scale SOEs) and the smallness of the country, regional problems tend to be much less severe than, e.g., in Hungary or Poland. Policy measures are focused on employment creation and establishing special economic zones in less developed regions.

Slovenia's manufacturing industry is largely dependent both on capital goods and raw material imports, as well as on exports of its final products given the smallness of the home market. Against this background the Slovene *trade policy* has focused on liberalising foreign trade relations. By the end of 1994, 98 per cent of imports were free from quantitative restrictions. The estimated rate of effective protection amounts to 4 per cent.[341] The government is committed to further liberalise its trade particularly with the EU as stipulated by its Association Agreement with the Union. Certain import restrictions remain for agricultural products. Since trade relations are geographically heavily concentrated (trade with the EU accounted for over 65 per cent of total exports in 1996), efforts are undertaken to diversify them. The government intends to expand trade, particularly with the US and other republics of former Yugoslavia.

Given Slovenia's dependence on foreign markets, the *promotion of exports* is given high priority within the country's industrial policy framework. Policy measures comprise information services as well as financial assistance. The government in conjunction with the Chamber of Commerce supports and runs campaigns abroad to promote the Slovene economy and particular regions. The most important institution promoting exports is the Slovene Export Corporation (SEC). Its function is twofold: the SEC insures exports against non-commercial risks (both short- and long-term), and against short- and medium-term com-

---

[340] Beyond the growth of real wages the annual Social Agreements include various other issues such as social security, employment, pension-fund contributions, price stability, interest rates, etc. See OECD (1997a), p. 41 and Glismann, Horn and Stanovik (1995), pp. 108ff.

[341] See EBRD (1996) and EBRD (1997b).

mercial risks. On the other hand, it provides loans to exporters who are refinanced through commercial banks and issues export guarantees. In addition to the SECs' activities, tax incentives exist for banks which grant export loans on concessionary terms. The Office for Economic Promotion and Foreign Investment offers institutional and logistic support to exporters and Slovene enterprises investing abroad.[342]

Slovenia's industrial policy strategy establishes the goal of an ecologically sustainable economic development.[343] The Ecological Development Fund finances investment in the protection of the environment and supports rehabilitation programmes for polluted areas. It also secures credits for enterprises earmarked for the modernisation of production aimed at reducing environmental pollution. *Environmental policies*, moreover, offer various tax incentives to induce firms to adopt environmentally friendly methods of production.

Table 5.4 summarises our analysis.

---

[342] Republic of Slovenia (1996b), pp. 32ff.

[343] Republic of Slovenia (1995), pp. 108f.

Policy Area	Measures
• *Promotion of industrial investment*	Tax concessions
• *R&D & technology policy*	Technological Development Fund
• *Employment measures*	Employment subsidies; incentives for re-employment and self-employment
• *Privatisation*	Mix of internal buy-outs and voucher scheme; Privatisation Agency and Development Fund
• *SME policy*	Fund for the Development of SMEs; Small Business Development Centre
• *Regulatory reform & competition policy*	Anti-Monopoly Office
• *Regional development policies*	Fund for Regional Development; Special Economic Zones
• *Environmental & energy policies*	Ecological Development Fund
• *FDI*	Office for Economic Promotion of Slovenia and Foreign Investment
• *Trade policies & export promotion*	Tariffs in line with EU Association Agreement; Slovene Export Corporation
• *Management of state enterprises*	Development Fund

Table 5.4: The industrial policy of Slovenia

5.4.2 Institutional Aspects

Compared to the Czech Republic, Hungary and Poland, Slovenia has a more *coherent industrial policy strategy*. The 'Strategy for the Economic Development of Slovenia' outlines the general sense of direction by defining the overall goals for the country's economic development and presents, in broad terms, the mainly horizontal policy measures to achieve them. From this white paper were derived subsequently separate strategies for key industrial policy areas. By this *top-down approach to the design of industrial policy*, starting from an overall vision for development and then proceeding step-by-step to the formulation of more and more detailed policies, both a greater coherence of industrial policies and a better co-ordination of different policy areas may be expected. This approach may thus help to reduce inefficiencies arising from counteracting policy measures and lead to a more focused application of available scarce public resources. The publication of these strategies, moreover, increases the transparency of government action and intentions and hence may help to reduce uncertainty rampant in transition economies. A key question to be answered, however, is how to legally and institutionally bind a government and its administration to strategies defined.

The *small size* of Slovenia both in terms of territory and population increases the ethnic, social, economic and regional homogeneity and cohesion both of society and the country. Between members of the government administration, academics and the business community exists a dense network of informal relationships and personal friendships. As an outsider visiting Slovenia one gets the impression of the Slovenes living together as one 'big family'. Under such circumstances it may be easier to reach a social consensus on the general direction of transition. More specifically, it may be the basis for a more cohesive approach to industrial policy.

The Slovenes opted for an individual mix between decentralised (i.e., insider) and centralised (i.e., mass) *privatisation methods*. There are both advantages and disadvantages to the chosen procedure. On the negative side, the late start of the Slovene privatisation process needs to mentioned. A further disadvantage is the retarding effect of the ensuing dominant insider control on the pace of enterprise restructuring. These disadvantages, however, do at the same time have positive aspects: first, Slovene officials could use the extra time resulting from the late start of privatisation to learn from the experiences of those transition economies more advanced in terms of ownership transfer and restructuring. Second, the chosen combination of internal management and employee buy-outs and voucher privatisation is tailored to the idiosyncratic historical, social and economic circumstances of Slovenia. As a consequence of the decentralised economic system of former Yugoslavia and the principle of social ownership, the feeling was deeply ingrained in the work force that they had a right to their respective enterprise. As a political compromise this approach may therefore reflect much better than other solutions the social realities in the Slovene transition process.

A strength of the Slovene institutional arrangements for its industrial policies is the *Development Fund*. This state agency of highly trained consultants and business analysts facilitates an institutionally focused and therefore consistent crisis management, restructuring and liquidation of formerly socially owned enterprises.

5.5 Synthesis IV

What can be learnt from the early experiences of the leading transition countries? In what follows we extract from the above analysed industrial policies three categories of lessons: first, we present general insights related to the issue of industrial policy in the process of transition. Second, we turn to more particular guidelines regarding the design of these policies. And, finally, we consider lessons that may be derived for the institutional framework of industrial policies in PSEs.

5.5.1 General Lessons

- *Lesson 1*: *All four leading PSEs do have an industrial policy.* Even the most ardent neoliberals among CEE governments, i.e., the Czech government does not show a hands-off attitude vis-à-vis the industrial sector. Two broad *approaches* to industrial policy in the transition process emerge in the medium term: the first, a set of ad-hoc policy measures puts greater emphasis on the operation of the free market and does not attempt to place the policies it develops into a coherent framework. The second is a comprehensive industrial policy strategy. Both approaches are increasingly tending towards horizontal policies as systemic transformation progresses.

  It might come as a surprise that different approaches to industrial policy in PSEs emerge given the similarities they have in common (e.g., same major challenges of transition; ultimate goal of developing a modern, competitive market economy; EU Association Agreements). Yet the different *idiosyncratic patterns of industrial policy* in the four countries discussed reflect their particular historical experience, cultural background, political aspects of the respective transition process, and the concrete economic development. Differences primarily relate to the degree of government intervention and whether or not industrial policies are part of an overall policy framework.

Yet despite these differences there exist strong similarities across the four countries in broad industrial policy areas. Table 5.5 compares the level of state intervention in industrial policy areas between the Czech Republic, Hungary, Poland and Slovenia.[344] It emerges that all four countries operate policies in every policy area albeit to a varying extent. Moreover, our previous analysis has revealed that all four make use of selective industrial policy measures to achieve both economic as well as non-economic goals (e.g., the support of strategic sectors and crisis management).

Policy Areas	CZ	H	PL	SLO
• Promotion of industrial investment	□□	□	□□	□□
• Technology policies	□□	□	□	□
• Employment measures	□	□□□	□□□	□□
• Privatisation	□□□	□□□	□□	□□
• SME policy	□□□	□	□	□□□
• Competition policy	□□	□□	□□	□□
• Regional development policies	□	□□	□□	□□
• Environmental & energy policies	□	□□	□□□	□□
• FDI	□□	□□□	□□	□□
• Trade policies & export promotion	□□	□□	□	□□
• Management of state enterprises	□	□□	□	□□□

Notes:
1. CZ: Czech Republic; H: Hungary; PL: Poland; SLO: Slovenia
2. Level of state activity: □ = low; □□ = middle; □□□ = high

Table 5.5: Cross-country comparison of state activity in industrial policy areas

---

[344] It goes without saying that the level of state intervention as indicated in Table 5.5 cannot be more than a rough estimate.

- *Lesson 2*:   Regarding the *pattern of emergence of industrial policy* in the
transition process *three broad phases* may be distinguished (see Figure 5.1):
phase one is congruent with the phase of macroeconomic stabilisation. Dur-

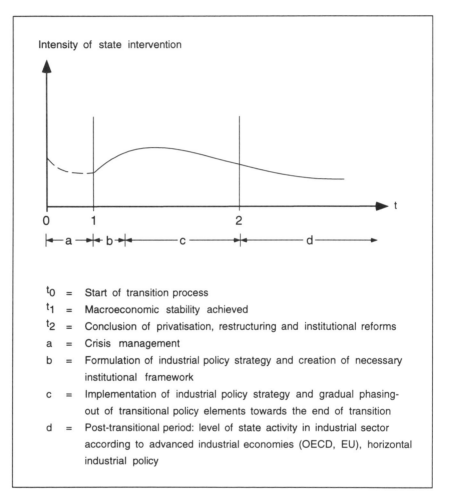

Figure 5.1: Pattern of emergence of industrial policy in the transition process

ing this period industrial policy is limited to *ad hoc* emergency measures assisting companies in acute crisis (phase a). The privatisation of SOEs, their
restructuring and institutional reforms stand at the heart of the second phase
(phases b and c). This period sees the emergence of an industrial policy either

in the form of a coherent strategy or a set of *ad hoc* measures. Both approaches make use of transitional (i.e., vertical) industrial policy measures which are continuously phased out towards the end of stage two. Advanced economic development and rapprochement with the EU and OECD countries implicate a shift to primarily horizontal, i.e., framework-oriented industrial policies and a reduced level of state intervention (phase d). Figure 5.1 sketches the approximate development of state intervention over time for a transition economy with a defined industrial policy strategy.

- *Lesson 3*:   Industrial policy in transition is evolving from a trial-and-error process and is based on on-going adaptive learning. Industrial policies have to be continuously adapted to changing circumstances and account for lessons learnt from past mistakes. This requires that policy effects are consistently monitored. Discrepancies between intended and actual results ought to be evaluated and should feed back into revised versions of respective policies. Hence industrial policy in transition is a *continuing process* and not settled with the passing of some white paper establishing an industrial policy strategy for the transition period.

- *Lesson 4*:   There are various *factors constraining industrial policy* in PSEs. The major constraints are:

  - macroeconomic instability (e.g., inflation, external balance and debt);
  - a state budget deficit;
  - frequent changes of government and political instability;
  - a deficient institutional framework (e.g., legal or administrative barriers to market entry);
  - influence of interest groups (e.g., excessive insider control, foreign investors);
  - lack of a professional and highly trained administration;[345]
  - unexpected developments (e.g., transition recession, external balance under pressure).

- *Lesson 5*:   Different industrial policy areas cannot be treated in isolation for two reasons: firstly, between different policy areas exist complementary and substituting interrelations which call for a co-ordination of policies. Sec-

---

[345] On this aspect refer also to Dabrowski (1994).

ondly, uncoordinated industrial policies involve major inefficiencies and a waste of scarce public funds. Thus a *comprehensive and systematic approach* to industrial policy is needed which integrates different policy areas in an overall context.

5.5.2 Industrial Policy Areas

5.5.2.1 Crisis Management

- *Lesson 6*:   Due to inherent moral hazard problems *crisis assistance* should be exceptional. It should be based on stringent conditionality and include some degree of risk sharing by the firms involved as well as a hard termination date.

5.5.2.2 Privatisation

- *Lesson 7*:   Despite *mass privatisation schemes* the state tends to retain a substantial influence on the private sector. Ensuing diffuse ownership structures and neglected ownership functions entail severe corporate governance problems.

- *Lesson 8*:   Corporate governance and the restructuring of privatised enterprises can be improved by *selling SOEs through standard methods at market prices*. It is vital to find 'real' owners for privatised companies that provide new management, technology and investment. FDI may play a crucial role.

- *Lesson 9*:   An *excessive influence of labour* on the political decision-making process in conjunction with self-managed SOEs may effectively retard or even stall restructuring and privatisation efforts altogether.

- *Lesson 10*:   In PSEs where both *privatisation and restructuring are blocked and foreign trade is fully liberalised* there evolves a twofold risk for the country's competitiveness: first, the capital and skill base of enterprises not yet privatised and restructured erodes because the modernisation of their production is precluded by the continued loss of market shares to foreign competitors. Second, PSEs are inclined to find themselves locked in a comparative advantage in sectors intensive in low-skilled labour and natural resources. This runs counter to the striven-for goal of transforming former planned economies into advanced industrialised market economies.

5.5.2.3 SME Policy

- *Lesson 11*: Given the overall importance of small and medium enterprises for dynamic growth and the adaptability of an economy, *SME promotion* should be a hall-mark of industrial policy in the process of transition. Support should encompass financial assistance (e.g., start-up loans) as well as information and consultancy services tailored to the specific needs of SMEs.

5.5.2.4 Competition Policy

- *Lesson 12*: In an emerging market economy where a plethora of state assets including public utilities are privatised, competition policy is a key to the *proper functioning of market forces*. The experience of the leading PSEs, however, reveals that anti-trust regulations are breached on different occasions where FDI is involved. Against this backdrop the position of regulatory bodies vis-à-vis other government agencies needs strengthening.

5.5.2.5 Investment Promotion

- *Lesson 13*: Given the prevailing deficiencies of financial intermediation in PSEs investment promotion may play a crucial role. A substantial leverage effect on investment demand can be expected from the *stimulation of complementary investment* in infrastructure.

5.5.2.6 FDI

- *Lesson 14*: The impact of FDI may be increased by promoting the creation of domestic *ancillary industries* clustered around larger enterprises under foreign ownership. In this respect local content rules of the EU Association Agreements do have a catalytic effect.
- *Lesson 15*: Major foreign direct investment projects turn out to be costly for host countries in terms of *substantial concessions* stipulated by foreign investors (e.g., high import tariff protection, tax reliefs, flouting anti-monopoly

regulations, etc.). The fact that important FDI projects are treated on a case-by-case basis implicates discretionary government action and thus a lack of transparency.

- *Lesson 16*: Increased competition to attract FDI among PSEs and with many other places in the world indicates the importance of domestic sources for investment. This implies that the most critical policies will be those that *stimulate domestic savings* and improve financial intermediation.

5.5.2.7 Export Promotion

- *Lesson 17*: Accession to multilateral trade agreements implies a shift from direct (i.e., exchange-rate devaluation, subsidies, etc.) to *indirect means of export promotion* (i.e., export-risk guarantees, information services, consultancy, etc.).

5.5.2.8 Science and Technology Policy

- *Lesson 18*: The neglect of R&D due to the lack of both private and public funds puts *indigenous technological and research capabilities in jeopardy*. To prevent research and development from further deteriorating a R&D policy is needed that in close co-operation with industry primarily supports applied research and development. These policies should be integrated into a larger industrial policy framework.

5.5.2.9 Regional Development Policies

- *Lesson 19*: Socialist economic policy entailed a high spatial concentration of industries. This makes *regional development policies* in transition a matter of urgency. Since the regional dimension extends to several other policy areas (e.g., unemployment measures, environmental policies, infrastructure policies, SOE management, crisis assistance, FDI, etc.) it should be a centrepiece of industrial policy.

5.5.2.10 Employment Measures

- *Lesson 20*: *Vocational training and retraining* are not sufficiently supplied in PSEs due to the lack of financial resources and their public good character. This has three major implications: first, it causes an erosion of the economy's skill base. Second, the pressing problem of youth unemployment is further exacerbated. Third, it aggravates the fundamental stock-flow problem inherent to the transition process by impeding the reallocation of labour between industries and sectors.

The importance of vocational training schemes and more general education in the process of transition cannot be overstated: by creating the skills and know-how needed in a free market economy the gap between the old and the new system is bridged. Thus "reform of vocational training is now a matter of urgency, crucial to public service quality, successful privatisation and industrial competitiveness."[346]

5.5.2.11 Environmental and Energy Policies

- *Lesson 21*: Ecological concerns need to be dovetailed with industrial policy for two reasons: first, the industry of the socialist economy caused severe ecological damage which now requires vast clean-up efforts. Since the latter touch on various industrial policy areas an inter-ministerial approach is called for. Second, new industrial capacities should be encouraged to utilise environmentally friendly production technologies through progressive legislation as well as fiscal incentives.

- *Lesson 22*: The contrast between the lack of public funds on the one hand and the resources required to clean up the ecological aftermath of the centrally planned economy on the other may be eased to some extent by *innovative financial instruments*, such as debt-for-environment swap agreements with foreign creditors.

---

[346] OECD (1994), p. 104

5.5.3 Institutional Aspects

- *Lesson 23*: *Institutional consolidation and a better co-ordination* of industrial policies is paramount for the efficient and focused application of limited resources. Overlapping competences between government bodies involved in the implementation of industrial policy due to not clearly assigned tasks and responsibilities result in inefficiencies and a waste of scarce resources. This finding is further aggravated if no single agency has been charged with the task of co-ordinating industrial policy measures. The lack of an institutional *primus inter pares* bears the risk of a general lack of direction of these policies.

- *Lesson 24*:   In transition economies, where uncertainty is wide-spread, government policies and actions should be predictable and transparent for market participants. This argues in favour of an institutional structure in which *rules* dominate discretionary decision-making by the government.[347] Industrial policy making based on rules also limits the extent to which well-organised special-interest groups can exert their influence and hence reduces rent-seeking: "The degree of autonomy and *accountability* of a government, being part of the institutions constituting the political order, are the main determinants of the extent of rent-seeking."[348]

- *Lesson 25*:   A *top-down approach to the design of industrial policies* may help to increase the coherence of industrial strategies. Starting from an overall vision for the economic development of a given transition economy, subsequently separate strategies for respective industrial policy areas are derived.

- *Lesson 26:*   A *professional and highly trained administration* is key to a successful transformation of the socio-economic system in general and to the design and implementation of industrial policy in particular:

  Economic restructuring and development thus depend on an efficient public administration that is capable of taking the right economic and industrial

---

[347] On the importance of rules-based policy-making in the context of East European transition see also Buchanan (1994).

[348] Blommestein (1994), p. 32, emphasis added

decisions when they are needed, and that derives its policies from a forward looking viewpoint. It is in the Government's interest to ensure that the civil service remains attractive, above all in the upper echelons where economic and industrial policies are shaped.[349]

- *Lesson 27*: The example of Poland elucidates that to secure the political sustainability of the transition process the *historical experience* of a PSE may require substantial concessions in terms of speed and efficiency of reforms.

- *Lesson 28*: Industrial policy should focus on the elimination of *legal and administrative barriers* that act as impediments to the emergence of a buoyant private sector.

* * *

This chapter's analysis and discussion of the leading transition economies has revealed that all four countries do operate a wide array of *de facto* industrial policies irrespective of the weak theoretical foundations of such government interventions.[350] This finding, moreover, stands in contrast to the advice given to PSE governments stemming from international financial institutions and Western consultants.

Industrial policies seem rather to evolve as a pragmatic answer to the pressing problems emerging in the transition process. As the transformation of the economic system progresses and with the rapprochement with the EU, horizontal policies become more and more important and an alignment with the latter's industrial policy concept can be observed. This confirms our contention made in Chapter 4 that the European Union's industrial policy approach exerts a strong influence on the policy design in PSEs.

The analysed industrial policies of the Czech Republic, Hungary, Poland and Slovenia reveal a plethora of policy areas. For an efficient and focused allocation of scarce public funds and in order to improve the effectiveness of operated policies industrial policy priorities need to be established. In the next chapter we attempt to identify these key policy areas.

---

[349] OECD (1994), p. 99

[350] See Chapter 3.

6 An Industrial Policy for Countries in Transition

In this chapter we develop a synthesis of the findings we elaborated in the preceding chapters. The eclectic approach applied hitherto allowed us to derive various lessons and gain insights related to our topic. We now join together the pieces of the puzzle and draw up a framework of industrial policy in transition. It has been stressed throughout the exposition that policy advice should account for the specific idiosyncratic mix of historical, social, political and economic factors. Our framework, thus, neither offers a magic formula for solving problems related to industrial restructuring in transition economies nor is it complete. On the contrary, we intend to develop a concept that leaves ample room to account for country-specific circumstances. Yet neither is our approach to industrial policy noncommittal: it does contain normative elements which we regard as of great importance for the successful governance of industrial restructuring. Its key features address issues pertaining to all transition economies under scrutiny and are thus of general validity. Hence the framework developed here may serve as a benchmark or a starting-point for the design of industrial policy in the process of transition.

The chapter is structured as follows: the first section elaborates on the policy agenda and examines the key issues that industrial strategies in Central and Eastern European (CEE) economies should target. Section two discusses the central policy areas. These are treated in order of descending priority, starting with those where the need for immediate action is most pressing. The concluding section finally considers institutional aspects.

6.1 The Policy Agenda

The core issues on the industrial policy agenda in transition economies stand at the heart of this section. In a first step we broach the basic rationale that can justify government interventions in the industrial sector. Next we turn to the foundations on which industrial policies should rest. Our analysis of the European and East Asian Newly Industrialising Economies' (NIEs') industrial policies has shown that these fundamentals ought to be considered indispensable for successful modernisation strategies. The following section looks into the major policy objectives. According to their degree of urgency we distinguish between short-term and medium-term objectives. Finally, those factors are discussed that constrain the role and scope of industrial policies in the transition process.

6.1.1 The Basic Rationale for Industrial Policy

This section takes up four arguments that support the notion of industrial policy in CEE transition economies. It is argued that government interventions in the industrial sector may be justified based on: (1) market failures; (2) highly concentrated market structures and barriers to entry and exit; (3) political economy arguments; and finally (4) on *de facto* industrial policies. In what follows we examine each of these arguments in turn. The following discussion is, however, not simply a summary of aforementioned arguments since the latter are applied to the specific circumstances of systemic transformation and expanded upon.

6.1.1.1 Market Failures

It lies in the nature of fundamental systemic change, as witnessed in Central and Eastern Europe, that the emergence of markets is a slow and cumbersome process. For many years to come, rudimentary ill-functioning and thin markets will co-exist with more developed ones. Against this background market failures will be dominating CEE economies for the foreseeable future. In transition economies market failures act as impediments both to the proper functioning of emerging markets as well as to the process of industrial restructuring. From a more *static* neoclassical perspective markets fail in two key areas, namely infrastructure and the environment (i.e., environmental clean up and protection). Both areas do have a public good character and require huge financial resources after forty years of neglect. Since market forces alone would lead to suboptimal results a case can be made for corrective policy interventions. This does not, however, imply that the state itself should produce the insufficiently provided for goods. On the contrary, lacking the necessary resources – both in terms of available capital and know-how – the state has to seek co-operation with private business. Alternatively, the provision of public goods may be completely transferred to the private sector via licences or the privatisation of state-owned enterprises (SOEs) as in the case of telecommunication.

With a view to industrial restructuring and the concomitant reallocation of resources *dynamic* market failures[351] may justify policy interventions. The transition from a centrally planned economy to a market-type economic system requires a process of far-reaching learning. To successfully compete in a market economy, existing know-how must be adapted to the changed circumstances and new skills and capabilities have to be acquired. We have repeatedly stressed the dangers of eroding skill bases in transition economies and pointed to the public good character of training, education and research and development (R&D). Against this background, and since human capital is a key factor determining the future competitive advantage of CEE economies, state action in this area is both necessary and urgent.

We have identified a third category of market failures that are prominent in the context of systemic transformation. Given emerging and above all incomplete markets *information* related market failures (i.e., incomplete markets, adverse selection and moral hazard) are rampant and industrial policy may play an important complementary role. Hence a case for the mixed economy can be made. We have also revealed that this type of market failure is related to the stage of economic development and is particularly acute in transition economies. Here they have major implications for the process of Schumpeterian creative destruction because they stand at the heart of the fundamental stock-flow problem:[352] the deficient system of financial intermediation hampering the

---

[351] 'Dynamic' market failures are those that impede economic development and thus retard the process of catching up.

[352] In Chapter 2 we identified the *stock-flow problem* as a major impediment to the process of industrial restructuring that Joseph Schumpeter called *creative destruction* and which stands at the heart of the second stage of economic transition. In this process, existing production capacities (i.e., the stock of allocated resources) that are the result of the past allocation mechanism of central planning ought to be closed down or revamped and new capacities should emerge. Notwithstanding the growing shares in GDP and in overall employment of the private sector, state-owned enterprises in CEE continue to contribute substantially to gross domestic product and are still among the biggest employers in the region. The employed resources are to a large extent misallocated and the assets obsolete. The application of strict market criteria would entail a dramatic closure of plants and enterprises with the concomitant large-scale shedding of workers in a very short time. The

reallocation of existing resources and depriving small and medium enterprises of fresh capital for the most part has to be ascribed to information-related market failures. Yet these market failures may not only slow down the adjustment process and defer some of its benefits, they may also cause the process of industrial restructuring to deviate from the optimal path and thus reduce the long-term potential for growth. Without support from a well developed financial system, a number of potentially viable enterprises might fail to adapt and be forced to close down and new business might find it excessively difficult to get investment funds.

Hence in cases such as financial markets and the small- and medium-sized enterprise (SME) sector well identifiable information-related market failures can vindicate industrial policies. Yet based on information economics a role for the state may be justified which transgresses the boundaries of merely corrective policy measures. In periods of rapid and fundamental socio-economic change, which is characteristic for the transition from a centrally planned to a market economy, the state may act as a *manager of the necessary adjustment process*.[353] As such, the government has a twofold function: first, it works as an information-clearing agency by systematically gathering and disseminating information on domestic and global markets. It thus forms a complement to the market mechanism and may help to substantially reduce transaction costs.

Second, industrial policies are made instrumental so as to accelerate structural adjustment. In other words, they provide catalysts which speed up the process of creative destruction. Following the European Union (EU) approach to industrial policy these catalysts pertain to policies focused on R&D, technology diffusion, small- and medium-sized enterprises, training and education and, finally, on business services.

---

flow part of the stock-flow problem relates to the building-up of new capacities and skills as well as to the reallocation of those resources allocated in the state sector which could be made viable in a market environment.

[353] We return to the notion of managing structural adjustment below, where we discuss the institutional set up of industrial policies in the transition process.

6.1.1.2 Market Structure and Barriers to Entry

From our discussion of economic aspects of systemic transformation it emerges that key markets in Central and Eastern Europe are still highly concentrated. Under these circumstances competition does not yet exert the necessary disciplining pressures that would induce industrial restructuring on a scale large enough. Even worse, as the analysis of industrial policies operated in leading transition economies reveals existing anti-trust legislation is all too often and too easily subordinated to attract foreign direct investment (FDI). In this way the stock-flow problem is further exacerbated. Collusive behaviour and monopolistic or oligopolistic market structures in transition economies have two effects, both highly detrimental to the progress of structural adjustment: first, barriers to market entry and the associated lack of competition in factor markets means that resources set free in the course of creative destruction may not be reallocated to their most efficient use. Second, it precludes that competition can develop its full spurring effect on innovation. The creation of novelty and its application in new products, thus, remain behind their potential. Taken together, this leads to a slower pace of industrial restructuring with the concomitant negative consequences for economic growth.

Thus the lack of competition not only justifies but urgently calls for policy interventions. Yet competition policy should not focus on market structure alone. Rather, policies also ought to be targeted on barriers to market entry so as to increase competitive pressures from potential new domestic and foreign entrants. Both deregulation, above all the simplification of procedures regulating the formation of firms, and an open-trade policy should work to this end. But to speed up the process of creative destruction these measures will not suffice. It, moreover, requires that nonviable firms irrespective of private or public ownership are forced into bankruptcy. Only if exit is a real and credible threat to incumbent firms may their operations finally become efficient.

6.1.1.3 Political Economy of Transition

Beyond economic rationale a strong case for industrial policy in transition can be made based on political economy arguments. These rest on the insight that for systemic transformation to be sustainable in the medium and long term an *ex ante* social consensus on the distribution of the costs and benefits of this process is vital. In the short to medium run, the negative aspects of socio-economic reforms in CEE for the majority of the population prevail. Inflation, mass redundancies and concomitant long-term unemployment and the slower than expected improvement of living standards lead to wide-spread frustration, discontent and open protest.

The transition to a pluralistic democracy in most CEE countries progresses at a faster pace than do economic reforms. This allows disadvantaged social groups to increasingly exert their influence on the political process. There is the potential risk that disadvantaged social groups (e.g., young unemployed, former employees of SOEs, and pensioners) may effectively retard economic reforms and pose a threat to political stability by voicing their discontent. Thus the challenge of successfully governing the transition process consists of finding the right balance between concerns for economic efficiency on the one hand and social aspects on the other. Following the East Asian NIEs' principle of shared growth, PSEs in order to secure political stability as the *conditio sine qua non* for a successful transition should make sure that the costs of adjustment are shared by all social groups. A highly unbalanced distribution of transition sacrifices bears the inherent risk of social instability. The *principle of shared adjustment costs*, and once these economies take off of *shared growth*, may add to the government's legitimacy and help to win the support of society at large. Under these circumstances industrial policy can play a pivotal role by striking a compromise between allocative efficiency and social aspects of transition. As a hinge it moderates between potentially conflicting interests and thus helps to secure the feasibility of transition.

To this end for some time to come state-owned enterprises will have to be kept in operation despite their being not viable in a market environment. Given that these firms are as yet among the largest employers in CEE and that entire regions are still highly dependent on these industrial conglomerates, their management and binding plans for their phased closure ought to form a core element of industrial policy strategies in transition. By spreading adjustment costs over time and cushioning the adverse effects of economic transition industrial policy thus significantly contributes to the political sustainability of transition strategies.

6.1.1.4 De facto Industrial Policy

Our analysis of the leading CEE transition economies in Chapter 5 has revealed that industrial policy, irrespective of official rhetoric, is a central element of the economic policies' repertoire of the governments in the region. Once this is acknowledged it becomes apparent that naive policy prescriptions calling for state minimalism in CEE transition falls short of reality. It not only misses the point but also means leaving alone governments of post-socialist economies (PSEs) with the design of such policies. Hence a pragmatic approach to the subject matter is required, based on the insight that these policies form an indisputable part of real-life policy making both in advanced industrial countries as well as in emerging market economies.

Yet if industrial policy is a reality then its covert operation, i.e., a *de facto* industrial policy that runs counter to the government's official free market stance, becomes pointless. On the contrary, an official industrial policy strategy would help to reduce uncertainty in the transition by defining the government's political course. It would, moreover, limit the room for discretionary policy making prone to under-the-table rent-seeking activities. An open industrial policy, finally, is subject to democratic control and thus reflects a social consensus on the development priorities rather than being driven by particularist interests on an *ad-hoc* basis.

6.1.2 The Foundations of Industrial Policy

The analysed industrial policy strategies of both the European Union as well as of the East Asian newly industrialising economies divulged that for industrial policies to be successful a number of fundamental prerequisites must be met. Adapted to the context of CEE transition, industrial policies should rest on: (1) macroeconomic stability; (2) political stability; (3) high skill levels; (4) an outward orientation of the economy; and finally (5) domestic and international competition.

If an economy is in complete disarray industrial policy is not a feasible option. A minimal degree of *macroeconomic stability* is required to manage the process of industrial adjustment. Only a stable macroeconomic framework will allow economic actors both private and public to form long-term plans. This long-term orientation and the trust in the stability of the economic system is indispensable for investment in industrial restructuring to occur. Large external imbalances, high foreign debt and persistent household deficits, moreover, do not leave any room to manoeuvre for active industrial policies.

Frequently changing governments, strikes and demonstrations all impinge on the speed of economic reforms. Political instability not only slows down the process of structural adjustment it also implies that public policies are likely do lack the necessary continuity and consistency. Repeated reversals of or major changes to the political course are detrimental to the credibility of transition strategies and stand in the way of achieving long-term development goals. *Political stability* consequently has to be considered an important prerequisite for industrial policy.

The experience of the East Asian NIEs proves the importance of investment in human capital for catching up with advanced industrial economies. *High skill levels* are a key to successfully mastering the process of industrial restructuring because they largely determine the extent to which an economy may adjust to change. Furthermore, the design and implementation of comprehensive industrial policy strategies are demanding with regard to administrative capabilities. Continued investment in skill and capability formation is thus an important pillar on which industrial policy must be based.

Although interventionist variants of the East Asian export push model are no option for PSEs, an unconditional *outward orientation* of these economies nevertheless seems vital. Only by actively encouraging and supporting domestic firms to produce for sophisticated export markets of advanced industrial countries will they eventually become internationally competitive. The success or else on these markets ought to be the yard-stick for government support. Without this outward orientation, industrial policies all too easily come to a dead end with the concomitant waste of scarce resources. Eastern European transition economies should create a national export culture along the lines of the NIEs, i.e., focus long-term policy strategies on the penetration of sophisticated export markets of advanced economies.

Domestic and foreign *competition*, or rather the lack thereof, not only may serve as a vindication for government interventions it is also decisive for the success of industrial policies. Only competitive pressures force firms in transition economies to effectively restructure and thus to increase efficiency in production. Highly concentrated markets which, in addition, are shielded from international competition are not an environment conducive to the maturation of government-assisted business. Thus competition in home markets and/or from abroad is an important prerequisite for the success of proactive industrial policies.

It emerges from our discussion that both macroeconomic and political stability have to be regarded as *indispensable preconditions* for the success of industrial policies in the transition. The remaining three fundamentals, namely high skill levels, outward orientation and competition, while not essential are yet factors *highly conducive* to the effectiveness of industrial policy interventions in transition economies. Figure 6.1 shows the three pillars of industrial policy in the transition process.

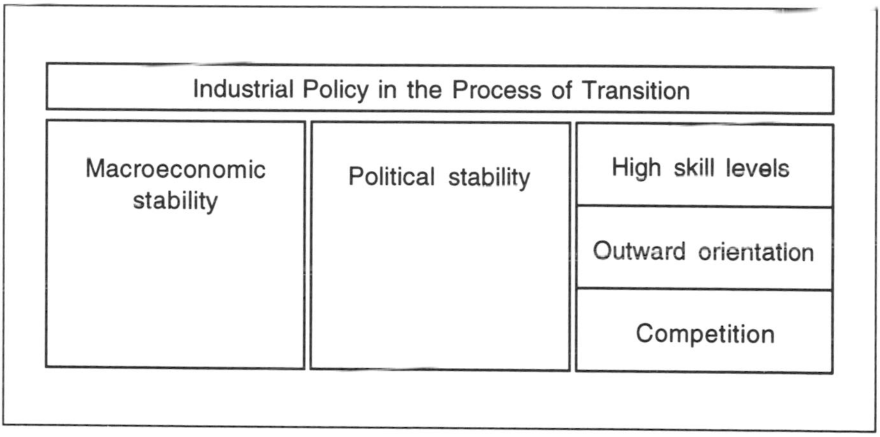

Figure 6.1: The pillars of industrial policy in transition

6.1.3 Objectives

The general objectives of industrial policy in the transition process have to be embedded in the overall goals of systemic transformation.[354] Hence a fundamental economic objective is to facilitate the emergence of a market economy. To

---

[354] Refer to Table 1.1 in the introductory chapter where we identified the respective goals for the economic, institutional, political and social subsystems.

this end, industrial policy should be aimed both at strengthening emerging markets and at paving the way for industrial restructuring. Once the final phase of economic transition is reached the objectives should shift toward the consolidation of reforms and target sustained long-term growth.[355] Contributing to the goal of a democratic constitutional state industrial policy, moreover, ought to be focused on modernising and strengthening those institutions that are involved in its design and implementation. Finally, industrial policies must be subject to democratic control and ought to be carried by a broad social consensus, thus helping to secure the political sustainability of transition.

Given that the scope of industrial policies in transition economies is constrained by various factors, which we discuss below, the government must weigh the urgency of policy issues and establish a time schedule for attaining set policy objectives. In what follows we draw a line between short-term and medium- to long-term objectives. The former category is a matter of urgency and requires immediate policy action.

6.1.3.1 *Short-Term Objectives*

Our analysis of economic aspects of systemic transformation identified the fundamental stock-flow problem as the Gordian knot that obstructs the process of creative destruction.[356] The stock-flow problem retards or even stalls the necessary reallocation of capital and human resources between firms and sectors. In this way it hampers industrial restructuring and impedes the emergence of a buoyant SME sector. Yet the stock-flow problem not only causes a delay of economic transition it also implies an erosion of the economy's capital and skill base. Finally, it bears the risk of deviating from the optimal long-term development path.

---

[355] In the introductory chapter we distinguished between three *phases of economic transition* and respective key reforms: in phase I macroeconomic stabilisation stands at the top of the policy agenda, while in phase II large-scale privatisation and economic restructuring are the primary policy issues. Phase III finally stands for the consolidation of economic reforms and the take-off to sustained growth. See Box 1.1 in the Introduction.

[356] See Chapter 2.1 on the economics of transition.

Against this background, alleviating the stock-flow problem has to stand at the top of the policy agenda. The two starting points for industrial policy should be (1) *corporate governance* problems and (2) the deficient financial intermediation in transition economies. The management of both state-owned and privatised enterprises must be controlled effectively and the insider coalition against restructuring must be broken up. To this end industrial policies must above all focus on:
- the entanglement between (state) banks, investment funds and privatised enterprises;
- improving the supervision of SOE management;
- accumulated inter-enterprises debts;
- enforcing bankruptcy legislation;
- increasing labour mobility;
- cushioning the adverse effects of structural adjustment on employment.

The second key area of short-term policy objectives pertains to *financial intermediation* whose functioning is of paramount importance for the process of structural adjustment. We have shown that investment capital does not flow to its most productive use for several reasons. In this context industrial policies should be targeted at:
- the vicious circle of non-performing loans between (state) banks and industrial firms;
- improving the supervision of banks;
- the privatisation of remaining state banks;
- giving start-up businesses, in particular SMEs, access to venture capital.

Hence the primary short-term objective of industrial policy in transition is to speed up the process of creative destruction by defusing the stock-flow problem.

6.1.3.2 Medium- to Long-Term Objectives

When both privatisation of SOEs and industrial restructuring are well under way, the consolidation of economic reforms and the catching up with EU member states move to the top of the transition agenda. This coincides with a shift of industrial policy objectives towards medium- to long-term targets. The combined effect of a number of factors such as huge investment requirements, the time needed to effectively tackle a given problem, and political opposition entail that the following objectives can only be targeted in the medium to long run:

- the phased closure of nonviable SOEs;
- the formation of human capital;
- the promotion of both investment and exports;
- the restructuring and modernisation of infrastructures;
- to strengthen the R&D base;
- to redress the most acute regional imbalances;
- to initiate environmental clean-up programmes.

The single most important long-term policy goal is the adoption of the EU industrial policy approach[357] and its adaptation to the specific circumstances and needs of a given transition economy.

6.1.4 Constraints

A number of factors constrain and thus determine the scope and type of industrial policies that can be operated in transition economies. Part of these constraints are the inversion of the above mentioned foundations of industrial policy, i.e., if these preconditions are not met. Others are based on the neoliberal critique of government interventions or relate to the specific conditions of systemic transformation.

The first and foremost important constraint is the great *financial stringency* in transition economies. Public households in CEE are under constant pressure from two sides: on the one hand, financing demands are huge. Reforms of the social safety net, infrastructure investment projects, environmental clean-up programmes, and agricultural policies, to mention but a few areas, all require vast amounts of finance. On the revenue side, the fiscal system is not yet work-

---

[357] The European Union's approach to industrial policy was presented in Chapter 4. European industrial policies are targeted on an open and competitive environment that is conducive to industrial change. The approach is primarily based on horizontal schemes open to all industries and firms qualifying for support. The key areas of these horizontal policies include: infrastructure, skills and training, small- and medium-sized enterprises, and R&D and technology policy.

ing efficiently and does not generate sufficient funds. Albeit initiated tax re-forms, this situation cannot be expected to change soon. The introduction of a value-added tax will not significantly alleviate the situation and an increase of revenue taxes would likely choke off economic recovery.

Directly related to the limited public funds is the preservation of *macro-economic stability*. The neglect of this primacy means that industrial policies rather sooner than later will get out of hand, i.e., lead to the inefficiency of pol-icy measures and the associated waste of resources. Hence it would be highly counterproductive to finance extensive structural adjustment programmes via budget deficits, external debt or, worse even, via the money press. With its dest-abilising effects on macroeconomic balance such an approach would put the progress of economic transition seriously at risk.

Another potential limitation of industrial policy in the process of transition arises from *political instability*. The lack of clear political majorities, frequent changes of government, and widespread public opposition against policy strategies are all detrimental to the long-term orientation and sustainability of industrial policy.

A deficient *institutional framework* may also greatly constrain the room to ma-noeuvre available to policy makers. There are several aspects to this point: first, regulations and cumbersome administrative procedures may impede the swift and effective implementation of policy strategies. Second, the lack of policy co-ordination and the institutional dispersal of efforts largely reduce both the ef-fectiveness of industrial policy, as well as the efficiency with which public funds are used. Third, the design and implementation of comprehensive devel-opment strategies is a demanding task and requires substantial administrative capabilities. Without a professional and highly trained administration, industrial policy ought to be restricted to horizontal policy measures[358] and resort as little as possible to direct interventions. Fourth, the best policy strategy cannot be implemented without adequate policy instruments. Without these leverages on

---

[358] *Horizontal industrial policies* are framework-oriented: rather than targeting specific firms and/or industries, they seek to improve the business environment within which economic agents operate, i.e., to improve the functioning of the market process itself. An example for a primarily horizontally oriented industrial policy is that of the European Union (see Footnote 357 on page 224).

the economy industrial policies become pointless. Finally, where few highly organised interest groups and/or self-seeking bureaucrats are in the position to
capture the political process resources will be diverted from intended destina-
tions and industrial policy ultimately rendered ineffective.

The state's ability to intervene successfully is also limited by the *information* it
has available. Given the fast and fundamentally changing environment of transition economies and recalling that the process of systemic transformation in
CEE is unprecedented in history, one has to acknowledge that this information
cannot be more than patchy. Since more active versions of industrial policies
are also more information-intensive such policy interventions should be limited
to but a few key areas and have to be administered with great care. The information constraint is further fortified if unexpected developments are considered.
In many CEE countries the depth and length of the transition recession came as
a surprise. The same holds for external balances which unexpectedly come under speculative pressures and with regard to the slump in major export markets,
above all the European Union. Such developments can radically change the parameters of industrial policy and may have major repercussions on its impact.

International *trade agreements*, particularly the EU Association Agreements,
have a strong effect on the type of industrial policy operable in transition and
the instruments that may be employed to this end. This is especially so with regard to trade policy: several treaties preclude the operation of strategic trade
policies based on the infant industry argument. Thus an industrial policy along
the lines of the East Asian NIEs in transition economies is no realistic option.
This finding is further corroborated by the fact that these countries are highly
dependent on having access to the markets of advanced industrial economies.
This access is only granted on a reciprocal basis.

In sum, the type, extent and scope of industrial policy in transition are severely
constrained by several factors. Taken together, they argue for selective policy
interventions only to be applied in those cases where key areas, such as financial intermediation, are affected by major market deficiencies.

6.2 Policy Areas and Instruments

Based on the agenda of industrial policy in transition this section examines the policy areas and instruments. As with the above discussed policy objectives a distinction is made between the short-term and the medium- to long-term. Although the order in which the different policy areas are treated does reflect the priority we ascribe to them, the temporal differentiation should not be misinterpreted. It is patently not so that in the short-run no efforts should be devoted to medium- to long-term policy areas. Given binding constraints the two categories are rather to mirror the shifting major thrust of industrial policy in transition over time.

Before we come to the structure of this section two qualifications are worth mentioning: first, the clear-cut distinction between the different areas of industrial policy is analytical. In reality they are overlapping and various interrelations between them exist. Second, against the background of our broad definition of industrial policy[359] the list of policy areas is not complete. We only examine those policy areas which we deem most important and accordingly should receive prominence.

In what follows we first discuss those policy areas which should be given immediate priority since they target the stock-flow problem. Next we turn to the medium- and long-term policy areas that are also important but where major efforts may be deferred until later. The final section touches on the observable convergence of CEE industrial policies with the EU approach to industrial policy.

6.2.1 Industrial Policies in the Short Term

For the alleviation of the stock-flow problem as the primary short-term objective industrial policy measures should focus on the following areas: (1) financial intermediation; (2) the promotion of small- and medium enterprises; (3)

---

[359] Recall at this stage the definition of industrial policy as presented in Chapter 1.1: "Industrial policy embodies measures formulated and implemented by the state which are targeted at industry to achieve given sector-specific objectives."

competition policy; (4) labour market policies; (5) state-owned enterprises; and finally (6) privatisation. Each of these policy areas is discussed in turn.

6.2.1.1 Financial Intermediation

Both to resolve the vicious circle existing between undercapitalised (state) banks and illiquid SOEs and to facilitate the intermediation between savers and investors, a competitive network of commercial banks should be made a top priority. This calls for the immediate and swift recapitalisation of banks. Their balance sheets must be cleaned of non-performing bad loans that have been accumulated between them and large state-owned industrial enterprises. This requires the state to socialise some risk so as to counter the danger of financial instability in the economy.

Freeing banks of their portfolios of bad debts, however, will not suffice. The largest banks which even in the most advanced CEE transition countries hitherto have remained in state property ought to be privatised without delay. This should be accomplished preferably involving strategic foreign investors who can guarantee the necessary transfer of know-how and influx of fresh capital. In addition, to ensure the stability of the financial system, tight bank regulation and supervision of their operations is needed.

Beyond this firm level intervention the state should promote a bank-based financial system. Particularly with regard to the SME sector, a bank-based financial system may help to instil a long-term perspective of co-ordinated investment decisions. Relationship banking involves a long-term commitment by the creditor (either the state and/or private banks) to the borrowing company. The former needs the latter to do well so as to enable him to repay his loans over the long term. The lender has a genuine interest in the performance of debtor companies and will allocate capital accordingly. Thus, from a bank-based financial intermediation an improvement of corporate governance problems in PSEs may finally be expected. A financial intermediation along these lines ultimately puts banks due to their engagement across sectors and industries in a position to better co-ordinate investment decisions and to encourage a more rapid sectoral mobility in anticipation of structural changes.

A bank-based financial system requires, however, that suppliers of credit must get involved with the company management. Only in this way will they be able to effectively co-ordinate investment decision in the economy and ameliorate corporate governance of firms. Industrial policy should therefore create the necessary incentives for banks to actively participate in firms' restructuring.

6.2.1.2 Small- and Medium-Sized Enterprises

For at least three reasons the promotion of small- and medium-sized enterprises should be a centre of gravity of industrial policies in transition: first, SMEs are most disadvantaged by the stock-flow problem which effectively drives them out of financial markets. Second, the socialist strategy of forced growth totally neglected this enterprise sector which resulted in an unbalanced industrial structure. Third, the overall significance of small- and medium-sized enterprises for dynamic growth and the adaptability of an economy is by now widely acknowledged.

A major task of industrial policy in transition should therefore be to assist SMEs in gaining access to finance, in particular to venture capital. Problems of asymmetric information and the dominant position of large industrial conglomerates in the credit market means that SMEs find the access to investment capital blocked and, consequently, have to rely on retained earnings alone. Under these circumstances two different policy measures may help to diffuse the situation: first, various forms of tax allowances may induce private business to increase capital expenditures by increasing retainable profits.[360] Second, the state may directly or indirectly act as a provider of investment funds. To this end either a development bank or a special fund for the development of SMEs may be established, providing on the one hand subsidised bank loans and loan guarantees and equity finance on the other.

Beyond financial assistance, support should also encompass information and consultancy services tailored to the specific needs of SMEs. Measures *inter alia* may include setting up science and technology parks to foster the diffusion of modern technologies in the SME sector, establishing training centres for modern business practices and information and counselling services on how to gain access to export markets. Yet industrial policy in transition economies should

---

[360] One may think, for example, of provisions broadening the deductibility of investment expenses from income taxes and tariff reductions on capital goods and raw material imports.

also focus on existing regulations and administrative procedures that act as barriers to entry for SMEs, particularly where the starting up of new businesses is concerned.

A comprehensive SME policy, moreover, is in several ways complementary to other areas of industrial policy which should be exploited. Two important examples are FDI and labour market policies: first, in combination with major foreign direct investments SME promotion could be made instrumental for building industrial clusters which may serve as growth poles in the economy. Second, SME policy measures may be used to actively create employment opportunities.

6.2.1.3 Competition Policy

In an emerging market economy, where a plethora of state assets including public utilities are privatised and where private businesses coexist with giant state-owned industrial conglomerates, competition policy is a key to the proper functioning of market forces. This is all the more so since key markets in transition economies are still highly concentrated. Empirical data shows that those branches most affected by high concentration are fuel, energy and basic metal industries. These sectors are dominated by large state enterprises, 'white elephants' which in most cases have not yet been privatised. The lack of competition points to the existence of major barriers to entry and calls for an effective competition policy.

Adopting anti-trust legislation and establishing anti-monopoly offices, however, is not enough. Our analysis of the leading PSEs in transition revealed that all of them have already established such institutions. Yet existing laws and regulations are not strictly enforced and the position of respective governments bodies is too weak. Taken together, competition in emerging market economies of Central and Eastern Europe is under constant threat. Particularly where attempts are made to attract major foreign direct investments anti-trust regulations are often sacrificed and concessions are made that go as far as temporary protection from import competition.

Against this backdrop, and in order to mitigate the stock-flow problem, it is essential that competition policy becomes a corner-stone of industrial policy in transition. This requires that the position of anti-trust offices is strengthened vis-à-vis other government agencies and that existing regulations are strictly enforced. Competition policy should be focused on:

- a stable legal framework allowing markets to emerge;
- barriers to market entry erected both by incumbent firms as well as by regulation and administrative procedures;
- a body of legislation allowing for market exit, i.e., a bankruptcy law which is enforced;
- properly functioning markets;
- ensuring international competitive pressures.

6.2.1.4 Labour Market Policies

Insider resistance to restructuring can largely be explained by a deficient labour market infrastructure and the fact that the majority of the jobless share a perspective of long-term unemployment.[361] Similar to financial intermediation, labour markets should fulfil the pivotal function of a transmission belt in the process of systemic transformation: individuals who are set free in the course of creative destruction must be reallocated to new employment. This process involves the adaptation to changing skill requirements of industry and increasing the responsiveness of labour supply to industrial change. Hence labour market policies should facilitate and simultaneously accelerate the necessary transition of skill profiles.

The reallocation of labour across enterprises, occupations, sectors and regions is one of the most challenging tasks of transition. What makes the problem such an intricate one is that to reduce the rigidity of labour markets, and so increase the mobility of labour, a number of distortions in other markets must be tackled. As a case in point, the spatial mobility of the unemployed is largely limited both by a rigid housing market as well as by a deficient public transport infrastructure. To fight long-term unemployment from getting out of hand and thus to contribute to the political sustainability of transition, a comprehensive approach to labour market and more generally social-security policy is required. Emphasis, however, should be on active policy measures such as retraining programmes, counselling services and job-creation schemes.

---

[361] See also Barr (1994) and OECD (1996a).

6.2.1.5 State-Owned Enterprises

Despite the hitherto considerable progress achieved with privatisation a number of large state-owned enterprises still exist. The remaining SOEs have either been deemed 'strategic' or could not yet be privatised. Finding and implementing a strategy on these extant state firms turns out to be one of the most delicate challenges for industrial policy makers in transition. In the current situation SOEs have neither the means nor the incentives to restructure. Against this background governments face a dilemma: strengthening incentives would require above all imposing hard budget constraints through the threat of bankruptcy. However, this approach involves the twofold risk of (1) provoking social resistance in enterprises concerned and (2) initiating a chain reaction leading to the closure of viable as well as non-viable firms. If the state on the other hand accepts relative softness of budget constraints, as a substitute for measures to compensate for market failures, and if it hesitates to put non-viable enterprises into bankruptcy on a scale sufficient to signal a new policy, it enlarges the structural adjustment gap with cascading negative effects on the privatisation, the financial system, the state budget, and more generally, macroeconomic performance.

Under these circumstances an incentive system needs to be created that can serve as *de facto* substitute for the private economy. This system should make administrative officers in government enterprises face the consequences of their actions and will influence the decisions they take through signals comparable to the natural effect of market forces. Only in this way may SOE managers be stopped from pursuing their strategy of muddling through and their wait-and-see attitude be changed. The state must as quickly as possible, move away from its role as absentee owner of SOEs, and radically improve the supervision of management.

For those remnant giant industrial conglomerates that have no future in a market environment political and economic objectives must be balanced. As mentioned above, the immediate closure of these firms for political economy reasons it not a tenable option. Yet a politically realistic plan of action for unpromising enterprises needs to be spelled out. This must be explicit about a binding schedule for the phased closure of non-viable production units and formulate compensatory measures such as early retirement schemes and retraining programmes. However, an industrial policy strategy in transition should not only define a clear-cut timetable for the temporary support of these firms it ought, moreover, to identify the motives behind this policy. The experience of leading transition economies showed that under the guise of implicit and explicit support to SOEs a *de facto* industrial policy is often operated. This leads to inherent moral hazard problems and opens the door to discretionary policy making.

6.2.1.6 Privatisation

The CEE experience with mass privatisation schemes has made it clear that the privatisation of state assets is not merely about a transfer of property rights from the public to the private sector. Rather should the process be aimed at finding genuine private owners in order to improve the corporate governance of privatised enterprises. Although give-away privatisation may be justified on the basis of moral justness, that is to say to compensate those who had to endure four decades of socialism, i.e., the people of Central and Eastern Europe, this method of ownership transfer suffers from a number of serious shortcomings. The most important are that (1) the privatisation did not involve the injection of fresh capital and (2) that it led to both dispersed and unclear ownership structures. In other words, the privatisation of SOEs did not entail an improvement of corporate governance.

For the remaining SOEs which are to be privatised, this implies that they should be disposed of by selling them through standard methods at market prices preferably to outside core investors. In this way, not only could much needed financial resources be generated to relieve some strain on the budget but also the chances may thus be increased to find 'real' owners who will provide new management, technology and investment. This pertains in particular to two categories of enterprises which still await privatisation, i.e., state banks and public utilities. In both cases substantial capital and know-how is required for their modernisation and restructuring. In addition, against the background of the stock-flow problem the privatisation of both types of enterprises should not be further delayed.

As to those SOEs that have been privatised using investment funds as intermediate holding companies, the entanglement between these funds and banks needs to be redressed as soon as possible to cut short the continued indirect influence of the state. The operations of investment funds, moreover, should be monitored more closely.

6.2.2 Industrial Policies in the Medium- to Long-Term

As industrial restructuring gains momentum and the most acute obstacles to the process of creative destruction are removed, the consolidation of systemic reforms and the integration with the European Union move up the policy agenda. Accordingly, the focus of industrial policy should shift to: (1) investment promotion; (2) export promotion; (3) education; (4) infrastructure projects; (5) research, science and technology policy; (6) foreign direct investment; (7) regional development policies; and finally (8) environmental issues.

6.2.2.1 Investment Promotion

The experience of the high-performing East Asian NIEs divulges that investment promotion is a key to overcoming imperfections of the financial system and capital markets. This holds particularly at early stages of development. These market imperfections above all affect SMEs which find it difficult to raise the needed investment funds. It is crucial that PSE governments by offering concessionary credits or credit guarantees substitute for malfunctioning financial intermediation and incomplete capital markets. Yet our analysis of the East Asian NIEs underlines the importance of *quid-pro-quo* conditions, i.e., the strict conditionality of state assistance. Industrial investment promotion, whether as concessionary credits or fiscal incentives, cannot mean an indiscriminate all-round distribution of subsidies. Instead, state assistance ought to be granted based on selective performance criteria (e.g., export performance) and for fixed periods only.

Yet a far greater challenge for industrial policy in transition arises from the divide between the huge and growing demand for long-term investment finance on the one hand and the general lack of capital on the other. The high propensity to consume in PSEs and the fact that foreign direct investment has not come up to initially high expectations imply that the mobilisation of household savings should be made a policy priority. A basic instrument to increase savings are fiscal incentives that both penalise consumer credits and stimulate long-term saving deposits. A more effective alternative is the reform of the pension system. Such reforms may lead to the replacement of the current pay-as-you-go pensions by a two or three pillar pension system.[362] Beyond stimulating the demand for such pension schemes by offering various tax incentives, the state should provide for a stable regulation and strict supervision of contractual savings.

6.2.2.2 Export Promotion

The importance of exports in the context of economic transition has been stressed throughout the exposition. Yet interventionist versions of export promotion which significantly contributed to the successful catching up of East Asian NIEs with advanced industrial economies for various reasons are no palpable option for PSE governments. Both the EU Association Agreements and multilateral trade agreements (e.g., GATT and WTO) largely preclude direct government interventions such as major devaluations, import protection of export industries or subsidies to exporters. Against this background CEE governments have to resort to more indirect means of promoting exports. Above all, emphasis should be given to opening and securing access to export markets for domestic producers.

Another important area of indirect export promotion relates to information and counselling services. It is here where our analysis of leading transition economies divulged a major shortcoming of industrial policies. In co-operation with business associations a network of trade missions in major export markets should be set up. These offices promote domestic products and firms by organising trade fairs and serving as fora for business contacts. They are supplemented by institutions at home whose function it is to provide information on export markets, trade regulations and international technical standards. As

---

[362] In pay-as-you-go schemes, current pension benefits are paid out of current (payroll) taxes without necessarily building reserves except for short-term liquidity. Shortfalls would be covered by budgetary transfer. A second pillar is based on mandatory, privately managed and funded pensions. A third pillar offers voluntary, privately funded pension plans, supported within certain limits by tax incentives or subsidies. [EBRD (1996), p. 94]

SMEs find it usually most difficult to access export markets, policies should particularly be focused on this enterprise sector.

6.2.2.3 Education and Training

Given the public good character of education and training, the formation of capabilities must be made a corner-stone of every policy strategy aimed at industrial upgrading and ultimately successful catching up with advanced economies. The lack of financial resources and strained state budgets entail that insufficient funds are earmarked for education and vocational training. This systematic neglect has major consequences: first, it leads to the continuous erosion of the economy's skill base. Second, it compounds the stock-flow problem by impeding the reallocation of labour between industries and sectors. Third, it leads to one of the most worrying aspects of unemployment in CEE transition economies, the rising number of young jobless. This phenomenon calls for urgent remedial action. It has been shown that without adequate policy interventions professional training for the young is not sufficiently provided. To put the training and education of school leavers on a systematic basis an apprenticeship system along the Swiss and German lines should be institutionalised and supported by the state.

Beyond increased funding both education and vocational training must be geared towards the needs of industry. Given the lack of finance, the focused application of available funds is all the more imperative. Against this background curricula should be set in close co-operation with business and professional associations.

The importance of education and training in the process of systemic transformation cannot be overstated: the transition from socialism to a market economy and pluralistic democracy requires large-scale learning on all systemic levels. Industrial policy may be made instrumental in creating the skills and know-how needed to bridge the gulf between the old and the new system. The continued negligence of human capital formation would be highly detrimental to the future international competitiveness of a transition economy.

6.2.2.4 Infrastructure

An efficient, reliable and user-oriented infrastructure is a key determinant and precondition for the proper functioning of a market economy. The infrastructure inherited from the command economy mirrors the particular development priorities of central planners with an emphasis on heavy goods production, a neglect of consumer preferences and an indifference to the environment. The transport network, telecommunications system, water supplies and electricity production all urgently need to be revamped and require major new investment. Against this background it emerges that the transformation of infrastructure is a crucial element of transition and, as such, should be made a central area of industrial policy. That efficient infrastructure networks, and particularly interconnections with trans-European infrastructures, will become increasingly important with the progressing EU integration corroborates this finding.

The modernisation and restructuring of infrastructures should also encourage a more commercial approach to infrastructure involving cost-consciousness, demand-oriented production and careful pricing of services. Since the task at hand exceeds the financial means of public households the state must seek the cooperation and participation of private business. This does not necessarily imply private ownership of infrastructure. It is just one option. In cases of continued state-ownership, other forms of private contributions may be resorted to such as, for example, the contracting out of certain services.

Regardless of the degree of private participation industrial policy will have to establish the regulation of infrastructure. A major challenge will be to draw the line between those areas where competition may reign and those which must be regulated. The experience of the UK, for example, with regard to infrastructure privatisation demonstrates that for a credible regulation both independent and accountable regulatory bodies are required. This certainly holds for the context of transition.

6.2.2.5 Science and Technology Policy

Regarding science, technology, research and development most CEE economies – at least in some areas – had a rather good starting position at transition's inception. Yet since then the situation has rapidly deteriorated due to cuts in budgets of enterprise R&D departments and public research institutes and because some of the brightest scientists and researchers transferred to advanced industrial economies. This development must be urgently brought to a halt and has to be reversed if the competitive edge of transition economies is not to erode. By the same token, consumer products must become a field of major R&D activities, an area which was systematically neglected by central planners.

PSEs need to develop R&D policies that complement private sector initiatives or substitute them where necessary. These policies should be developed in close co-operation with industry and given limited public funds be above all focused on applied research. Emphasis should, moreover, be on the fast dissemination and commercialisation of research results. To this end it is vital to establish close links between academia, research institutes and industry in order to initiate a lively dialogue and exchange of ideas between them. Another important aspect of R&D policies should be to warrant small- and medium-sized enterprises the access to the latest technologies.[363]

SMEs are but one area with which R&D policies overlap. Important interrelations also exist with education, investment and public procurement policies. Hence R&D policies ought to be a centrepiece of a comprehensive industrial policy in transition closely tied in with other policy areas. Only in this way can potential synergies be exploited and a co-ordinated approach be secured.

Technology policy should be aimed at the acquisition of technological capabilities to speed up the process of technological change. Successful industrial reforms not only call for the impoverishment of the science and technology infrastructure to be stopped but also for continuous efforts to upgrade it. To alleviate pressures on heavily strained public finances, new forms of co-operation between the state and private business in terms of, for example, jointly financed S&T institutions may be found. This may particularly be an option in the case of basic research. Beyond institutional factors, technology policy should also offer incentives for firms to step up their own technological efforts.

---

[363] On the notion of a strategic technology policy for PSEs see Radosevic (1994).

6.2.2.6 Foreign Direct Investment

The experience of most CEE transition economies shows that early high expectations relating to the influx of foreign direct investment have been disappointed. At the start of systemic transformation it was hoped that with the fall of the iron curtain substantial inflows of foreign capital would help to swiftly restructure and modernise the economy. Yet, despite some major foreign direct investments, finance from abroad has hitherto played only a marginal role when compared to the economy-wide investment requirements. Patently obvious CEE transition economies are just one alternative destination for transnational corporations globally seeking investment opportunities. PSEs not only compete with emerging market economies in Latin America and East Asia, they also contend with neighbouring transition countries to attract foreign investors.

Under these circumstances, foreign investors have a very strong position in negotiations with CEE governments. The latter are easily played off by the former against alternative investment locations. Against this background major foreign investment projects turned out to be very costly for host countries in terms of substantial concessions stipulated by foreign companies (e.g., high import tariff protection, generous tax allowances, flouting anti-trust regulations, etc.). Most importantly, many of the large foreign investment projects were dealt with on a case by case basis. This implied discretionary government action and thus a lack of transparency. To us the attempt to provide overly generous incentives seems unwise as they can lead to the capture of industrial policies by foreign investors and tend to undermine a major objective of economic transition, namely the creation of a competitive market economy.

Thus FDI policies should be rules-driven and follow a clear line of action. Foreign direct investment, moreover, cannot be expected to compensate for the lack of domestic sources of investment finance.[364] Despite the weak bargaining position of PSE governments vis-à-vis foreign investors, FDI policies should, nevertheless, try to attract investment from abroad that (1) produces for export markets and (2) from which significant spill-over effects can be expected. Besides, given the rather limited amount of FDI, its impact on the host economy

---

[364] This corroborates the finding that industrial policy must stimulate and tap household savings as a primary source for investment finance.

needs to be increased. This may be accomplished by actively promoting the creation of domestic ancillary industries clustered around larger enterprises under foreign ownership. In this area a co-ordinated approach with measures both to promote SMEs and to reduce regional imbalances may be fruitful.

6.2.2.7 Regional Development Policies

Regional development policies extend to various other industrial policy areas. Aspects of regional development are intimately blended with issues such as labour market infrastructures, environmental clean-up programmes, the future of nonviable SOEs and the location of foreign direct investment. Moreover, regional imbalances in transition economies are acute. The high special concentration of industries as a legacy of socialist development strategies is a major challenge of CEE systemic transformation. Hence regional policies should form a central element of medium- to long-term industrial policies.

Regional problems should be solved at a decentralised level and require a comprehensive approach that accounts for all relevant aspects. The tasks at hand are politically highly delicate: in a number of cases, entire regions depend on a single industrial white elephant which is by far the greatest employer in the area. The closure of this state enterprise and the ensuing mass redundancies might lead to fierce public protest and could easily spread to epidemic country-wide proportions. Thus an active industrial policy aimed at selectively revitalising such regions is needed. One possible starting-point would be to assist the start up of new SMEs and the establishment of enterprise networks. The latter could be charged with regional public initiatives, such as infrastructure works, environmental clean up, and other projects that contribute to the resumption of regional growth.[365]

6.2.2.8 Environmental Policies

The socialist strategy of forced growth[366] totally disregarded environmental aspects. For decades the environment was ruthlessly exploited and no heed paid to

---

[365] A regional programme along these lines was operated in Spain. See OECD (1992), p. 117.

[366] See Chapter 1.3.1 on the socialist development strategy.

the disastrous pollution, contamination and exhaustion of natural resources. The entire extent and degree of environmental degradation become apparent only over time and border on ecological disaster. The pollution of air, water and soil seriously restrains transition economies' growth prospects. Cautious estimates of income losses associated with ecological problems in PSEs range between two to three per cent of GDP.[367] Since environmental clean-up programmes entail horrendous costs which will accrue over the coming decades, environmental policies should be made an integral part of any long-term industrial policy strategy in transition economies. Beyond removing damages to the environment ecological concerns ought moreover to be dovetailed with industrial policy, since new industrial capacities must be encouraged to utilise environmentally friendly production technologies both by means of progressive regulation as well as fiscal incentives.

Given the dimensions of the ecological aftermath of central planning and that environmental considerations potentially stand in conflict with other industrial policy goals[368], innovative and pragmatic solutions ought to be developed. Hence, for example, the tensions between the resources required for environmental rehabilitation programmes on the one hand and the strained situation of public households on the other may be alleviated to some extent by innovative financial instruments, such as debt-for-environment swap agreements with foreign creditors. Moreover, information campaigns ought to be aimed at changing people's mentality and thus create a environmental consciousness both among producers and consumers. Finally, a clear and stable regulatory framework is required that sets reasonable standards and provides for their effective monitoring.

6.2.3 Convergence of Industrial Policies

With regard to the long-term development of industrial policy in transition economies, a convergence with the European Union's framework oriented in-

---

[367] OECD (1992), p. 117

[368] Consider as an example the environmental rehabilitation of heavy industries: environmental considerations dictate that these enterprises are immediately shut down while political-economy considerations argue for a gradual approach.

dustrial policy approach is foreseeable. Three major factors reinforce this trend: firstly, horizontal industrial policies primarily aimed at improving competitiveness during the last fifteen years have become the acceptable 'face' of industrial policy in the West. Secondly, the European Union expects prospective members to take over its *acquis communautaire* to which the EU approach to industrial policy has to be counted. With the Phare programme and the pre-accession strategy the Commission disposes a powerful leverage on the policy design in transition economies. Thirdly, PSE governments eager to out-perform neighbouring CEE countries by fulfilling accession criteria ahead of schedule are keen to adapt their industrial policies to those of the Union.

Yet the EU approach to industrial policy corresponds to the specific Western European historical experience and is tailored to the particular socio-economic circumstances of the Union. Our analysis of economic transition revealed that for years to come PSEs may have quite different needs which require a distinct focus of industrial policies. This pertains in particular to the role of government: the dimensions of structural change with which transition economies are confronted and have to master, suggests that PSE governments may have to play a greater role in managing the direction of industrial change than the European approach to industrial policy would permit.

Hence an indiscriminate adoption of the European industrial policy conception that does not account for the idiosyncratic problems of systemic transformation has to be rejected. When designing their industrial policy strategies PSE governments must take heed of their historical, cultural, and socio-economic background and adapt Western policies accordingly. In fact, since the European industrial policy is only vaguely defined it actually leaves ample room for a different emphasis on appropriate types of policies and their respective design. All things considered, the medium- to long-term adoption of the Union's *acquis communautaire* does not save PSE governments from formulating and designing their own industrial policy strategies.

6.3 Institutional Aspects

This section looks at industrial policies in transition from an institutional angle and is structured as follows: first, we comment on the general principles on which these policies should rest. Next, the process of designing an industrial policy strategy is considered before we finally discuss issues pertaining to its implementation.

6.3.1 Principles

An important finding of our analysis is that industrial policies in transition should be based on *rules*. In CEE systemic transformation key economic parameters are changing rapidly and radically. Under these circumstances uncertainty is rife and short-termism and concomitant highly speculative investment behaviour are widespread. Against this background industrial policy in transition economies ought to be embedded into a stable institutional structure in which rules dominate discretion. By countervailing governmental arbitrariness industrial policy may help to reduce uncertainty and by giving entrepreneurs a long-term vision of economic development extend their decision-making horizon.

Government policies, moreover, must be transparent for market participants. Policy measures and administrative procedures ought to be both clear and comprehensible to the public. The *transparency* of industrial policies will run counter to illicit, under-the-table deals and thus may help to reduce rent-seeking activities. Additionally, it subjects policy measures to democratic control and thereby may help to increase their legitimacy. Transparent industrial policies, finally, are more predictable and may serve as a basis for the improved formation of expectations by private agents.

Another primacy of industrial policies in transition relates to the government's *credibility*. The credibility of policy strategies cannot be decreed into existence. It can only evolve over time and roots in the government's reputation of keeping to a political course of action once publicly announced and embarked upon. The importance of a credible political strategy in the process of transition cannot be overstated: if the government, for example, intervenes as a lender of last resort for enterprises in acute crisis despite its repeatedly proclaimed hands-off approach to industrial policy such behaviour seriously undermines its credibility.[369] The government, in other words, ought to committ itself or be committed by legislation to its industrial policy strategy.[370] The deviation from an official position entails serious moral hazard problems: in our example, the threat of bankruptcy largely loses its deterring effect and enterprise management accordingly reduces its efforts to avoid financial default.

Political *accountability* and the *autonomy* of the state administration vis-à-vis the economy are another two important factors determining the effectiveness of industrial policies. The primacy of accountability has two aspects: firstly, it requires that clearly assigned responsibilities for different industrial policy areas are defined and secondly, that government officials and/or institutions may be held liable for their respective policy actions. An autonomous state on the other hand must have strong government institutions that show little susceptibility to political pressures of well-organised special interest groups. Where political accountability is absent and state institutions are 'weak', industrial policy will easily be captured by rent-seeking actors both private and public.

A final principle can be derived from the previously mentioned ones and pertains to the *explicitness* of industrial policies. The primacies of rules-based policy-making, transparency, credibility and political accountability all call for industrial policies to be defined explicitly. *De facto* industrial policies as operated in some of the analysed leading CEE transition economies conflict with all of the principles we have elaborated in this section and thus ought to be avoided. Instead industrial policy strategies should be elaborated and published that define (1) the policy goals, (2) the ways and means to achieve them and finally (3) the respective time horizons. We regard the primacy of explicitly defining an industrial policy strategy as a *conditio sine qua non* for the success of such policies. Against this background we are convinced that an official hands-off approach combined with an industrial policy through the back door is un-

---

[369] Another example is the phased closure of remaining nonviable state-owned enterprises whose operations should be completed by a predetermined date. Departing from such a schedule on any occasion would have serious repercussions for carrying through similar plans in the future.

[370] On the inherent difficulties of a binding (self-) committment see Stiglitz (1989), pp. 49f. and Mueller (1993).

democratic and both highly detrimental and counterproductive to the progress of economic transition. This leads us to Figure 6.2 which summarises our discussion and shows the hexagon of industrial policy principles in transition.

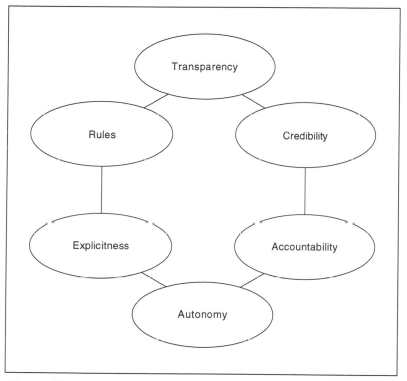

Figure 6.2: Hexagon of industrial policy principles in transition

6.3.2 Designing an Industrial Policy Strategy

After having examined the principles that should guide industrial policies in transition we now turn to the issue of how to design such a policy strategy. First, we discuss the notion of an institutionalised dialogue between the state, employers and employees to find a social consensus on the general direction of industrial policy. This long-term vision of economic development forms the core preoccupation of the second section. Finally, we argue for a comprehensive approach to industrial policy that does justice to the multi-dimensional nature of transition.

6.3.2.1 Institutionalised Dialogue

We have shown that for the transition process to be politically sustainable an *ex ante* social consensus on the distribution of its costs and benefits is required. This argument may be extended to include a social agreement on the general direction of socio-economic development, on the 'final' destination of the transition process and how to get there. From an institutional perspective, a mechanism is needed which can serve as a platform for moderating between interests and where as a compromise a consensus may be reached. In other words, a more encompassing dialogue between the government, business and the wider public is needed which allows to build a coalition for change between these parties. A learning process has to be initiated in which policy makers, private and state managers and labour representatives begin to interact in a way that lays the foundations for a sustainable transition path that leads from economic recovery to longer-term growth and technological catching-up.[371] The design of industrial policy should be understood as a joint-problem solving process in which the state acts as a co-ordinating and information gathering *primus inter pares*.

Deliberation councils are an institutional arrangement that may act as an interface for the tripartite dialogue between the state, business and labour. These consultation fora not only assure the exchange of information between the parties involved, they are also instrumental to interest conciliation. The corporatist nature of deliberation councils has several advantages: first, working as an information-clearing forum they may help to lower transaction costs. Second, in so far as the information flow between the parties involved works, the councils may allow the government to formulate better policies since the latter is better informed. Third, deliberative processes may add to the democratic legitimacy of industrial policies since they are based on a social consensus. Fourth, involving major interest groups in the process of industrial policy design they fulfil the primacy of transparency of public policies. Finally, due to the repeated interaction a deliberation council may help to build confidence between the parties involved.

---

[371] On the required learning process see also Kozul-Wright and Rayment (1996) and Kozul-Wright and Rayment (1997).

For deliberation councils to work in the context of transition a number of pre-conditions ought to be met: first, the council members must have mutual respect for each other. Second, representatives of the state, business and labour must enjoy a high degree of respect among their peers to be able to deliver on the commitments made in the negotiations. Third, for the continuity of consultation fora some reasonable degree of longevity of the policy regime is important. Fourth, a minimum level of trust between the government and the private sector is indispensable.

If these requisites are met an institutional dialogue along these lines between the government, business and labour in transition economies may be of paramount importance since it can help to bridge the hiatus between economic efficiency and social justice. Deliberation councils can mediate the uneasy tensions between unrestricted market forces and social peace. They may be harnessed to buffering the costs of socio-economic transformation while at the same time allowing structural adjustments to occur. This is particularly the case with such sensitive issues as the future of nonviable industrial conglomerates. Consultation fora may help to reach a compromise between countervailing interests and, thus, define an agreed-upon plan of action. Yet a primary function of deliberation councils is it to find an agreement on the long-term vision of the industrial policy strategy.

6.3.2.2 Long-Term Vision

Industrial policy strategies ought to provide a long-term vision of socio-economic development to give the process of structural change a general sense of direction. As an overall vision it should articulate an image of the society to which the transition is moving.[372] As the example of the East Asian NIEs illustrates, such a longer-term orientation of industrial policy can be made instrumental to bundle economy-wide structural adjustment efforts: the jointly elaborated vision of socio-economic development provides a focal point around which concerted efforts can be organised. The notion of a focal point, however,

---

[372] As an example one may think of a 'Soziale Marktwirtschaft' (social market economy) along the German lines with banks playing a major co-ordinating role. The vision may also identify particular areas such as biotechnology or environmental technologies whose development is to be assisted by government support.

should not be confounded with some variant of central planning: first of all, the vision for industrial policy is based on a social consensus and not decreed by some central planning agency. The vision, moreover, does not define any minute output targets which have to be achieved within predetermined periods. Rather its function is twofold: first, it should serve as a point of reference in the process of systemic transformation. Second, it forms the starting-point from which an industrial policy strategy for the transition is derived.

A top-down approach to the design of industrial policies may help to increase the coherence of industrial strategies. Starting from the overall vision of socio-economic development subsequently separate strategies for respective industrial policy areas are deduced. In this way a long-term industrial policy programme for the transition process can be drawn up which may serve as a focus for popular support. Apart from helping to secure the political sustainability of transition, deriving a coherent industrial policy programme along these lines is likely to have a positive impact on entrepreneurial expectations.

6.3.2.3 Comprehensive Approach

We have repeatedly stressed that an industrial policy strategy for transition economies must account for the multi-dimensional nature of systemic transformation. An industrial policy that narrows the task at hand to economic phenomena alone would certainly fall short of reality and would thus at best have limited success. Instead, an industrial policy strategy must be tailored to the specific historical, social, cultural and economic circumstances of a particular PSE. The idiosyncratic character pertains both to the country-specific weighting of political priorities as well as to the institutional arrangements of respective industrial policy strategies. Thus the particular historical experience of a PSE, for example, may require that a substantial share of state assets is distributed to insiders (i.e., to the management and employees) rather than being sold to core (outside) investors although this privatisation method would improve corporate governance. As divulged by the Polish experience, such a necessary compromise may require substantial concessions in terms of economic efficiency and speed of economic reforms.

A comprehensive policy strategy, moreover, must co-ordinate the various industrial policy measures for two reasons: firstly, between different policy areas exist complementary interrelations which call for their co-ordination in order to exploit potential synergies. Secondly, uncoordinated industrial policies involve major inefficiencies and a waste of scarce public funds because policy areas are overlapping. Thus a comprehensive and systematic approach to industrial policy is needed which integrates different policy areas in an overall context.

6.3.3 Implementing Industrial Policy

Based on our analysis we consider two institutional aspects pertaining to the implementation of an industrial policy strategy as important: first, the consolidation of institutional arrangements and second, to interpret the operation of industrial policies as an adaptive learning process.

6.3.3.1 Institutional Consolidation

The industrial policies of the European Union and the CEE transition economies both suffer from a lack of co-ordination and institutional dispersal. Due to not clearly assigned tasks and responsibilities, overlapping competences between government bodies result in inefficiencies and a waste of scarce resources. Our findings reveal that the effectiveness of industrial policies is further reduced if no single agency has been charged with the task of co-ordinating industrial policy measures. The lack of an institutional *primus inter pares* bears the risk of a general lack of direction of these policies. Thus against the background of strained public households in PSEs the institutional consolidation and better co-ordination of industrial policies should be made a priority.

The experience of the East Asian NIEs divulges that for an industrial policy to be effective one or two government agencies should steer the formulation and application of policy instruments. The policy heartland of this *pilot agency* within the central bureaucracy is the industrial and trade profile of the economy and its future growth path. It should be assigned the paramount task of co-ordinating the work of the different ministries involved in the implementation of industrial policies and hence ensure that the various policy areas are complementary. To accomplish this task the pilot agency must be given far-reaching authority to issue directives vis-à-vis other ministries and government agencies so that its interventions have binding character. To this end, the pilot agency ought to be directly subordinated to the Prime Minister (see Figure 6.3). Since this bundling of power is vulnerable to attempts by interest groups to exert their influence on industrial policies, the pilot agency ought to be shielded as far as possible from day-to-day political interference.[373]

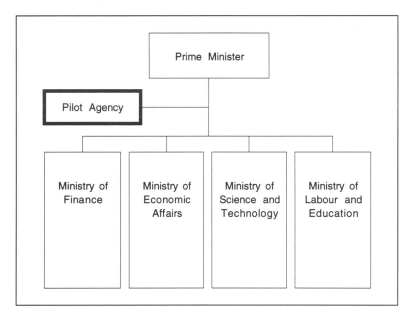

Figure 6.3: The pilot agency's position within government administration

To illustrate our point we chose the example of SME promotion: the pilot agency based on the industrial policy strategy has to bring in line the policies of those ministries that have a major impact on the development of small business. *In concreto* this could pertain to the Ministry of Finance (e.g., tax policy), Ministry of Economic Affairs (e.g., small business networks, infrastructure and regional development), Ministry of Science and Technology (e.g., science and technology parks, technology access for SMEs), and the Ministry of Labour and Education (e.g., job-creation programmes and apprenticeship system). The pilot agency should dovetail respective policy measures and focus them on the pro-

---

[373] Note that it is the *implementation* of the industrial policy strategy that in contrast to its *design* should be protected from interfering influences.

motion of SMEs so as to increase the overall effectiveness of industrial policy and to assure the efficient application of resources.

Thus the first function of the pilot agency is to co-ordinate efforts within a particular industrial policy area that falls in the realm of more than one ministry or government agency. Its second function is it to make sure that the different policy areas conform with the industrial policy strategy and do not run counter to overall development goals. Finally the pilot agency ought to systematically collect and assess information on the impact of industrial policies. This should put it into the position of the early revision of policy strategies if these lead to undesired or unintended results, or of adapting them to changing circumstances. The pilot agency, in other words, has a key function to play with respect to industrial policy understood as an on-going adaptive learning process.

It goes without saying that the task of the pilot agency in terms of administrative capabilities is very demanding. A professional and highly trained administration is key to the successful centralised management of industrial policies. Thus the government has to ensure that the civil service remains attractive to be able to recruit the necessary technocratic staff from among the best. Moreover, the creation of a sense of national mission among the economic general staff should be attempted, combined with a meritocratically based *esprit de corps*.

Although establishing a pilot agency that co-ordinates and manages industrial policies may turn out to be a difficult task it should, nevertheless, be introduced without delay: if operated successfully, it may help to consolidate the institutionally dispersed responsibilities for industrial policy and increase both the effectiveness of policy measures and the efficiency with which resources are used.

6.3.3.2 Learning

Many challenges in the transition process are historically unprecedented and require policy makers to follow new avenues. Ready-made policy recipes and ideologically biased fixed-point ideas are of little use. Rather for the successful catching up with advanced industrial economies a flexible and pragmatic approach to industrial policy making is called for. This approach has to be based on an open process of trial-and-error, which is not *ex ante* restricted by any rules or values and, therefore, allows for different policies to be tried out. Given the fundamental systemic change facing policy makers, emphasis needs to be on as wide a choice of policies as possible to encourage the development of market and non-market institutions.

Hence industrial policy in the transition from a centrally planned to a market economy ought to be understood as a process of non-linear discovery entailing on-going adaptive learning. Industrial policies have to be continuously adapted to changing circumstances and account for lessons learnt from past mistakes. This requires that policy effects are consistently monitored. Discrepancies between intended and actual results ought to be evaluated and should feed back into revised versions of respective policies.[374] It follows that industrial policy in transition is a continuing process and not settled with the passing of some white paper establishing an industrial policy strategy for the transition period.

Policy makers in transition economies should, moreover, attempt to learn from the experience of other transition economies and from advanced industrial countries. We regard the willingness and openness to learn from others as a key factor in determining the success of catching-up strategies. The yard-stick for assessing industrial policies ought not to be dogmatic ideas but rather whether policy instruments under consideration worked successfully and whether they could be applied under different circumstances elsewhere.

* * *

Table 6.1 summarises as an overview the essential elements of the industrial policy framework we have developed in this chapter for countries in transition.

---

[374] In the previous section we assigned this task to the pilot agency that ought to co-ordinate and steer the implementation of the industrial policy strategy.

Policy Agenda	
☐ Rationale for industrial policy	
– Market failures – Market concentration and barriers to entry and exit	– Political sustainability of transition – De facto industrial policy
☐ The foundations of industrial policy	
– Macroeconomic stability – Political stability – High skill levels	– Outward orientation – Domestic and international competition
☐ Policy objectives	

Short-term:
  – Stock-flow problem
	Medium- to long-term:
	  – Consolidation of economic reforms
	  – Catching-up with advanced industrial economies

☐ Policy constraints	
– Strained public households – Macroeconomic stability – Political stability	– Institutional framework – Available information – Trade and EU Association Agreements
Policy Areas and Instruments	
☐ Short-term	☐ Medium- to long-term
– Financial intermediation – SME policy – Competition policy – Labour market policies – SOEs – Privatisation	– Investment promotion – Export promotion – Education and training policies – Infrastructure policy – R&D and S&T policies – FDI policy – Regional development policy Environmental policy
☐ Long-term convergence with EU industrial policy	
Institutional Aspects	
☐ Principles	
– Rules-based policy making – Transparency – Credibility	– Accountability – Autonomy – Explicit industrial policy strategy
☐ Designing industrial policies	
– Institutional dialogue – Long-term vision	– Comprehensive Approach
☐ Implementing industrial policies	
– Institutional consolidation and pilot agency	– Industrial policy making as an adaptive learning process

Table 6.1: An industrial policy framework for countries in transition

7 Conclusions

This final chapter is structured as follows: first, we come back to the working hypotheses which we formulated at the beginning of this thesis and see to what an extent they have been verified or falsified. Next we reflect on the role of the state in the process of systemic transformation as it emerges from our analysis. The chapter ends with questions being raised for further research.

In the introductory chapter we put forward six working hypotheses that guided our research. We are now in the position to confront these contentions with the results of our analysis and to scrutinise their validity in turn.

> *Hypothesis 1*
>
> *The theory of systemic transformation has not yet satisfactorily dealt with the issue of industrial policy. This gap should be closed since industrial policy ought to be a key element of transition strategies.*

This first hypothesis is corroborated by our analysis. The in-depth study of the available body of literature on the transition from a centrally planned economy to a market-type system shows that the issue of industrial policy has hitherto received only little attention. The present paper, moreover, confirms that this omission is a major shortcoming of the theory of systemic transformation for a number of reasons: first, to deny outright the desirability, let alone the necessity of industrial policy in the transition and to maintain that 'no industrial policy is the best industrial policy' means leaving alone the governments in the region with the design of such policies. Our analysis clearly indicates that a hands-off approach under the circumstances of fundamental systemic change as experienced in Central and Eastern Europe is no realistic option. Second, that the issue of industrial policy has been neglected is all the more disturbing since the transition process must not imply deserting the state. On the contrary, the political and social aspects of systemic transformation require that not only the centralised coordination of economic activity is replaced by a decentralised solution via the market. At the same time a new role for the state must be found.

Finally, it is a great fallacy to believe or to hope that a market economy in Eastern Europe would arise without substantial government assistance like a phoenix from the ashes of the socialist system. Rather has it been shown that the state has a pivotal role to play as far as the emergence of a market-type economy is concerned. Industrial policy as broadly defined in the present paper ought to be a key element of any transition strategy. Put in pithier terms, one might say that "[a] country in transition is a mixed economy, whether it likes it or not."[375]

Hypothesis 2

The transition from a command economy to a market economy that is internationally competitive requires a process of far-reaching economic restructuring.

The early experience of the leading transition economies revealed that once a degree of macroeconomic stability is achieved and the privatisation of state-owned assets is well under way a slow and lengthy process of economic restructuring must be initiated. The socialist strategy of forced growth with its overemphasis on heavy industries and its notorious neglect of services and consumer goods resulted in a highly distorted economic structure. To catch up with advanced industrial economies a process of creative destruction is requisite, implying the dismantling or modernisation of existing capacities and the creation of new capacities.

Hypothesis 3

The need for restructuring is especially pressing in the industrial sector where socialist production structures and state-ownership have to be overcome.

This hypothesis is also verified by our analysis: large state-owned industrial enterprises as a legacy of central planning burden the budget and pose a risk to social and political stability as the *conditio sine qua non* for a successful transi-

---

[375] Lavigne (1995), p. 251

tion. Many of these white elephants are not vital if strict market criteria were applied while others require large-scale restructuring in order to have a chance for survival in a market environment. The need for restructuring in the industrial sector is pressing since large SOEs continue to contribute a major share to GDP and due to their dominating role on regional labour markets.

Hypothesis 4

This enormous task and the as yet underdeveloped nature of emerging markets require an active role of the state.

The dimensions of both the task at hand and the resources necessary for the structural adjustment process, combined with the deficient and incomplete nature of emerging markets in transition economies, means that the state has to play a corrective and complementary role. Without government interventions these nascent markets would lead to the rapid closure of both vital and non-vital production capacities and the concomitant large-scale shedding of labour. Together, this would put the entire transition process seriously at risk. In addition, such an early retreat of the state would have serious consequences for the emergence of new enterprises, above all for small- and medium-sized businesses which ought to form the competitive backbone of every advanced industrial economy. This is what we called the *transition paradoxon*, i.e., the state has to play a more active role during the transition process in order to reduce its influence on the economy in the future.

Hypothesis 5

For state action to be predictable, goals and the measures to attain them need to be explicitly outlined. An industrial policy strategy has to define the role of the state in this field.

The analysis both of the East Asian newly industrialising economies and the leading countries in transition have substantiated this contention. In times of rapid and fundamental change, such as the transition from a centrally planned to a market-type economy, uncertainty is rife. Under these circumstances investment behaviour tends to be dominated by short-termism rather than by a much

needed long-term orientation. Against this background *de facto* industrial policies that are both *ad-hoc* and erratic are highly detrimental to the overall
framework of economic decision making since they further heighten the already
rampant uncertainty. We come to the conclusion that in the process of transition
a long-term perspective of policies is vital. Moreover, government action and
interventions in the economy need to be predictable and thus help create a stable economic framework. To this end, the state ought to formulate an industrial
policy strategy that stipulates the goals and the corresponding policy measures
to achieve them. In addition, it should clarify the role of the state in the transition process vis-à-vis the industrial sector.

Hypothesis 6

*Guidelines for the design of such a strategy can be eclectically de-
rived from economic theory, from industrial policies of advanced industrial countries and, finally, from the early industrial policy
experiences of leading countries in transition.*

A major difficulty pertaining to the issue of industrial policy in general and to
the discussion of such policies in the process of transition in particular is the
lack of a coherent theoretical basis. At the outset of our analysis we, therefore,
chose an eclectic approach. With its help we hoped to be able to derive from
economic theory on the one hand and from practical experiences on the other
guidelines for the design of industrial policy in the transition. The industrial
policy framework developed in the previous chapter seems to corroborate hypothesis six. Indeed, our thesis seems to confirm the idea that an eclectic approach to the subject matter of industrial policy is the most promising. We have
shown that both the willingness and the flexibility to learn from a horizon as
wide as possible is a key success factor for transition strategies and for industrial policy interpreted as an on-going adaptive learning process. In sum, all of
the working hypotheses formulated in the introductory chapter have been verified by our analysis.

Having scrutinised the validity of our working hypotheses, we now turn to the
question of what functions the state according to our policy framework ought to
fulfil in the transition process. Of primary importance is the interface function

of industrial policy between the primacy of economic efficiency and distributional concerns. As a *manager of conflict* the state has to moderate and mediate
between counteracting and diverging interests. Building a social consensus on
the distribution of benefits and, above all, of the costs associated with systemic
transformation across social strata and over time is a key to the political sustainability of the transition process.

With regard to the emergence of markets, several functions fall upon the state:
first, government interventions have to act as a *corrective* for deficient
(complementary role) and missing markets (substituting role). Second, by establishing the necessary legal and regulatory framework the state as an *institution builder* sets the rules of the game and secures a level playing-field. Third,
the state acts as *catalyst* to a emerging market economy because (1) by investing in accelerators (e.g., infrastructure, education, science and technology,
small- and medium-sized enterprises, business services, etc.) it facilitates the
process of structural adjustment, and (2) because it speeds up industrial restructuring. Fourth, transition economies suffer from a plethora of information-
related market failures. In our industrial policy concept the state systematically
gathers and disseminates information on domestic and global markets and,
thus, lowers transaction costs.

The state, moreover, serves as a *manager and co-ordinator of change* since it
gears separate industrial policies towards the overall development objectives as
defined by the industrial policy strategy. This function corresponds to a folk
theorem which holds that, in crisis situations, state involvement tends to increase – not decrease – even in developed market economies.[376] In addition, it
coincides with a finding on the interrelation between the state and the market in
historical perspective: historical literature[377] on industrialisation patterns in the
19th and 20th centuries reveals the different paths taken by successful, newly
industrialising economies. Yet in all cases – albeit to different degrees and with
different policy measures – the process of catching up has involved guidance
from the state.

---

[376] Kádár (1994), p. 17 and Stiglitz (1994), p. 168.

[377] See, for example, Abramovitz (1986), Gershenkron (1962), Polanyi (1957) and Armstrong, Glyn and Harrison (1991).

The state finally has a *modernising role* to play since the public administration must be adapted to the requirements of an advanced market economy. To this end, existing ministries and government agencies need to be revamped and re-organised. The governance of the transition and an industrial policy based on the primacy of the market, moreover, demand new administrative capacities to be created.

As was stressed throughout the exposition, we do not intend to offer the ultimate solution for the issue of industrial policy in transition. Our discussion should rather serve as a starting-point for a theoretical debate and the framework developed as a benchmark for the design of such policies. Against this background our analysis evidently and necessarily leaves many questions unanswered. An important next step for *further research* would be to develop an industrial policy strategy for a specific country in transition which would imply putting our general policy framework into a concrete form. This would obviously entail a plethora of new questions and problems to be solved relating to the various policy areas which we subsumed under the term industrial policy. Another aspect relates to the process of political decision making and interest reconciliation. How to establish deliberation councils, how to organise a corporatist dialogue, and whom to include in these consultations, are but a few questions to be investigated in this context. The proposed pilot agency as the institutional *primus inter pares* responsible for the co-ordinated implementation of the industrial policy strategy, moreover, points to constitutional issues. Another area for further research centres on the question of how to finance industrial policy programmes in transition economies.

* * *

It emerges from our analysis that the dichotomy between the state and the market is artificial. Surmounting the legacies of forty years of central planning cannot mean deserting the state. Rather, based on the primacy of the market and on a pluralistic constitutional order beyond fixed-point ideas, a balance must be struck between the centralised power of the state and the decentralised co-ordination of the price mechanism. To overcome the challenges of systemic transformation a modern mixed economy is essential. In fact, a central task of systemic transformation is to redefine the role of the state along these lines.

Against this background it is high time that economists no longer disregard the matter and equip Central and Eastern European policy-makers with proper analytical tools and the necessary policy instruments to successfully master the transition to an advanced market economy.

Appendix

Appendix to Chapter 4: Western Industrial Policy

Table A.1: Priority sectors and support of Phare

Sector	Phare support
• *Privatisation*	– Work on strategies and policies – Legal and institutional framework for privatisation – Initiated the first pilot privatisation transactions – Co-operation and co-ordination with international financial institutions (IFIs) – Clearing-house for information on privatisation projects
• *Bank restructuring*	– Diagnostic studies and assessment of bad-loan problem within bank portfolios – Policy recommendations for central banks and banks themselves – Assistance with prudential regulations – Co-operation with IFIs
• *Enterprise restructuring*	– Industry sector studies – Financing of turnaround management teams and special restructuring programmes – Co-operation with EBRD and IBRD – Transfer of management and restructuring skills
• *Developing markets for goods, services & production factors*	– Technical assistance for development of the legal and regulatory framework – Institutional framework for competition policies (e.g., Anti-Monopoly Offices, Competition Commissions, etc.) – Agencies advocating consumer interests (e.g., Consumer Protection Agencies, etc.) – Labour market institution-building at national, regional and local levesl

Sector	Phare support
• *SME development*	– Creation of new national support institutions and support to ministries for strategy and policy development – Stimulation of local initiatives (i.e., local and/or regional development agencies, etc.) – Creation of regional business consulting centres – Support to entrepreneur associations and to entrepreneurs themselves
• *Agricultural restructuring & reform*	– Development of reform strategies and policies – Restructuring and privatisation of state enterprises and farms – Development of rural finance schemes – Land reforms and registration systems
• *FDI & export promotion*	– Development of strategy and policy formulation – Assistance to set up FDI agencies – FDI promotion programmes – Export promotion programmes
• *Infrastructure*	– Developing policies and strategies – Infrastructure development and investment programmes – Technical support for the telecommunications and post sector – Public investment financing programmes – Developing regulatory framework – Co-financing of infrastructure projects with IFIs
• *Energy*	– Conventional energy programmes – Energy infrastructure development programmes
• *Environment*	– Support for legislative, policy and institutional work – Provision of equipment for monitoring pollution – Setting up environmental funds – Technical feasibility studies and pilot projects for urgent environmental programmes
• *Fiscal policy*	– Assistance to introduce VAT legislation and implement its introduction – Support for improvements in budget management

Sector	Phare support
• *Monetary & financial policies*	– Support for central banks especially to strengthen their supervisory capacities – Introduction of commercial bank management to new techniques of financial management and strategy development – Banking training institutes and training activities
• *Public administration*	– Training programmes for civil servants – Developing informatics policies – Assistance for decentralisation of government and local government development – Support to improve public procurement – Assistance to State Audit Offices – Restructuring of ministries
• *Customs & statistical services*	– Help to prepare customs legislation compatible with EU legislation – Training staff and computerisation of customs offices – Training programmes for statistical offices – Provision of computer systems and software
• *Democracy & civil society*	– Development of NGOs, charities, foundations, professional associations, political parties, mass media outlets, etc.

Based on CEC (1997b) and Mergos and Tsantis (1997).

Appendix to Chapter 5: Early Experiences – The Leading Countries in Transition

Table A.2: Macroeconomic data for the Czech Republic 1990-1996

	1990	1991	1992	1993	1994	1995	1996[5]
• GDP at constant prices[1]	-0.4	-14.2	-6.4	-0.9	2.6	4.8	4.1
• Industrial production[1]	-3.5	-22.3	-7.9	-5.3	2.1	8.7	6.9
• Gross fixed investment at constant prices[1]	n.a.	n.a.	8.9	-7.7	17.3	16.1	17.5
• Consumer prices (annual average)[1]	10.8	56.6	11.1	20.8	10.0	9.1	8.8
• Wages in industry (annual average)	4.5	16.7	19.6	23.8	15.7	17.0	18.4
• Unemployment rate (end of period)	0.8	4.1	2.6	3.5	3.2	2.9	3.5
• Trade balance[2]	-0.8	-0.4	-1.9	-0.3	0.9	-3.7	-6.1
• Current account balance[2]	-1.1	0.4	-0.3	0.1	-0.1	-1.4	-4.1
• Capital account balance[2]	n.a.	n.a.	n.a.	2.5	3.4	8.2	n.a.
• External debt[2,3]	7.7	8.3	3.5	2.3	1.8	-0.9	1.2
• General government balance[4]	0.1	-2.0	-3.3	1.4	0.5	-0.8	-0.5
• General government expenditure[4]	60.1	54.2	52.8	50	50.7	50.4	45.0

Note: Figures in bold type pertain to the Czech Republic whereas figures in normal type pertain to the former CSFR. 1: Percentage change, 2: In billions of US dollar value, 3: Net of reserves of the banking system (end-year), 4: In percent of GDP, 5: Estimate; n.a. = not available

Source: EBRD (1997a), p. 41

Table A.3: Macroeconomic data for Hungary 1990-1996

	1990	1991	1992	1993	1994	1995	1996[4]
• GDP[1]	-3.5	-11.9	-3.1	-0.6	2.9	1.5	0.5
• Industrial gross output[1]	-9.3	-18.4	-9.7	4.0	9.6	4.8	2
• Gross fixed investment[1]	-7.1	-10.4	-2.6	2	12.5	1	4
• Consumer prices (annual average)[1]	28.9	35.0	23.0	22.5	18.8	28.2	23.7
• Gross monthly earnings per employee in manufacturing[1]	22.9	25.6	25.9	24.7	21.5	21.3	20.4
• Unemployment (in per cent of labour force)	1.9	7.5	12.3	12.1	10.4	10.4	10.5
• Trade balance[2]	0.3	0.2	0.0	-3.2	-3.6	-2.4	-2.7
• Current account balance[2]	0.1	0.3	0.3	-3.5	-3.9	-2.5	-1.7
• External debt[2], net of reserves	20.2	18.7	17.1	17.9	21.8	19.6	17
• General government balance[3]	0.4	-2.2	-5.5	-6.8	-8.2	-6.5	-3.5
• General government expenditure[3]	53.5	54.3	61.6	62.2	62.1	56.1	50.5

Note: 1: Percentage change, 2: In billions of US dollar value, 3: In percent of GDP, 4: Estimate

Source: EBRD (1997a), p. 45

Table A.4: Macroeconomic data for Poland 1990-1996

	1990	1991	1992	1993	1994	1995	1996[1]
• GDP at constant prices[1]	-11.6	-7.0	2.6	3.8	5.2	7.0	6.0
• Industrial production[1]	n.a.	-8.0	2.8	6.3	12.1	9.9	8.0
• Gross fixed investment at constant prices[1]	-10.6	-4.4	2.3	2.9	9.2	18.5	n.a.
• Consumer prices (annual average)[1]	585.3	70.3	43.0	35.3	33.2	27.8	20.0
• Wages and salaries (annual average)[1]	398.0	70.6	39.2	33.6	36.8	32.9	25.0
• Unemployment (in per cent of labour force, end-year)	6.1	11.8	13.6	15.7	16.0	14.9	n.a.
• Trade balance[2,3]	2.2	0.1	0.5	-2.3	-0.8	-1.8	-7.2
• Current account balance[2]	0.6	-2.0	0.9	-1.3	0.8	5.5	-0.1
• External debt[2]	48.9	48.3	48.2	48.7	40.9	39.4	n.a.
• State budget balance[5]	0.7	-7.0	-6.9	-3.4	-2.5	-2.8	-2.7
• State budget outlays[5]	32.7	32.7	33.7	32.8	31.9	32.0	30.3

Note: 1: Percentage change, 2: In billions of US dollar value, 3: Official balance which excludes unrecorded border trade, 4: Estimate, 5: in percent of GDP

Source: EBRD (1997a), p. 51

Table A.5: Macroeconomic data for Slovenia 1990-1996

	1990	1991	1992	1993	1994	1995	1996[4]
• GDP in constant prices[1]	-4.7	-8.1	-5.4	2.8	5.3	3.9	3.5
• Industrial production[1]	-10.5	-12.4	-13.2	-2.5	6.1	2.4	1.5
• Retail prices (annual average)[1]	550	117.7	201.3	32.3	19.8	12.6	9.7
• Nominal wages, net of tax (annual average)[1]	379	82.5	198.5	52.0	28.3	18.6	3
• Unemployment (in per cent of labour force)	4.7	8.2	11.6	14.4	14.4	13.9	13.5
• Trade balance[2,6]	-0.61	-0.26	0.8	-0.15	-0.34	-0.96	-1.2
• Current account[2,6]	0.53	0.13	0.93	0.15	0.54	-0.04	-0.3
• External debt[2,5]	n.a.	1.7	1.0	1.1	0.8	1.2	1.7
• General government balance[3]	-0.3	2.6	0.3	0.3	-0.2	-0.03	-0.6
• General government expenditure[3]	49.6	41.1	46.2	46.8	47.3	46.2	45.5

Note: 1: Percentage change, 2: In billions of US dollar value, 3: In per cent of GDP, 4: Estimate; 5: Net of official foreign exchange reserves and excluding non-allocated federal Yugoslav debt; 6: For 1990 91 excluding trade with former Yugoslavia.

Source: EBRD (1997a), p. 55

Bibliography

Abel, I. and M. Landesmann (1994): 'The Transition in Eastern Europe: The Case for Industrial Policy' in H. J. Chang and P. Nolan: *The Transformation of the Communist Economies: Against the Mainstream*, Basingstoke: Macmillan, 136-161.

Abramovitz, M. (1986): 'Catching Up, Forging Ahead, and Falling Behind' *Journal of Economic History*, vol. 46, no. 2, 385-406.

Aghion, P. and N. Stern (eds.) (1994): *Obstacles to Enterprises Restructuring in Transition*, London: EBRD, Working Paper, no. 16, December.

Aghion, P. and O. J. Blanchard (1993): *On the Speed of Transition in Central Europe*, London: EBRD, Working Paper, no. 6, July.

Aghion, P. and W. Carlin (1997): 'Restructuring Outcomes and the Evolution of Ownership Patterns in Central and Eastern Europe' in S. Zecchini (ed.): *Lessons from the Economic Transition: Central and Eastern Europe in the 1990s*, Dordrecht, Boston and London: Kluwer Academic Publishers and OECD, CCET, 241-262.

Aghion, P., Blanchard, O. J. and R. Burgess (1993): *The Behaviour of State Firms in Eastern Europe: Pre-Privatisation*, London: EBRD, Working Paper, no. 12, October.

Aghion, P., Blanchard, O. J. and R. Burgess (1994): 'The Behaviour of State Firms in Eastern Europe: Pre-Privatisation' *European Economic Review*, vol. 38, no. 6.

Albert, M. (1992): *Kapitalismus contra Kapitalismus*, Frankfurt and New York: Campus.

Alter, R. (1994): 'The Economic Role of Government' in H. Blommestein and B. Steunenberg (eds.): *Governments and Markets: Establishing a Democratic Constitutional Order and a Market Economy in Former Socialist Countries*, Dordrecht, Boston and London: Kluwer Academic, 115-128.

Amsden, A. (1989): *Asia's next Giant: South Korea and Late Industrialization*, New York: Oxford University Press.

Amsden, A. (1991): 'Diffusion of Development: The Late-Industrializing Model and Greater East Asia' *American Economic Review*, vol. 81, no. 2, 282-286.

Amsden, A. (1994): 'Can Eastern Europe Compete by «Getting Prices Right»? Contrast with East Asian Structural Reforms' in M. I. Blejer, A. Solimano and O. Sunkel (eds.): *Rebuilding Capitalism: Alternative Roads after Socialism and Dirigism*, Ann Arbor: University of Michigan Press, 81-107.

Amsden, A., Kochanowicz, J. and L, Taylor (1994): *The Market Meets its Match: Restructuring the Economies of Eastern Europe*, Cambridge, Mass. and London: Harvard University Press.

Andersen, E. S. (1994): *Evolutionary Economics: Post-Schumpeterian Contributions*, London: Pinter Publishers.

Aoki, M., Murdock, K. and M. Okuno-Fujiwara (1996): 'Beyond the East Asian Miracle: Introducing the Market-Enhancing View' in Aoki, M., Kim, H.-K. and M. Okuno-Fujiwara (eds.): *The Role of Government in East Asian Economic Development*, Oxford: Oxford University Press, 1-37.

Armstrong, P., Glyn, A. and J. Harrison (1991): *Capitalism Since 1945*, Oxford: Basil Blackwell.

Arnott, R. and J. E. Stiglitz (1988): 'The Basic Analytics of Moral Hazard' *Scandinavian Journal of Economics*, vol. 90, 383-413.

Arnott, R. and J. E. Stiglitz (1989): 'The Welfare Economics of Moral Hazard' in H. Louberge (ed.): *Risk, Information and Insurance: Essays in the Memory of Karl H. Borch*, Norwell, MA: Kluwer Academic Publishers, 91-122.

Arrow, K. J. and G. Debreu (1954): 'Existence of an Equilibrium for a Competitive Economy' *Econometrica*, vol. 22, no. 2, 265-290.

Balassa, B. (1988): 'The Lessons from East Asian Development: An Overview' *Economic Development and Cultural Changes*, vol. 36, no. 3, Supplement.

Balcerowicz, L. (1993): *Common Fallacies in the Debate on the Economic Transition in Central and Eastern Europe*, London: EBRD, Working Paper, no. 11, October.

Balcerowicz, L. (1995): *Socialism, Capitalism, Transformation*, Budapest: Central European University Press.

Balcerowicz, L. (1997): 'The Interplay Between Economic and Political Transition' in S. Zecchini (ed.): *Lessons from the Economic Transition: Central and Eastern Europe in the 1990s*, Dordrecht, Boston and London: Kluwer Academic Publishers and OECD, CCET, 153-167.

Baldwin, R. E. (1969): 'The Case Against Infant-Industry Tariff Protection' *Journal of Political Economy*, vol. 77, no. 3, 295-305.

Bangemann, M. (1992): *Meeting the Global Challenge: Establishing a Successful European Industrial Policy*, London: Kogan Page.

Barr, N. (ed.) (1994): *Labor, Markets and Social Policy in Central and Eastern Europe*, Oxford: Oxford University Press.

Bartlett, W. (1995): *Industrial Policy in Slovenia: Pioneering the Transition to a Market Economy*, Bristol: School for Advanced Urban Studies, University of Bristol, August, Unpublished Manuscript.

Bartlett, W. and J. Prašnikar (1995): 'Small Firms and Economics of Transformation in Slovenia' *Communist Economies and Economic Transformation*, vol. 7, no. 1, 83-103.

Bator, F. M. (1958): 'The Anatomy of Market Failure' *Quarterly Journal of Economics*, vol. 72, 351-379.

Baumer, J. M. (1994): *Das Strukturanpassungsprogramm Boliviens*, Synthesebericht, Nationales Forschungsprogramm 28, Einsiedeln.

Baumol, W. (1993): *Welfare Economics and the Theory of the State*, 2nd Edition, Aldershot: Gregy Revivals.

Baumol, W., Panzar, J. and R. Willig (1982): *Contestable Markets and the Theory of Industry Structure*, New York: Harcourt Brace Jovanovich.

Begg, D. and R. Portes (1992): *Enterprise Debt and Economic Transformation: Financial Restructuring of the State Sector in Central and Eastern Europe*, London: CEPR, Discussion Paper, no. 695.

Belka, M. and S. Krajewski (1995): *Industrial Policy in Poland*, mimeo.

Bell, M., Ross-Larson, B. and L. E. Westphal (1984): 'Assessing the Performance of Infant Industries' *Journal of Development Economics*, vol. 16, 101-128.

Bianchi, P., Cowling, K. and R. Sudgen (1995): *Europe's Economic Challenge: Analysis of Industrial Strategy and Agenda for the 1990s*, London and New York: Routledge.

Bicanic, I. (1992): 'Privatisation in Small European Soviet-Type Economies. Options, Strategies and Consequences for Industrial Structure' in K. Cowling, Keith and R. Sudgen (eds.): *Current Issues in Industrial Economic Strategy*, Manchester: Manchester University Press, 243-259.

Blanchard, O. J., Dornbusch, R., Krugman, P., Layard, R. and L. Summers (1991): *Reform in Eastern Europe*, Cambridge, Mass. and London: MIT Press.

Blejer, M. I., Calvo, G., Coricelli, F. and A. Gelb (eds.) (1993): *Eastern Europe in Transition: from Recession to Growth?: Proceedings of a Conference on the Macroeconomic Aspects of Adjustment*, Washington: World Bank, Discussion Paper no. 196.

Blommestein, H. J. (1994): 'Markets and Governments in Advanced Market Economies: Experiences and Lessons' in H. Blommestein and B. Steunenberg (eds.): *Governments and Markets: Establishing a Democratic Constitutional Order and a Market Economy in Former Socialist Countries*, Dordrecht, Boston and London: Kluwer Academic, 15-37.

Blommestein, H. J. and B. Steuneberg (1994): 'Governments and Markets: An Introduction' in H. Blommestein and B. Steunenberg (eds.): *Governments and Markets: Establishing a Democratic Constitutional Order and a Market Economy in Former Socialist Countries*, Dordrecht, Boston and London: Kluwer Academic, 1-14.

Bohatá, M. and J. Mladek (1996): *Industrial Policy in the Czech Republic*, London, Prague: CERGE-EI, Academy of Sciences, January.

Bornstein, M. (1994): 'Privatization in Central and Eastern Europe: Techniques, Policy Options and Economic Consequences' in L. Csaba (ed.): *Privatization, Liberalization and Destruction: Recreating the Market in Central and Eastern Europe*, Aldershot: Dartmouth, 233-258.

Boulding, K. (1991): 'What is Evolutionary Economics?' *Journal of Evolutionary Economics*, vol. 1, 9-17.

Brabant, J. M. van (1993): *Industrial Policy in Eastern Europe: Governing the Transition*, Dordrecht and London: Kluwer Academic.

Brabant, J. M. van (1996): 'Behaviour in Labour Markets during Transition in Eastern Europe' in C. H. A. Verhaar, P. M. de Klaver, M. P. M. de Goede, J. A. C. van Ophen and A. de Vries: *On the Challenges of Unemployment in a Regional Europe*, Aldershot and Brookfield: Avebury, 25-44.

Brown, A. A. and E. Neuberger (1979): 'Basic Features of a Centrally Planned Economy' in M. Bornstein (ed.): *Comparative Economic Systems. Models and Cases*, 4th Edition, Homewood, Ill.: Richard D. Irwin, 185-195.

Buchanan, J. M. (1986): *Liberty, Market and State. Political Economy in the 1980s*, Brighton: Wheatsheaf Books.

Buchanan, J. M. (1994): 'Democracy Within Constitutional Limits' in Blommestein, H. and B. Steunenberg: *Governments and Markets: Establishing a Democratic Constitutional Order and a Market Economy in Former Socialist Countries*, Dordrecht, Boston and London: Kluwer Academic, 39-47.

Buchanan, J. M., Tollison, R. and G. Tullock (eds.) (1980): *Toward a Theory of Rent-Seeking Society*, College Station: Texas A&M University Press.

Burton, J. (1983): *Picking Losers?: The Political Economy of Industrial Policy*, London: Institute of Economic Affairs.

Carlin, W., Reenen, J. van and T. Wolfe (1994): *Enterprise Restructuring in the Transition: an Analytical Survey of the Case Study Evidence from Central and Eastern Europe*, London: EBRD, Working Paper, no. 14, July.

CEC (1993): 'White Paper on Growth, Competitiveness and Employment' *Bulletin of the European Communities*, Supplement, June.

CEC (1996): *Central and Eastern Eurobarometer. Public Opinion and the European Union (19 Countries' Survey)*, no. 6, March [Online], Available: http:/www.cec.lu/en/comm/dg10/infocom/epo/ceeb6/en/index.htm [16 August 1996]

CEC (1997a): *Agenda 2000 - Volume I - Communication: for a Stronger and Wider Union*, Doc/97/6, 15. July, Strasbourg: CEC.

CEC (1997b): *Agenda 2000 - Volume II - Communication: Reinforcing the Pre-Accession Strategy*, Doc/97/7, 15. July, Brussels: CEC.

CEC (1997c): *Agenda 2000 - Volume II - Communication: The Effects of the Union's Policies of Enlargement to the Applicant Countries of Central and Eastern Europe (Impact Study)*, Brussels: CEC.

CEC (1997d): *The Union's Policies - Industrial Policy* [Online], Available: http://europa.eu.int/pol/ind/en/info.htm [11 April 1997].

CEC, DG 1A (1996): *The Phare Programme. Annual Report 1995*, Com (96) 360, Brussels: Office for Official Publications of the European Communities.

CEC, DG 1A (1997a): *Pre-Accesssion Strategy for the Associated Countries of Central Europe* [Online], Available: http://europa.eu.int/comm/dg1a/preaccession/strategy.htm [11 April 1997].

CEC, DG 1A (1997b): *What is Phare?* [Online], Available: http://europa.eu.int/comm/dg1a/phare/general/what_is_phare.htm [11 April 1997].

Chang, H. J. (1993): *The Political Economy of Industrial Policy*, London: Macmillan Press.

Chang, H. J. (1994a): 'Return to Europe?: Is there Anything for Eastern Europe to Learn from East Asia?' in H. J. Chang and P. Nolan (eds.): *The Transformation of the Communist Economies: Against the Mainstream*, Basingstoke: Macmillan, 382-399.

Chang, H. J. (1994b): 'State, Institutions and Structural Change' *Structural Change and Economic Dynamics*, vol. 5, no. 2, 293-313.

Chang, H. J. (1995): 'Explaining «Flexible Rigidities» in East Asia' in T. Killick (ed.): *The Flexible Economy. Causes and Consequences of the Adaptability of National Economies*, London and New York: Routledge, 197-221.

Chang, H. J. and P. Nolan (1994): *The Transformation of the Communist Economies: Against the Mainstream*, Basingstoke: Macmillan.

Charap, J. and A. Zemplinerova (1993): *Restructuring in the Czech Economy*, London: EBRD, Working Paper, no. 2, March.

Chowdhury, A. and I. Islam (1993): *The Newly Industrialising Economies of East Asia*, London and New York: Routledge.

Clark, N. (1988): 'Some New Approaches to Evolutionary Economics' *Journal of Economic Issues*, vol. 22, no. 2, June, 511-531.

Coase, R. H. (1988): *The Firm, the Market, and the Law*, Chicago: University of Chicago Press.

Colander, D. C. (ed.) (1984): *Neoclassical Political Economy*, Cambridge, Mass.: Ballinger Publishing.

Commander, S. and A. Tolstopiatenko (1997): 'Unemployment, Restructuring and the Pace of Transition' in S. Zecchini (ed.): *Lessons from the Economic Transition: Central and Eastern Europe in the 1990s*, Dordrecht, Boston and London: Kluwer Academic Publishers and OECD, CCET, 331-350.

Cowling, K. (1990): 'A New Industrial Strategy: Preparing Europe for the Turn of the Century' *International Journal of Industrial Organisation*, August, 165-183.

Crampton, R. J. (1994): *Eastern Europe in the Twentieth Century*, London and New York: Routledge.

Csaba, L. (1995): *Capitalist Revolution in Eastern Europe: Contribution to the Economic Theory of Systemic Change*, Aldershot: Edward Elgar.

Cullis, J. and P. Jones (1987): *Microeconomics and the Public Economy: A Defence of Leviathan*, Oxford: Basil Blackwell.

Dabrowski, M. (1994): 'The Role of the Government in Postcommunist Economies' in L. Csaba (ed.): *Privatization, Liberalization and Destruction: Recreating the Market in Central and Eastern Europe*, Aldershot: Dartmouth, 21-34.

Dahrendorf, R. (1990): *Betrachtungen über die Revolution in Europa*, Stuttgart: Deutsche Verlags-Anstalt.

Dasgupta, P. and J. E. Stiglitz (1988): 'Learning-by-Doing, Market Structure and Industrial and Trade Policies' *Oxford Economic Papers*, vol. 40, 246-268.

Dewatripont, M. and R. Gérard (1992): 'The Virtues of Gradualism and Legitimacy in the Transition to a Market Economy' *Economic Journal*, March, vol. 102, no. 411, 291-300.

Deyo, F. (ed.) (1987): *The Political Economy of the New East Asian Industrialism*, Ithaca and London: Cornell University Press.

Dietrich, M. (1992): 'The Foundations of Industrial Policy' in K. Cowling, Keith and R. Sudgen (eds.): *Current Issues in Industrial Economic Strategy*, Manchester: Manchester University Press, 16-32.

Dopfer, K. (1990): 'Elemente einer evolutorischen Ökonomik' in K. Dopfer and U. Witt (eds.): *Studien zur evolutorischen Ökonomik*, Berlin: Duncker and Humblot, 19-40.

Dosi, G. and R. R. Nelson (1994): 'An Introduction to Evolutionary Theories in Economics' *Journal of Evolutionary Economics*, April, 153-172.

EBRD (1994): *Transition Report 1994*, London: EBRD.

EBRD (1995): *Transition Report 1995. Investment and Enterprise Development*, London: EBRD.

EBRD (1996): *Transition Report 1996. Infrastructure and Savings*, London: EBRD.

EBRD (1997a): *Transition Report Update*, April, London: EBRD.

EBRD (1997b): *Transition Report 1997. Enterprise Performance and Growth*, London: EBRD.

Elsner, W. and J. Huffschmid (1994): 'Industrial Policy' in G. M. Hodgson, W. Samuels and M. R. Tool (eds.): *Elgar Companion to Institutional and Evolutionary Economics, A-K*, vol. 1, Aldershot: Edward Elgar Publishing, 343-350.

Estrin, S. (1983): Self-Management: *Economic Theory and Yugoslav Practice*, Cambridge: Cambridge University Press.

Evans, P. B., Rueschemeyer, D. and T. Skocpol (1985): 'On the Road Toward a More Adequate Understanding of the State' in P. B. Evans, D. Rueschemeyer and T. Skocpol (eds.): *Bringing the State Back In*, Cambridge: Cambridge University Press, 347-366.

Feldmann, A. M. (1987): 'Welfare Economics' in J. Eatwell, M. Milgate and P. Newman (eds.): *The New Palgrave: A Dictionary for Economics*, vol. 4, New York: Macmillan, 889-895.

Ferguson, P. R. and G. J. Ferguson (1994): *Industrial Economics. Issues and Perspectives*, 2nd Edition, New York: New York University Press.

Frydman, R. and A. Rapaczynski (1993): 'Insiders and the State: Overview of Responses to Agency Problems in East European Privatization' *Economics of Transition*, vol. 1, no. 1, 39-59.

Frydman, R. and A. Rapaczynski (1994): *Privatization in Eastern Europe: Is the State Withering Away?*, Budapest, London and New York: Central European University Press.

Frydman, R. and A. Rapaczynski (1997): 'Corporate Governance and the Political Effects of Privatization' in S. Zecchini (ed.): *Lessons from the Economic Transition: Central and Eastern Europe in the 1990s*, Dordrecht, Boston and London: Kluwer Academic Publishers and OECD, CCET, 263-274.

Frydman, R., Phelps, E. S., Rapaczynski, A., and A. Shleifer (1993): 'Needed Mechanism of Corporate Governance and Finance in Eastern Europe' *Economics of Transition*, vol. 1, no. 2, 171-207.

Funke, N. (1993): *Timing and Sequencing of Reforms: Competing Views and the Role of Credibility*, Kiel: Institut für Weltwirtschaft an der Universität Kiel, Kiel Reprints, no. 42.

Fuster, T. (1998): *Die «Good Governance» Diskussion der Jahre 1989 bis 1994. Ein Beitrag zur jüngeren Geschichte der Entwicklungspolitik unter spezieller Berücksichtigung der Weltbank und des DAC*, Bern, Stuttgart and Wien: Haupt.

Gelb, A. (1994): 'Socialist Transformations: An Overview of Eastern Europe and Some Comparators' in M. I. Blejer, A. Solimano and O. Sunkel (eds.): *Rebuilding Capitalism: Alternative Roads after Socialism and Dirigism*, Ann Arbor: University of Michigan Press, 111-140.

Gerschenkron, A. (1962): *Economic Backwardness in Historical Perspective: A Book of Essays*, Cambridge, Mass.: Belknap Press of Harvard University Press.

Gerybadze, A. (1992): 'The Implementation of Industrial Policy in an Evolutionary Perspective' in U. Witt (ed.): *Explaining Process and Change: Approaches to Evolutionary Economics*, Ann Arbor: University of Michigan Press, 151-173.

Glismann, H. H., Horn, E. J. and P. Stanovik (1995): *Institutional Change in the Search of the Market: The Case of Slovenia*, Kiel: Institut für Weltwirtschaft, Working Paper, no. 706.

Gros, D. and A. Steinherr (1995): *Winds of Change: Economic Transition in Central and Eastern Europe*, London and New York: Longman.

Grossman, S. J. and O. D. Hart (1988): 'One Share - One Vote and the Market for Corporate Control' *Journal of Financial Economics*, vol. 20, 175-202.

Grossmann, G. (1990): ' Promoting New Industrial Activities: A Survey of Recent Arguments and Evidence' *OECD Economic Studies*, no. 14, 87-125.

Haggard, S. and J. Williamson (1994): 'The Political Conditions for Economic Reform' in J. Williamson (ed.): *The Political Economy of Policy Reform*, Washington D. C.: Institute for International Economics, 525-596.

Haggard, S. and R. R. Kauman (1995): *The Political Economy of Democratic Transitions*, Princeton, N.J.: Princeton University Press.

Haggard, S. and S. Webb (eds.) (1994): *Voting for Reform: Democracy, Political Liberalization, and Economic Adjustment*, Oxford and New York: Oxford University Press.

Hare, P. (1995): 'Industrial Policy and Structural Adjustment in Central and Eastern Europe' *Economist Intelligence Unit Country Forecast. 4th Quarter*, 5-13.

Harrold, P., Jayawickrama, M. and D. Bhattasali (1996): *Practical Lessons for Africa from East Asia in Industrial and Trade Policies*, Washington: World Bank, Discussion Paper, no. 310.

Hayek, F. A. (1944) [1993]: *The Road to Serfdom*, London: Routledge and Paul Kegan.

Hellmann, T., Murdock, K. and J. Stiglitz (1996): 'Financial Restraint: Toward a New Paradigm' in M. Aoki, H.-K. and M. Okuno-Fujiwara (eds.): *The Role of Government in East Asian Economic Development*, Oxford: Oxford University Press, 163-207.

Hennipmann, P., Walker, D. A., Heertje, A. and H. van den Doel (1995): *Welfare Economics and the Theory of Economic Policy*, Aldershot: Edward Elgar Publishing.

Hillman, A. L. (1994): 'The Transition From Socialism: An Overview From a Political Economy Perspective' *European Journal of Political Economy*, vol. 10, no. 1, May, 191-225.

Hobbes, T. (1651) [1985]: *Leviathan*, London: Penguin Classics.

Hodgson, G. M. (1991): 'Economic Evolution: Intervention Contra Pangloss' *Journal of Economic Issues*, vol. 25, no. 2, June, 519-533.

Hodgson, G. M. (1993): 'Theories of Economic Evolution' in G. M. Hodgson, W. J. Samuels and M. R. Tool (eds.): *Elgar Companion to Institutional and Evolutionary Economics, A-K*, vol. 1, Aldershot: Edward Elgar Publishing, 218-223.

Hodgson, G. M. and E. Screpanti (eds.) (1991): *Rethinking Economics: Markets, Technology and Economic Evolution*, Aldershot: Edward Elgar Publishing.

Hughes, K. (1996): *The Development of Industrial Policy in Transition Economies: A Comparative Analysis*, mimeo.

Jovanovic, M. (1995): 'The Asian-Pacific Region - Model for the Economic Transformation of Eastern European Countries' in T. Felvinczi (ed.): *The Path of Economic Development*, Budapest: Institute for World Economics of the Hungarian Academy of Sciences, Trends in World Economy, no. 77, 159-167.

Kaase, M. (1994): 'Political Culture and Political Consolidation' in H. Blommestein and B. Steunenberg (eds.): *Governments and Markets: Establishing a Democratic Constitutional Order and a Market Economy in Former Socialist Countries*, Dordrecht, Boston and London: Kluwer Academic, 71-114.

Kádár, B. (1994): 'Economies in Transition: Problems, Patterns and Policies' in Csaba, L. (ed.): *Privatization, Liberalization and Destruction: Recreating the Market in Central and Eastern Europe*, Aldershot: Dartmouth, 7-19.

Kappel, R. and O. Landmann (1997): *Die Schweiz im globalen Wandel*, Zürich: Verlag Neue Zürcher Zeitung.

Kirzner, I. M. (1987): 'Austrian School of Economics' in J. Eatwell, M. Murray and P. Newman (eds.): *The New Palgrave: A Dictionary of Economics*, vol. 1, New York: Macmillan, 145-151.

Kommission der Europäischen Gemeinschaften (1991): 'Industriepolitik in einem offenen und wettbewerbsorientierten Umfeld: Ansätze für ein Gemeinschaftskonzept' *Bulletin der Europäischen Gemeinschaften*, Beilage, no. 3.

Kommission der Europäischen Gemeinschaften (1993): 'Wachstum, Wettbewerbsfähigkeit, Beschäftigung: Herausforderungen der Gegenwart und Wege ins 21. Jahrhundert: Weissbuch' *Bulletin der Europäischen Gemeinschaften*, Beilage, no. 6.

Kommission der Europäischen Union (1994): 'Eine Politik der industriellen Wettbewerbsfähigkeit für die Europäische Union. Mitteilung der Kommission an den Rat und das Parlament sowie an den Wirtschafts- und Sozialausschuss und den Ausschuss der Regionen' *Bulletin der Europäischen Gemeinschaften*, Beilage, no. 3.

Kornai, J. (1980): *The Economics of Shortage*, Amsterdam: North Holland.

Kornai, J. (1986): 'The Soft Budget Constraint' *Kyklos*, vol. 39, 3-30.

Kornai, J. (1992): *The Socialist System: The Political Economy of Communism*, Oxford: Clarendon Press.

Kornai, J. (1994): 'Transformational Recession: The Main Causes' *Journal of Comparative Economics*, vol. 19, no. 1, 39-63.

Kornai, J. (1995): *Highways and Byways. Studies on Reform and Post-Communist Transition*, Cambridge, Mass. and London: MIT Press.

Kozul-Wright, R. and P. Rayment (1996): ' Closing the Institutional Hiatus in Economies in Transition: Beyond the «State versus Market» Debate' in M. Knell (ed.): *Economics of Transition: Structural Adjustments and Growth Prospects in Eastern Europe*, Cheltenham: Edward Elgar Publishing, 210-240.

Kozul-Wright, R. and P. Rayment (1997): ' The Institutional Hiatus in Economies in Transition and its Policy Consequences' *Cambridge Journal of Economics*, vol. 21, 641-661.

Krueger, A. O. (1974): 'The Political Economy of the Rent-Seeking Society' *American Economic Review*, vol. 64, no. 3, 291-303.

Krueger, A. O. (1990): 'Government Failures in Development' *Journal of Economic Perspectives*, vol. 4, no. 3, 9-23.

Laffont, J.-J. (1989): *The Economics of Information and Uncertainty*, Cambridge, Mass.: MIT Press.

Lal, D. (1983): *The Poverty of Development Economics*, London: Institute of Economic Affairs.

Lall, S. (1990): *Building Industrial Competitiveness in Developing Countries*, Paris: OECD Development Centre.

Lall, S. (1992): 'Technological Capabilities and the Role of Government in Developing Countries' *Greek Economy Review*, vol. 14, no. 1, 1-36.

Lall, S. (1994): *Industrial Policy: The Role of Government in Promoting Industrial and Technological Development*, Geneva: UNCTAD.

Landesmann, M. A. (1993): *Industrial Policy and the Transition in East-Central Europe*, Vienna: Wiener Institut für Internationale Wirtschaftsvergleiche, Forschungsbericht, no. 196, April.

Landesmann, M. A. and I. P. Ábel (1995): 'Industrial Policy in the Transition' in M. Landesmann and I. P. Székely (eds.): *Industrial Restructuring and Trade Reorientation in Eastern Europe*, Cambridge and New York: Cambridge University Press, 313-336.

Landesmann, M. A. and I. P. Székely (eds.) (1995): *Industrial Restructuring and Trade Reorientation in Eastern Europe*, Cambridge and New York: Cambridge University Press.

Lavigne, M. (1995): *The Economics of Transition. From Socialist Economy to Market Economy*, Basingstoke and London: Macmillan Press.

Levcik, F. (1995): 'Economic Transformation in the East: A Critical Appraisal of its Developments and Suggestions for a Possible Way Out' in C. T. Saunders (ed.): *Eastern Europe in Crisis and the Way Out*, Basingstoke: Macmillan, 13-28.

Lipton, D. and J. D. Sachs (1990): *Creating a Market Economy in Eastern Europe: The Case of Poland*, Washington D. C.: The Brookings Institution, Brookings Papers on Economic Activity, no. 1.

Little, I. (1982): *Economic Development*, New York: Basic Books.

Lösch, D. (1992a): 'The Road to a Market Economy. Elements of a Normative Theory of System Transformation' *Intereconomics*, November / December, 255-260.

Lösch, D. (1992b): *Das «Timing» als zentrales Problem der Systemtransformation. Überlegungen zur Klärung der Kontroverse um «Schocktherapie» versus «Gradualismus» beim Übergang zur Marktwirtschaft*, Hamburg: HWWA-Institut für Wirtschaftsforschung, Report, no. 99.

Lydall, H. (1984): *Yugoslav Socialism*, Oxford: Clarendon Press.

Mas-Colell, A. (1987): 'Non-Convexity' in J. Eatwell, M. Milgate and P. Newman (eds.): *The New Palgrave: A Dictionary of Economics*, vol. 3, New York: Macmillan, 653-661.

McCloskey, D. N. (1994): *Knowledge and Persuasion in Economics*, Cambridge: Cambridge University Press.

Meier, G. M. (1987): 'Infant Industry' in J. Eatwell, M. Milgate and P. Newman (eds.): *The New Palgrave: A Dictionary of Economics*, vol. 2, New York: Macmillan, 828-830.

Mencinger, J. (1993): 'Lessons from the Transition Process' *Empirica*, vol. 20, 189-204.

Mencinger, J. (1994): 'Privatization Dilemmas in Slovenia' in L. Csaba (ed.): *Privatization, Liberalization and Destruction: Recreating the Market in Central and Eastern Europe*, Aldershot: Dartmouth, 153-166.

Mergos, G. and A. Tsantis (eds.) (1997): *The Phare Programme: An Interim Evaluation*, Brussels: CEC, DG 1A F/5.

Metcalfe, J. S. (1994): 'Evolutionary Economics and Technology Policy' *The Economic Journal*, vol. 104, July, 931-944.

Milgrom, P. and J. Roberts (1992): *Economics, Organization, and Management*, Englewood Cliffs, NJ.: Prentice Hall.

Mueller, D. C. (1993): 'Choosing a Constitution in East Europe: Lessons from Public Choice' in D. C. Mueller (ed.): *The Public Choice Approach to Politics*, Aldershot: Edward Elgar Publishing, 77-100.

Murrell, P. (1991): 'Can Neoclassical Economics Underpin the Reform of Centrally Planned Economies?' *Journal of Economic Perspectives*, vol. 5, no. 4, 59-76.

Murrell, P. (1992): 'Evolutions in Economics and in the Economic Reform of the Centrally Planned Economies' in C. Clague and G. C. Rausser (eds.): *The Emergence of Market Economies in Eastern Europe*, Oxford: Basil Blackwell, 35-53.

Nelson, R. R. and S. G. Winter (1982): *An Evolutionary Theory of Economic Change*, Cambridge, Mass.: Belknap Press.

Neue Zürcher Zeitung (1997a): *Ungarns Privatisierer im Endspurt. Die Eigentumsreform als Erfolg trotz allem*, no. 106, May 10/11, 25.

Neue Zürcher Zeitung (1997b): *Zweites tschechisches Stabilisierungspaket. Dramatische Selbstkritik der Regierung Klaus*, no. 122, May 30, 21.

Neue Zürcher Zeitung (1997c): *Der tschechische Königsweg wird steinig. Unwirsche Marktreaktionen auf den Wahlausgang*, no. 126, June 4, 3.

Neue Zürcher Zeitung (1997d): *Endet Prags Königsweg in einer Sackgasse? Was in der Tschechischen Republik seit der Transformation schiefgelaufen ist*, no. 127, June 5, 23.

Neue Zürcher Zeitung (1997e): *Polen bricht Bank-Ausschreibung ab. Börsengang der PBK als Alternative*, no. 163, July 17, 21.

Neue Zürcher Zeitung (1997f): *Das bittere Aus für den Prager Musterschüler*, no. 279, December 1, 3.

Neue Zürcher Zeitung (1998): *Mächtige Manager und störende Aktionäre. Noch unvollendete Eigentumsreform in Slowenien*, no. 37, February 14/15, 22.

Newbery, D. (1991): *Sequencing the Transition*, London: CEPR, Discussion Paper, no. 575.

Nicolaides, P. (ed.) (1993): *Industrial Policy in the European Community: A Necessary Response to Economic Integration?*, Dordrecht and Boston: Martinus Nijhof.

Niehans, J. (1987): 'Transaction Costs' in J. Eatwell, M. Milgate and P. Newman (eds.): *The New Palgrave: A Dictionary of Economics*, vol. 4, New York: Macmillan, 676-679.

Nozik, R. (1974): *Anarchy, State, and Utopia*, Oxford: Basil Blackwell.

Nunnenkamp, P. (1995): *The German Model of Corporate Governance: Basic Features, Critical Issues, and Applicability to Transition Economies*, Kiel: Institut für Weltwirtschaft.

OECD (1992): *Industry in Poland. Structural Adjustment Issues and Policy Options*, Paris: OECD, CCET.

OECD (1994): *Industry in the Czech and Slovak Republics*, Paris: OECD, CCET.

OECD (1995): *Review of Industry and Industrial Policy in Hungary*, Paris: OECD, CCET.

OECD (1996a): *Lessons from Labour Market Policies in the Transition Countries*, Paris: OECD, CCET.

OECD (1996b): *OECD Economic Surveys: Poland 1997*, Paris: OECD.

OECD (1997a): *Labour Market Policies in Slovenia*, Paris: OECD, CCET.

OECD (1997b): *OECD Economic Surveys: Slovenia 1997*, Paris: OECD.

Pelikan, P. (1992): 'The Dynamics of Economic Systems, or How to Transform a Failed Socialist Economy' *Journal of Evolutionary Economics*, vol. 2, 39-63.

Pinto, B., Belka, M. and S. Krajewski (1993): *Transforming State Enterprises in Poland: Evidence on Adjustment by Manufacturing Firms*, mimeo.

Pleskovic, B. and J. D. Sachs (1994): 'Political Independence and Economic Reform in Slovenia' in O. J. Blanchard, K. Froot and J. D. Sachs (eds.): *The Transition in Eastern Europe. Vol 1: Country Studies*, Chicago: University of Chicago Press, 191-200.

Polanyi, K. (1957): *The Great Transformation: The Political and Economic Origins of Our Time*, Boston: Beacon Press.

Porter, M. (1991): *Nationale Wettbewerbsvorteile. Erfolgreich konkurrieren auf dem Weltmarkt*, Munich: Droemersche Verlagsanstalt.

Radosevic, S. (1994): 'Strategic Technology Policy for Eastern Europe' *Economic Systems*, vol. 18, no. 2, 87-116.

Raiser, M. (1993): 'Old Habits Die Hard. A Note on the Nature of the Crisis in Central Eastern Europe' *Intereconomics*, July / August, 170-177.

Rausser, G. and L. Simon (1994): 'The Political Economy of Transition in Eastern Europe: Packaging Enterprises for Privatization' in C. Clague and G. C. Rausser (eds.): *The Emergence of Market Economies in Eastern Europe*, Oxford: Basil Blackwell, 245-270.

Republic of Slovenia (1993): *Annual Report for 1993*, Ljubljana: Development Fund.

Republic of Slovenia (1995): *Approaching Europe. Growth, Competitiveness and Integration. The Strategy for the Economic Development of Slovenia*, Ljubljana: Institute of Macroeconomic Analysis and Development.

Republic of Slovenia (1996a): *Strategy for Increasing the Competitiveness Capabilities of Slovenian Industry*, Ljubljana: Ministry of Economic Affairs.

Republic of Slovenia (1996b): *Strategy for International Economic Relations. From Associated to Full-Fledged Membership in the European Union*, Ljubljana: Ministry of Economic Relations and Development.

Rodrik, D. (1993): *Trade and Industrial Policy Reform in Developing Countries: A Review of Recent Theory and Evidence*, Cambridge, Mass.: NBER, Working Paper, no. 4417.

Rodrik, D. (1994): *King Kong Meets Godzilla: The World Bank and the East Asian Miracle*, London: CEPR, Discussion Paper, no. 944.

Rodrik, D. (1996): 'Understanding Economic Policy Reform' *Journal of Economic Literature*, vol. 34, no. 3, 9-41.

Rojec, M. (1992): *Investing in a Small Ex-Socialist Economy: Foreign Investor's Considerations. The Case of Slovenia*, Ljubljana: Centre for International Co-operation and Development.

Rojec, M., Jasovic, B. and I. Kusar (1994): *Privatization Through Foreign Investment in Slovenia. Concepts, Experiences and Policy Options*, Ljubljana: Centre for International Co-operation and Development.

Roland, G. (1993): 'Political Economy of Restructuring and Privatisation in Eastern Europe' *European Economic Review*, vol. 37, no. 2/3, April, 533-540.

Roland, G. (1994a): *On the Speed and Sequencing of Privatization and Restructuring*, London: CEPR, Discussion Paper, no. 942, April.

Roland, G. (1994b): *The Role of Political Constraints in Transition Strategies*, London: CEPR, Discussion Paper, no. 943.

Roland, G. (1997): 'Political Constraints and the Transition Experience' in S. Zecchini (ed.): *Lessons from the Economic Transition: Central and Eastern Europe in the 1990s*, Dordrecht, Boston and London: Kluwer Academic Publishers and OECD, CCET, 169-187.

Ross, S. (1973): 'The Economic Theory of Agency: The Principal's Problem' *American Economic Review*, vol. 63, 134-139.

Roumasset, J. A. and S. Barr (eds.) (1992): *The Economics of Cooperation: East Asian Development and the Case for Pro-Market Invervention*, Boulder and Oxford: Westview Press.

Sachs, J. (1994): 'Life in the Economic Emergency Room' in J. Williamson (ed.): *The Political Economy of Policy Reform*, Washington D. C.: Institute for International Economics, 503-523.

Sacks, S. R. (1983): *Self-Management and Efficiency: Large Corporations in Yugoslavia*, London: George Allan and Unwin.

Saunders, C. (ed.) (1993): *The Role of Competition in Economic Transition*, London: Macmillan and Vienna Institute for Comparative Economic Studies.

Sawyer, M. C. (1991): *The Economics of Industries and Firms: Theories, Evidence and Policy*, 2nd Reprint, London: Routledge.

Sawyer, M. C. (1992): 'On the Theory of Industrial Policy' in K. Cowling, Keith and R. Sudgen (eds.): *Current Issues in Industrial Economic Strategy*, Manchester: Manchester University Press, 3-15.

Scholtès, P. R. (1996a): 'Economic Reforms, Industrial Restructuring and Multi-agent Decision-Making' in P. R. Scholtès (ed.): *Industrial Policies and Private Sector Development Branch: Industrial Economics for Countries in Transition. Evidence from Eastern Europe and Asia Pacific*, Cheltenham and Brookfield: Edward Elgar and UNIDO, 85-104.

Scholtès, P. R. (ed.) (1996b): *Industrial Policies and Private Sector Development Branch: Industrial Economics for Countries in Transition. Evidence from Eastern Europe and Asia Pacific*, Cheltenham and Brookfield: Edward Elgar and UNIDO.

Schumpeter, J. (1943): *Capitalism, Socialism and Democracy*, London: George Allan and Unwin.

Self, P. (1993): *Government by the Market? The Politics of Public Choice*, Basingstoke: Macmillan Press.

Socha, M. W. and U. Sztanderska (1994): 'Restructuring and Industrial Policy in Poland' *MOCT-MOST: Industrial Policy in the Transition*, Special Issue, 71-106.

Somoguyi, L. (ed.) (1993): *The Political Economy of the Transition Process in Eastern Europe*, Aldershot: Edward Elgar Publishing.

Spiegel, H. W. (1991): *The Growth of Economic Thought*, Durham and London: Duke University Press.

Stanovik, P. and L. Milan (1995): 'Privatisation in Slovenia and the Restructuring of Manufacturing Industries' in T. Felvinczi (ed.): *The Path of Economic Development. Trends in World Economy*, no. 77, Budapest: Institute for World Economics of the Hungarian Academy of Sciences, 9-23.

Stiglitz, J. E. (1987): ' Learning to Learn, Localized Learning and Technological Progress ' in P. Dasgupta and P. Stoneman (eds.): *Economic Policy and Technological Performance*, Cambridge: Cambridge University Press, 125-153.

Stiglitz, J. E. (1989): 'On the Economic Role of the State' in A. Heertje (ed.): *The Economic Role of the State*, Oxford and Cambridge, Mass.: Basil Blackwell, 10-85.

Stiglitz, J. E. (1994): *Wither Socialism?*, Cambridge, Mass.: MIT Press.

Svejnar, J. (1994): 'Obstacles to Restructuring Post Privatisation' in P. Aghion and N. Stern (eds.): *Obstacles to Enterprises Restructuring in Transition*, London: EBRD, Working Paper, no. 16, December, 15-20.

Thomas, S. (1994): 'The Political Economy of Privatization: Poland, Hungary, and Czechoslovakia' in C. Clague and G. C. Rausser (eds.): *The Emergence of Market Economies in Eastern Europe*, Oxford: Basil Blackwell, 279-295.

Tomer, J. (1993): 'A New Rationale for Industrial Policy: Developing the Capabilities of the Learning Firm' *International Review of Applied Economics*, vol. 7, no. 2, 208-222.

Török, A. (1994): 'A One-Sided Restructuring Process: Challenges for Hungary's Industrial Policy in the Nineties' *MOCT-MOST: Industrial Policy in the Transition*, Special Issue, 31-53.

Tullock, G. (1987): 'Rent Seeking' in J. Eatwell, M. Milgate and P. Newman (eds.): *The New Palgrave: A Dictionary for Economics*, vol. 4, New York: Macmillan, 147-149.

Tyson, L. D'A. (1979): *The Yugoslav Economic System and its Performance in the 1970s*, Berkley: University of California, Institute for International Studies.

Verša, D. (1996): 'Some Particularities of the Unemployed Population in Slovenia' in C. H. A. Verhaar, P. M. de Klaver, M. P. M. de Goede, J. A. C. van Ophen and A. de Vries: *On the Challenges of Unemployment in a Regional Europe*, Aldershot and Brookfield: Avebury, 67-86.

Vodopivec, M. (1995): *Unemployment Insurance and Duration of Unemployment: Evidence from Slovenia's Transition*, Washington D. C.: World Bank, Policy Research Department, Working Paper, no. 1552.

Vodopivec, M. and S. Hribar-Milic (1993): *The Slovenian Labor Market in Transition. Issues and Lessons Learned*, Washington D. C.: World Bank, Policy Research Department, Working Paper, no. 1162, July.

Wade, R. (1990): *Governing the Market: Economic Theory and the Role of Government in East Asian Industrialization*, Princeton, N.J.: Princeton University Press.

Wagener, H. (1994): *The Political Economy of Transition*, Heidelberg: Physica Verlag.

Westphal, L. E. (1990): 'Industrial Policy in an Export-Propelled Economy: Lessons from South Korea's Experience' *Journal of Economic Perspectives*, vol. 4, no. 3, 41-59.

White, G. (ed.) (1988): *Developmental States in East Asia*, London and Basingstoke: Macmillan.

Williamson, J. (1990): 'What Washington Means by Policy Reform' in J. Williamson (ed.): *Latin American Adjustment: How Much Has Happened?*, Washington D. C.: Institute for International Economics, 7-38.

Willig, R. D. (1987): 'Contestable Markets' in J. Eatwell, M. Milgate and P. Newman (eds.): *The New Palgrave: A Dictionary for Economics*, vol. 1, New York: Macmillan, 618-622.

Witt, U. (1991): 'Reflections on the Present State of Evolutionary Economics' in G. M. Hogdson and E. Screpanti (eds.): *Rethinking Economics: Markets, Technology and Economic Evolution*, Aldershot: Edward Elgar Publishing, 83-102.

Witt, U. (ed.) (1993): *Evolutionary Economics*, Aldershot: Edward Elgar Publishing.

World Bank (1979): 'The Decentralized Self-Managed Economic System of Yugoslavia' in M. Bornstein (ed.): *Comparative Economic Systems. Models and Cases*, 4th Edition, Homewood, Ill.: Richard D. Irwin, 154-181.

World Bank (1987): *World Development Report*, New York: Oxford University Press.

World Bank (1993): *The East Asian Miracle: Economic Growth and Public Policy*, New York and Oxford: Oxford University Press.

Wyplosz, C. (1993): 'After the Honeymoon. On the Economics and the Politics of Economic Transformation' *European Economic Review*, vol. 37, no. 2/3, April, 379-386.

Zeman, K. (1994): 'Industry-Related Policies in the First Phase of the Transition Towards a Market Economy in Czech and Slovak Republics' *MOCT-MOST: Industrial Policy in the Transition*, Special Issue, 55-69.

Bitte beachten Sie die folgenden Seiten!

Prof. Dr. Hans Schmid / Dr. Tilman Slembeck
(Herausgeber)

Finanz- und Wirtschaftspolitik in Theorie und Praxis

Festschrift zum 60. Geburtstag von Alfred Meier

«Schriftenreihe des Instituts für Finanzwirtschaft und Finanzrecht» Band 86

XII + 579 Seiten, 20 Abbildungen, 18 Tabellen, 12 Grafiken
gebunden Fr. 84.– / DM 94.– / öS 686.–
ISBN 3-258-05572-6

Die wissenschaftliche Durchdringung der staatlichen Finanz- und Wirtschaftspolitik erfordert einen umfassenden Überblick über die Finanz- und Wirtschafts-
theorie und deren jüngste Entwicklungen. Sie verlangt aber auch vertiefte Kennt-
nisse über die realen finanz- und wirtschaftspolitischen Abläufe. Einer der
wenigen, der beide Voraussetzungen erfüllt, ist Alfred Meier. Ihm ist diese Festschrift gewidmet. Sie enthält Beiträge von Autoren mit ähnlich gelagerten Inter-
essen.

Verlag Paul Haupt Bern · Stuttgart · Wien

Prof. Dr. Jürgen Pätzold

Stabilisierungspolitik

Grundlagen der nachfrage- und angebotsorientierten Wirtschaftspolitik

«Uni-Taschenbücher» Band 1353

6., vollständig überarbeitete und aktualisierte Auflage
463 Seiten, 54 Abbildungen, 8 Tabellen
kartoniert, Fr. 32.50 / DM 34.80 / öS 254.–
ISBN 3-258-05693-5 (Haupt)
ISBN 3-8252-1353-6 (UTB)

Den Gegenstand dieses erfolgreichen Lehrbuches bilden aktuelle Fragen der Wirtschaftspolitik. Ausgehend von den Ursachen von Inflation, Arbeitslosigkeit und Wachstumsschwäche werden unterschiedliche wirtschaftspolitische Strategien dargestellt und kritisch beleuchtet. Behandelt werden insbesondere:

– die postkeynesianische bzw. nachfrageorientierte Wirtschaftspolitik
– die neoklassische bzw. angebotsorientierte Wirtschaftspolitik
– die Lohn- und Einkommenspolitik
– die Struktur- und Arbeitsmarktpolitik
– die Politik der Arbeitsverkürzung
– Fragen der Vereinigung der beiden deutschen Staaten

Verlag Paul Haupt Bern · Stuttgart · Wien

Dr. Monica L. Perez dos Santos

Ordnungspolitische Bedingungen des Wirtschaftswachstums

«Beiträge zur Wirtschaftspolitik» Band 67

611 Seiten, 85 Abbildungen
gebunden, Fr. 52.– / DM 58.– / öS 424.
ISBN 3-258-05867-9

«Wirtschaftswunder», d. h. Perioden besonders hohen Wirtschaftswachstums, können mit Hilfe der herkömmlichen Wachstumstheorien kaum erklärt werden. Wenn man etwa feststellt, dass in diesen Perioden die Investitionsquote hoch und der marginale Kapitalkoeffizient niedrig bzw. die Restgrösse der makroökonomischen Produktionsfunktion hoch waren, so stellt sich unmittelbar danach die Frage: Warum waren in den Ländern mit «Wirtschaftswunder» Investitionsquote, marginale Kapitalproduktivität und totale Faktorproduktivität so hoch? Aufgrund umfassender theoretischer und empirischer Untersuchungen zeigt diese Arbeit, dass Wirtschaftsordnung und Wirtschaftspolitik die entscheidenden Bestimmungsfaktoren des Wirtschaftswachstums sind. Danach ist Wirtschaftswachstum (bzw. auf der anderen Seite: Stagnation und Rückschritt) von Politikern machbar.

Verlag Paul Haupt Bern · Stuttgart · Wien

Prof. Dr. Reinhold Biskup
(Herausgeber)

Dimensionen Europas

«Beiträge zur Wirtschaftspolitik» Band 68

349 Seiten, 2 Abbildungen, 4 Tabellen
gebunden, Fr. 53.– / DM 59.– / öS 431.–
ISBN 3-258-05812-1

Ein aktuelles Buch von interdisziplinärer Kompetenz, das über die prägenden Herkünfte der europäischen Integration ebenso informiert wie über die Probleme insbesondere der zukünftigen Gestaltung der Wirtschafts- und Währungsunion Europas.
Das Vorstossen der europäischen Integration in neue Bereiche ist eine grosse Herausforderung für die Politik. Damit sie erfolgreich gestaltet werden kann, ist es unerlässlich, ihre Risiken zu kennen, auf die dieses Buch hinweist.

Verlag Paul Haupt Bern · Stuttgart · Wien